Text Messages

Text Messages

Preaching God's Word in a Smartphone World

Edited by John Tucker

WIPF & STOCK · Eugene, Oregon

TEXT MESSAGES
Preaching God's Word in a Smartphone World

Copyright © 2017 Wipf and Stock. All rights reserved. Except for brief quotations in critical publications or reviews, no part of this book may be reproduced in any manner without prior written permission from the publisher. Write: Permissions, Wipf and Stock Publishers, 199 W. 8th Ave., Suite 3, Eugene, OR 97401.

Wipf & Stock
An Imprint of Wipf and Stock Publishers
199 W. 8th Ave., Suite 3
Eugene, OR 97401

www.wipfandstock.com

PAPERBACK ISBN: 978-1-5326-3022-4
HARDCOVER ISBN: 978-1-5326-3024-8
EBOOK ISBN: 978-1-5326-3023-1

Manufactured in the U.S.A.   DECEMBER 4, 2017

The images used in chapter 2 first appeared in an article by Darrell Johnson, "Preaching the Gospel with the Great Preacher: Ten Convictions after 40 Years of Trying to do it Well," *Theology Matters* 18:1 (2012): 1–16. Used with permission of the publisher.

For
Emma,
Sophie,
and Daniel.

Contents

Contributors | ix
Acknowledgments | xiii
Introduction | xv
   —John Tucker

What is Preaching? | 1
   —Paul Windsor

Part I: Text

The Transforming Power of Text: Seven Discoveries | 21
   —Darrell W. Johnson

Lost for Words: How to Read Scripture in a Smartphone World | 46
   —Geoff New

Karl Barth's Theology of Preaching | 65
   —Andrea McDougall

Part II: Society

Looking Backward to Look Forward: Insights from the Past for Preaching in the Future | 83
   —Marc Rader

Word Made Flesh: The Fundamentals of Cross-Cultural Preaching | 101
   —Robert Smith Jr

Preaching with Vulnerability: Self-disclosure in the Pulpit | 113
—Simon Moetara

Part III: Listener

Engaging the Listener: Passionate, Pointed, and Prophetic Preaching | 137
—Laurie Guy

Free-for-all: How a Culture of Giving Voice Shapes Preaching | 148
—Jody Kilpatrick

Part IV: Preacher

Spiritual Practices for Preachers: Making Space for a Continuing Conversation with the Living God | 163
—Lynne M. Baab

Depleted No More: Practices that Sustain and Invigorate Preaching Ministries | 182
—Philip Halstead

Upgrading Our Preaching: Professional Development for Preachers Today | 200
—John Tucker

Part V: Christ

Preaching Christ Crucified: Cruciformity in Content and Delivery | 217
—Mark Keown

Disturbed Words: The Holy Spirit and Preaching | 230
—William H. Willimon

Contributors

Lynne Baab was the Jack Somerville Senior Lecturer in Pastoral Theology at the University of Otago from 2007 to 2017. Currently based in Seattle, she continues to supervise postgraduate students for the University of Otago. She is the author of numerous books on Christian spiritual practices, including *Sabbath Keeping, Joy Together: Spiritual Practices for Your Congregation,* and *The Power of Listening*. She has also written many articles about spiritual practices, which can be found on her website, www.lynnebaab.com.

Laurie Guy has had a career as a lawyer, pastor, missionary, and lecturer in Church History and New Testament at Carey Baptist College, Auckland. Now retired, he "works" as a volunteer in both secular and Christian settings. He is the author of five books, including *Unlocking Revelation: Ten Keys to Unlocking the Bible's Final Words* (Paternoster, 2016).

Philip Halstead is a lecturer in Pastoral Care, Pastoral Counselling, Christian Inner Healing, Research Methods, and Applied Theology at Carey Baptist College, Auckland. He is also the pastoral care leader at St Augustine's Church, Auckland. His publications include a trilogy of forgiveness-related articles in *The Journal of Spirituality in Mental Health*.

Darrell W. Johnson is a retired preaching pastor; Teaching Fellow, Regent College; and Professor of Preaching and Scholar in Residence, Carey Theological College.

Andrea McDougall is an Anglican priest and vicar of the Oamaru-Maheno Parish in Otago, New Zealand. She has a PhD from Otago University on Karl Barth's theology of humility. Andrea has worked as a maths lecturer at AUT University, research scientist, truck driver, and caregiver for street kids and those staying in night shelters.

CONTRIBUTORS

Mark Keown is a Presbyterian minister and New Testament lecturer at Laidlaw College, Auckland. His publications include *Congregational Evangelism in Philippians* (2008), *What's God Up to on Planet Earth?* (2010), and *Philippians Commentary* (2016). His academic interests include the New Testament and missional theology.

Jody Kilpatrick is the minister at Ponsonby Baptist Church in Auckland, which she has served since 2005. She preaches most Sundays and is in demand as a preacher and speaker. Jody is married to Julian. They have four children.

Simon Moetara is senior lecturer in theology and biblical studies at Vision College, Hamilton, and a teaching pastor at Activate Church, Hamilton. His publications include "Maori and Pentecostal Christianity in Aotearoa New Zealand" in *Mana Maori and Christianity* (Wellington: Huia Publishers, 2012) and "Tutu te Puehu and the Tears of Joseph: Reflections and Insights on Conflict Resolution and Reconciliation," in *Living in the Family of Jesus: Critical Contextualization in Melanesia and Beyond* (Auckland: Archer Press, 2016).

Geoff New is the Dean of Studies at Knox Centre for Ministry and Leadership, Dunedin, New Zealand. He was the minister of Papakura East Presbyterian Church from 1997 to 2015. Geoff is a trainer for Langham Preaching in South Asia. He is also the director of Kiwimade Preaching which seeks to resource and encourage preachers in New Zealand. His publications include *Imaginative Preaching: Praying the Scriptures so God can Speak Through You* (Langham, 2015), and *Live, Listen, Tell: The Art of Preaching* (Langham, 2017).

Marc Rader is the Senior Pastor of Gymea Baptist Church, a multistaff, multicampus church in the southern suburbs of Sydney, Australia. He is also a faculty member at Morling College where he lectures in Biblical Studies, Homiletics, and Church History. His DMin project focused on the use of multisource feedback for the development of preachers. He is the current president of the Australasian Academy of Homiletics.

Robert Smith Jr. serves as Professor of Christian Preaching and holds the Charles T. Carter Baptist Chair of Divinity at Beeson Divinity School, Birmingham, Alabama. Dr. Smith is a contributing editor for a study of Christian ministry in the African American church, *Preparing for Christian Ministry*, and is co-editor of *A Mighty Long Journey*. He has served as an editor of *Our Sufficiency Is of God: Essays on Preaching in Honor of Gardner*

C. Taylor. His publications include *Doctrine that Dances: Bringing Doctrinal Preaching and Teaching to Life* and *The Oasis of God: From Mourning to Morning—Biblical Insights from Psalms 42 and 43*, along with articles and essays on preaching and racial reconciliation.

John Tucker is Principal of Carey Baptist College, Auckland, where he lectures in Homiletics and Church History. He is also the Director of the Carey School of Preaching. His publications include *A Braided River: New Zealand Baptists and Public Issues, 1882–2000* (Bern: Peter Lang, 2013) and several essays on the history and mechanics of preaching.

Will Willimon is Professor of the Practice of Christian Ministry at Duke Divinity School, Durham, North Carolina, and a United Methodist Bishop, retired. His recent publications include *How Odd of God: Chosen for the Curious Vocation of Preaching* (WJKP, 2015), and *Who Lynched Willie Earle?: Preaching to Confront Racism* (Abingdon, 2017). With Stanley Hauerwas he is author of *The Holy Spirit* (Abingdon, 2015).

Paul Windsor is the International Programme Director for Langham Preaching and Lecturer in Homiletics at the South Asia Institute of Advanced Christian Studies in Bangalore, India. His doctoral research explored the role of intrigue in communication with sceptics.

Acknowledgments

IN THE PRODUCTION OF this book I have incurred many debts. First, I want to thank the contributing authors. Most of the chapters in this book grew out of papers presented at a conference hosted by the Carey School of Preaching at Carey Baptist College, Auckland. Thank you to the authors who refined their presentations for publication. Thank you too to Darrell Johnson, Robert Smith Jr., and Paul Windsor for their additional and excellent contributions.

I am particularly indebted to Paul Windsor. Not only does his essay provide the conceptual framework for this book, but his preaching and teaching ministry has been foundational for mine. More than anyone else, Paul has shaped my convictions about preaching. I also want to thank Charles Hewlett, my predecessor as principal of Carey Baptist College, for his generous support of the Carey School of Preaching. Thanks are due too to Myk Habets, Director of Research at Carey, for his encouragement and advice with this project.

At the production end I am extremely grateful to Sarah Snell for formatting the manuscript and developing the bibliographies, and to Junie Jumig for his work on the illustrations. Thank you too to Matthew Wimer and Brian Palmer at Wipf and Stock for their partnership in this project.

Finally, I want to thank my family. Lorraine, you are such a beautiful and faithful friend. I deeply appreciate your support and encouragement, and graciousness. Emma, Sophie, and Daniel, thank you for making life so much fun. I pray that you would grow up—like Nana—to love the Word. May this book help you, and many like you, to experience transformative "text messages" from the Scriptures.

Introduction

JOHN TUCKER

THE BRITISH BAPTIST THEOLOGIAN, Steve Holmes, claims that "we live in a time when preaching is under more sustained attack . . . than any other point in history of which I am aware."[1] Holmes is no lone voice. Writing from a charismatic and evangelical context, Ian Stackhouse argues that there is a "crisis in preaching."[2] It is felt in the pews. Researchers at Durham University have found that only 17% of churchgoers in Britain believe that preaching changes their lives.[3] In other words, the overwhelming majority of churchgoers don't believe that sermons on Sunday change the way they live on Monday.

This crisis of confidence is not limited, however, to the pews. Often it is pastors themselves who express declining faith in the power of preaching. In one informal study of 30 New Zealand churches, a Sunday visit to each of those churches found that in only four cases was the sole or senior pastor actually preaching.[4] Most ministers, it seemed, had more important things to do than prepare a sermon. From a North American context, Kenton Anderson confesses, "I sometimes wonder whether preaching is worth the effort. I don't know whether it is any harder to get up a sermon today than it used to be, but it sure feels like it is."[5] Anderson, writing in 2006,

---

1. Holmes, "'Living Like Maggots,'" 154.
2. Stackhouse, *Gospel-Driven Church*, 80. See also Quicke, *360-Degree Preaching*, 34.
3. Ironside, "Are Sunday Sermons Really Effective?" 11.
4. Robertson, "Preaching Delivers Clear Biblical Vision," 7.
5. Anderson, *Choosing to Preach*, 15.

was referring to the impact of digital technology—before the rise of smartphones, Facebook, Twitter, and Snapchat.

There are many reasons for this crisis in preaching. The communications revolution, for one thing, has undermined confidence in words, the preacher's stock-in-trade. With the rise of visual media, the image has triumphed, the word has been humiliated.[6] One consequence, according to Neil Postman, is that we have moved from the "Age of Exposition" into the "Age of Showbusiness."[7] Listeners expect to be entertained. And biblical preaching doesn't often meet that expectation. The emergence of social media in the last ten years has also spawned a preference for dialogue over monologue, discussion over proclamation.

This extraordinary revolution in technology has been matched by an equally dramatic revolution in epistemology. Philosophical pluralism has undermined our confidence in Scripture. Fred Craddock articulated this development so well in his seminal work, *As One Without Authority*:

> Rarely, if ever, in the history of the church have so many firm periods slumped into commas and so many triumphant exclamation marks curled into question marks. Those who speak with strong conviction on a topic are suspected of the heresy of premature finality. Permanent temples are to be abandoned as houses of idolatry; the true people of God are in tents again. It is the age of journalistic theology; even the Bible is out in paperback.[8]

This suspicion of definitive interpretations and strong convictions is reflected in the preaching of many ministers:

> Their predecessors ascended the pulpit to speak of the eternal certainties, truths etched forever in the granite of absolute reality, matters framed for proclamation, not for discussion. But where have all the absolutes gone? The old thunderbolts rust in the attic while the minister tries to lead his people through the morass of relativities and proximate possibilities, and the difficulties involved in finding and articulating a faith are not the congregation's alone; they are the minister's as well.[9]

Listeners, then, are sceptical of authoritative pronouncements, and preachers are wary of them. Truth is now constructed or discovered

---

6. Ellul, *The Humiliation of the Word*, 155–82.
7. Postman, *Amusing Ourselves to Death*, 83–98.
8. Craddock, *As One Without Authority*, 11.
9. Ibid., 13.

collaboratively. Congregations want a "guide from the side," not a "sage on the stage." The sermonic monologue—or "speaching"—is seen as arrogant and outdated.[10]

The crisis in preaching can also be traced to a revolution in the way pastors understand their role. In the New Testament pastoral ministry was essentially a ministry of the word. "While one hesitates to go so far as to call [preaching] the one central activity of the apostolic ministry, clearly it was far more than simply one ministerial function among many."[11] Taking their cue from Scripture, the Protestant Reformers believed that the pastor was a *minister verbi divini*, or a servant of the word of God. In their view the church was a "creature of the word." Not only did God call it into being by his word, but "he maintains and sustains it, directs and sanctifies it, reforms and renews it through the same Word."[12] For the Reformers, therefore, the first and major mark of a true church was the faithful preaching of the word.[13] The church was, in Luther's words, a "mouth house."

In the modern Western church, however, and particularly in evangelical and charismatic circles, ministers have been encouraged to see themselves less as preachers, and more as business leaders, organizational executives, or entrepreneurs.[14] I recall one senior leader within the New Zealand Baptist movement saying to me, "I'm wondering if the pastor-preacher model of church leadership is out-of-date." He felt, in the face of ongoing numerical decline, that ministers needed to give less time to preparing sermons and more time to pioneering new missional initiatives. Now the Western church certainly needs pastoral leaders with apostolic giftings who can be "impatient instigators."[15] It definitely needs to train pastors who have the capacity to read our changing culture and develop new ways of being church that are both faithful to Scripture and appropriate to our society. But the church cannot survive without a commitment on the part of pastors to studying, teaching, and preaching the Scriptures.

Michael Ross observes that "a profound confusion exists in many pastors' minds about the purpose and place of preaching in the ministry."[16] Clearly, many "pastors have low expectations of what can be accomplished

---

10. Pagitt, *Preaching Re-Imagined*, 17–51.
11. Old, *The Reading and Preaching of the Scriptures*, 166.
12. Stott, *I Believe in Preaching*, 109.
13. Willimon, *Pastor*, 142.
14. Quicke, *360-Degree Preaching*, 41.
15. Willimon, "Making Ministry Difficult," 11–12.
16. Ross, *Preaching for Revitalization*, 62.

through preaching and subconsciously convey this to their congregations."[17] Consequently, they do not prepare as carefully as they might. They do not linger prayerfully and patiently in a passage of Scripture until they are gripped by a word worth sharing. They do not wrestle through the week with the implications of that word for our world. They do not agonize over the best way to communicate that word to their congregation. Most importantly, these pastors invest very little time and energy in their ongoing development as preachers of God's word. As a result, their preaching easily becomes stale, predictable, boring, thin. And the church starves.

P. T. Forsyth began his Lyman Beecher lectures with the bold claim that Christianity stands or falls with its preaching.[18] The last century, I think, has to a large extent proved him right. John Stott writes:

> I do not hesitate to say that a (even the) major reason for the Church's decline in some areas and immaturity in others is what Amos called a "famine of hearing the words of the Lord" (8:11). The low level of Christian living is due, more than anything else, to the low level of Christian preaching.... So, if the Church is to flourish again, there is no greater need than a recovery of faithful, powerful, biblical preaching. God still says to his people, "O that today you would listen to my Word" (cf. Ps 95:7) and to preachers "O that you would proclaim it."[19]

So what does faithful, powerful, biblical preaching look like today? How can preachers, in the face of such pressures, proclaim God's word effectively? This book attempts to answer that question by assembling essays from a wide range of leading voices on preaching today. The contributors are based in the United States, Canada, India, Australia, and New Zealand. They represent a range of denominational traditions: Baptist, Anglican, Presbyterian, Methodist, and Pentecostal. And they draw on a breadth of disciplines: biblical studies, systematic theology, church history, pastoral theology, educational theory, and pastoral counselling.

The opening essay by Paul Windsor argues that faithful biblical preaching is characterized by five key attributes: it opens the Scriptures, enters society, engages the listener, exposes the preacher, and exalts Christ. Windsor shows how these five dimensions—Scripture, society, listener, preacher, and Christ—are all rooted in Paul's classic description of preaching in 1 Corinthians 1:18–2:5. So many approaches to preaching today focus on just

---

17. Ibid., 62.
18. Forsyth, *Positive Preaching and the Modern Mind*, 1.
19. Stott, *I Believe in Preaching*, 116.

two or three of these tasks. But truly biblical preaching—complete preaching—weaves together all five elements.

These five elements or dimensions provide the structure for the book. Part I focuses on Scripture. Darrell Johnson, in his chapter, claims that the call to preach is the call to preach the word of another. And the only way to be sure we are speaking his word is to speak from his word, to open up a passage of Scripture. Johnson claims that the crisis of preaching in our day is quite simply a failure to do this. In this remarkable essay, therefore, Johnson reflects on his nearly five decades of preaching and highlights seven discoveries he has made about the preaching of texts.

In chapter 3, Geoff New observes that there is a famine of the word in many churches today. In some places it can be hard to hear a sermon that lingers in a biblical text. In this chapter he considers the ways in which digital technology might be responsible. History shows that technological developments have always affected the way we read and hear Scripture. New argues that smartphones and search engines, while increasing our access to Scripture, are actually limiting our engagement with Scripture and preventing us from hearing the word of God. After this diagnosis he offers by way of prescription two ancient prayer practices. He calls preachers to embrace *lectio divina*, or "divine reading," and Ignatian Gospel Contemplation in their sermon preparation in order to engage deeply and fruitfully with the biblical text.

In chapter 4, Andrea McDougall reflects on Karl Barth's theology of preaching. Barth claimed that in preaching, God is the primary preacher, and that the preacher's task is to simply let the Bible speak. This chapter examines three aspects of Barth's teaching on preaching: his contention that the preacher is to be guided by a text rather than a topic, the importance of the prayers which the preacher prays at the beginning and conclusion of the sermon, and the relationship of preaching to theology.

Part II turns to issues of culture. In his chapter, Marc Rader asks how preaching needs to change today. He observes from the history of preaching that the most effective preaching in any age reflects three contexts: the needs of the church, leading theological trends, and the hermeneutic emphases of the day. In light of this, he proceeds to suggest several directions for preaching in the coming days. He calls for sermons that reflect canonical and narrative hermeneutics in the pulpit, enable participation by the congregation, focus on ecclesiology and missiology as it relates to the missional movement, and teach the congregations to critically engage with and "exegete" their culture.

Writing from the African American church tradition, Robert Smith Jr. reflects on the ways in which the church often fails to communicate across cultures. He argues that this is a pressing issue for the church in the light of the massive levels of international migration occurring today. Weaving together biblical exegesis, cultural analysis, and personal narrative, he discusses and demonstrates what effective crosscultural preaching in this context looks like.

Chapter 7 examines the need for self-disclosure and vulnerability in preaching today. It does this by subjecting contemporary Western society to probing cultural exegesis. Simon Moetara discusses the temptation for Christians, in an age of social media, to construct virtual lives that don't represent who they really are. He reflects on the dominant cultural model of masculinity in a society like New Zealand, one that is afraid of showing weakness, views emotional expression as unmanly, and chooses to suffer in silence rather than ask for help. And he considers popular Pentecostal-Charismatic attitudes to leadership and suffering. In each case he shows how authenticity and transparency in the pulpit is not only biblically sound but culturally redemptive. The chapter concludes with some helpful guidelines for what is appropriate vulnerability, and what is not.

Part III focuses on the need for preaching to connect with and engage the listeners. Laurie Guy, a church historian and New Testament scholar, starts by arguing that preaching is more than biblical exegesis. Christian preaching is the proclamation or application of a particular word to a particular audience at a particular moment in time. To achieve this, every sermon requires three attributes: it must be delivered with genuine conviction, it must be focused around a single theme, and it must be addressed to the listeners' particular context. Guy critiques expository preaching that confines itself to merely explaining a biblical passage. True expository preaching is rooted in Scripture but is also pointed, passionate, and prophetic.

Chapter 9 explores the potential for listeners to participate in the act of preaching by sharing their reflections after the sermon has been preached. Jody Kilpatrick has done this with her congregation week in and week out for over ten years. Through a longstanding tradition of "free-for-all," every member of the congregation is given the opportunity to respond to the sermon or add their own voice to what has been preached. In this chapter, Kilpatrick describes this practice and shows how a plurality of voices can serve to deeply enrich the preaching event.

After highlighting the need to exegete the Scriptures, our culture, and our listeners, Part IV turns the focus onto the person of the preacher. Lynne Baab has written extensively on spiritual disciplines. In this chapter, she explains what constitutes a spiritual practice and why these practices are such an essential element in a preacher's life: they enable us to hear from God. The discussion focuses particularly on three disciplines: keeping the

Sabbath, listening to others, and communal discernment. Baab shows that, in the words of E. M. Bounds, "Preaching is not the performance of an hour, it is the outflow of a life."[20]

In chapter 11, Philip Halstead, a pastoral counselor, discusses the reality of burnout in ministry. He examines the experience of four seasoned pastors and their advice for sustaining vibrant preaching ministries. He then outlines three key pastoral counseling insights that have been successfully utilized to help preachers mitigate stress, recover from burnout, and find new inspiration for their preaching.

Chapter 12 addresses the issue of professional development for preachers in today's world. Drawing on insights from the field of educational theory, and interviews with a number of pastors, it maps the primary contours for an effective program of lifelong learning among preachers. The basic argument is that for preachers to acquire, nurture, and sustain the skills, character, and convictions required to discharge their ministry in a challenging world, they will need to give attention to five important relationships.

The ultimate goal of all Christian preaching is to exalt Jesus. Part V focuses on Christ as the one who we proclaim and the one who, in the end, does the proclaiming through us. In chapter 14, Mark Keown, a New Testament specialist, explores what it means to preach Christ by a careful analysis of Paul's preaching in Corinth. He shows how Paul subverts the cultural norms of his day by adopting an approach to preaching that might best be described as cruciform. Not only was the content of his proclamation Christ and his crucifixion, but in his delivery Paul sought to embody Christ crucified. This, Keown shows us, has significant implications for contemporary preaching in an environment enamored with image, celebrity, charisma, and entertainment.

The book closes with a compelling essay by William Willimon on the Holy Spirit's work in preaching. Reflecting on the Spirit's agency in the Incarnation and Pentecost, Willimon argues that the Spirit of Christ is the primary agent in the preaching event. We are not on our own, he argues. We are called and empowered by the invasive, disruptive Spirit of Jesus. He writes: "Just as the Spirit brooded over the waters at creation, faithful sermons are conceived and birthed by the Holy Spirit. Preparation for preaching requires the discipline of regularly standing before God empty-handed, mute, brashly begging God for words we cannot say on our own."[21] And through those words, through preaching, God somehow recreates the world.

20. Bounds, *E. M. Bounds on Prayer*, 104.
21. See p. 234.

Bibliography

Anderson, Kenton. *Choosing to Preach: A Comprehensive Introduction to Sermon Options and Structures*. Grand Rapids: Zondervan, 2006.
Bounds, E. M. *E. M. Bounds on Prayer*. Peabody, MA: Hendrickson, 2006.
Craddock, Fred. *As One Without Authority*. Rev. ed. St. Louis: Chalice, 2001.
Ellul, Jacques. *The Humiliation of the Word*. Grand Rapids: William B. Eerdmans, 1985.
Forsyth, P. T. *Positive Preaching and the Modern Mind*. New York: Hodder & Stoughton, 1907.
Holmes, Stephen R. "'Living Like Maggots': Is Preaching Still Relevant in the Twenty-First Century?" In *Truth That Never Dies: The Dr. G. R. Beasley-Murray Memorial Lectures, 2002–2012*, edited by Nigel G. Wright, 152–67. Eugene, OR: Pickwick, 2014.
Ironside, Aaron. "Are Sunday Sermons Really Effective?" *Challenge Weekly* (1 March 2010) 11.
Old, Hughes Oliphant. *The Reading and Preaching of the Scriptures, Vol. 1*. Grand Rapids: Eerdmans, 1998.
Pagitt, Doug. *Preaching Re-Imagined: The Role of the Sermon in Communities of Faith*. Grand Rapids: Zondervan, 2005.
Postman, Neil. *Amusing Ourselves to Death: Public Discourse in the Age of Show Business*. New York: Penguin, 1985.
Quicke, Michael J. *360-Degree Preaching: Hearing, Speaking, and Living the Word*. Grand Rapids: Baker Academic, 2003.
Robertson, Murray. "Preaching Delivers Clear Biblical Vision." *New Zealand Baptist* (November 2009) 7.
Ross, Michael F. *Preaching for Revitalization: How to Revitalise Your Church Through Your Pulpit*. Fearn, UK: Mentor, 2006.
Stackhouse, Ian. *Gospel-Driven Church: Retrieving Classical Ministries for Contemporary Revivalism*. Milton Keynes, UK: Paternoster, 2005.
Stott, John R. W. *I Believe in Preaching*. London: Hodder & Stoughton, 1982.
Willimon, William H. "Making Ministry Difficult: The Goal of Seminary." 130:4. *The Christian Century* (2013) 11–12.
———. *Pastor: The Theology and Practice of Ordained Ministry*. Nashville: Abingdon, 2010.

What is Preaching?

Paul Windsor

When I started teaching preaching the critique from students took me by surprise. Monologues? Attention spans? Learning styles? Questions abounded. Eventually it became clear what was happening. Students had their worst examples of preaching in mind, while I had my best ones in mind. We were talking about two different things with the same word. We needed to start again. I needed to be more student-centered and then to explore with them the possibilities of a refreshed description for preaching.

We moved on from the phrase "expository preaching," inhibited as it was by being identified so commonly with an exegetical preaching that is absorbed solely with an explanation of the *text*. We traveled back to the 1980s, sparked by John Stott and his *Between Two Worlds*,[1] and investigated the importance of an engagement with both the text and the contemporary *context*. We traveled even further back, to the 1870s, sparked by Phillips Brooks and his "truth through personality,"[2] and investigated the importance of both the text and the *preacher*.

In this essay we travel much further back in search of a fuller description of preaching. We will argue that preaching involves even more than the text, the contemporary context, and the preacher. In 1 Corinthians 1:18–2:5, a passage central to Paul's philosophy of preaching, we find the Apostle as a master chef at work, mixing the ingredients together that create his understanding of preaching.[3]

---

1. Stott, *Between Two Worlds*.
2. Brooks, *Lectures on Preaching*, 5.
3. Although I had been working with these ingredients for several years it was

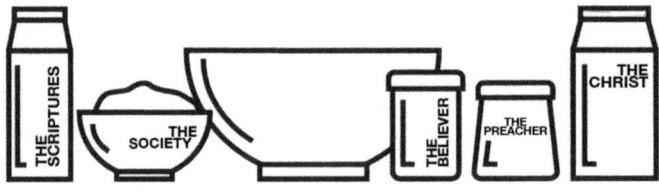

1. The Five Ingredients

The Scriptures (1:19; 1:31)

In the opening chapters of 1 Corinthians, Paul anchors his argument in the authoritative written Scriptures which he shares with his readers. He does this by threading "a series of Scripture citations into this section as evidence for the superiority of God's wisdom to all forms of human reasoning or calculation."[4] In doing so he asserts that these are not his own ideas, but God's.[5]

In the specific passage under consideration Paul appeals twice to these Scriptures. The first occasion is in 1:19 (quoting Isa 29:14) and it is preceded by "For it is written" (or, "As God says in the Scriptures," CEV), thereby asserting that the opening claim, the central proposition of his argument (in 1:18), finds its basis in the Old Testament. The second occasion is in 1:31 (quoting Jer 9:24) and is preceded by "Therefore, as it is written," thereby asserting that the climactic conclusion to his argument (in 1:18–30) also finds its basis in the Old Testament. As Richard Hays claims, it is the Old Testament which provides the "backbone" for this discussion.[6]

Moreover both the wider content and context of these Isaiah and Jeremiah passages demonstrate that these are not mere proof texts for which Paul reaches. Isaiah is in the midst of some Oracles of Woe, while Jeremiah is in the midst of some Oracles of Judgment. God is unimpressed by human boasting centered around wisdom, power, or wealth, and wherever such

---

Timothy Keller who alerted me, just two years ago, to the possibility of them all being found within this single biblical passage (see Keller, *Preaching*. See also Litfin, *Paul's Theology of Preaching*).

4. Perkins, *First Corinthians*, 49.

5. Paul's logic swings on the hinges provided by an array of explanatory, contrastive, and purposive conjunctions: "for/because" (1:18a; 1:19; 1:21; 1:22; 1:25; 1:26; 2:2); "but"(1:18b; 1:23; 1:24; 1:27; 1:30; 2:5); and "so that" (1:28; 1:29; 1:31; 2:5).

6. As quoted in Beale and Carson, *Commentary on the New Testament Use of the Old Testament*, 697. "As it turns out, the culminating pithy maxim in 1 Corinthians 1:31 is only the tip of the iceberg of scriptural dependence" (Ciampa and Rosner, *The First Letter to the Corinthians*, 111).

boasting is found, it is to be overthrown. In this way there is continuity in the biblical message across the testaments.

The Society (1:20–25)

Having appealed to the authoritative word he shares with his audience, Paul now steps into the society he inhabits with his audience. Three grammatical features in the text highlight this transition. The reader is drawn immediately into successive rhetorical questions: "Where are the wise . . . the scholars . . . the philosophers . . . Has not God made foolish the wisdom of the world?" (1:20, NIV). Then, in the verses which follow, two groups of people in the world are identified: Jews—for whom Paul's preaching is a "stumbling block"—are "asking for signs," and Greeks—for whom Paul's preaching is "foolishness"—are "searching for wisdom" (1:22–23). Finally, the vocabulary used by Paul supports this shift to a focus on the wider cultural context: "of the world" (1:20, 1:21, 1:27 (2x), 1:28; NRSV); "of this age" (1.20; NRSV); and "according to the flesh" (1:26, NASB).

So with the questions he asks, the people he identifies, and the vocabulary he uses, Paul, in 1:20–25, is drawing attention to the world beyond the gathered church community. More specifically, he engages with the elite in synagogue and society whom Garland refers to as the "professional experts."[7] These are the ones to whom people in any age turn for wisdom and advice. Whether it be with an idea, attitude, trend, or a tone, these are the ones who influence the worldview and behavior of people in a society. Much of the focus here in Corinth is on orator-celebrities whose influence and wisdom, for Paul, "is fatally flawed by egocentrism."[8] As with any cultural engagement a leading concern is with syncretism. It is no surprise to discover that this egocentrism seeps into this church and contributes to the conflict which lurks in the background to this letter:

> The Corinthians' quarreling reveals that they have absorbed, uncritically, the ideals and values of the pagan world around them, and Paul wants to replace pagan paradigms with the ideals and values exhibited in the cross.[9]

---

7. Garland, 1 *Corinthians*, 65.
8. Ibid., 67.
9. Ibid., 61.

Thus Paul's engagement with the world leads to a counter-cultural response that seeks to reverse, undermine, and subvert any damaging influence which the society has on the church.[10]

The Believer (1:26–31)

From the opening verse Paul makes clear that he has two groups in his sights: "those who are perishing" and "us who are being saved" (1:18). The former group includes the Jews and the Greeks, the "professional experts," and the syncretized Corinthians. With the second group, the textual evidence mounts rapidly when the pronouns "you" and "us/we," as well as the familial "brothers and sisters," are identified and the activities associated with them are accumulated. These are the ones who listen and believe.

God has done great things for these Corinthian believers. At different points the passive voice surfaces as they are included among "those who are being saved" (1:18) and "those who are called" (1:24). This is the fourth reference to calling in the letter already, emphasizing the initiative of God.[11] At other points the active voice reveals how "God saves those who believe" (1:21) and "God chooses" (1:27 (2x); 1:28). The saving, calling, choosing God is at work and this work rests on the power of God (2:5). It is little wonder that just prior to the concluding comment in 1:31, Paul asserts that "it is by *God's* doing you are in Christ Jesus" (1:30, emphasis mine). God is the mind behind it all and so there can be no boasting other than in God.

For Paul, this "calling" (1:26) is something to consider as he clothes it in a series of antitheses, with verbs making way for adjectives as the central grammatical feature. Rather than being characterized as the wise, the mighty, or the noble ("not many of you," 1:26), these believers are the foolish, the weak, and the base (1:27–28). "Throughout the biblical narrative God consistently chooses the most unlikely figures."[12] Channeling a little bit of *The Message*, Paul affirms that the somebodies are nobodies and the nobodies are somebodies in the eyes of God:

> God chose the foolish because the wise thought the cross was sheer folly as a means of saving the world, the weak because the

---

10. "Above all, [the wisdom of God] stands in antithetical opposition to the wisdom of this world order, which is fallible, temporary, short-term, and self-absorbed." (See Thiselton, *The First Epistle to the Corinthians,* 169).

11. See also 1:1; 1:2; and 1:9.

12. Garland, 1 *Corinthians,* 77. For example, consider Hannah's prayer in 1 Samuel 2 and Mary's song in Luke 1. The responsiveness of the Dalit people to the gospel here in India from where I write is one such contemporary example.

strong thought they were powerful enough without God, and the low and despised because the high and mighty did not care to debase themselves by attaching themselves to a crucified God. The foolish, weak, and despised, however, respond more readily to the shame of the cross because they themselves are already shamed. Unlike the powerful, those who are deemed foolish and weak are amenable to receiving the paradox of divine weakness that conveys strength. They respond more readily to the shame of the cross because they themselves belong to the shamed.[13]

The Preacher (2:1–4)

A pattern is emerging. There is foolishness and weakness all the way through this passage. "Not only is the message singularly unimpressive in the world's estimation (1:18–25), so are the majority of the members of the church of God in Corinth (1:26–31)!"[14] And now we discover that the preacher is also unimpressive.

In 2:1–4, Paul is "picking up where he left off in 1:17"[15] with a return to the first person pronoun ("me/I/my"), giving us the opportunity to assess his self-awareness as a preacher. Each verse makes a contribution. In his "coming" among them he makes no claim to "superiority of speech or of wisdom" (2:1, NASB). This was because his determination is "to know nothing among you except Jesus Christ, and Him crucified" (2:2, NASB). His presence with them is marked by "weakness . . . fear . . . trembling" (2:3, NASB), while his preaching was characterized by a "demonstration of the Spirit and of power," rather than with "persuasive words of wisdom" (2:4, NASB).

This suggests that Paul considers himself to be a herald. "The herald's task is not to create a persuasive message at all, but to convey effectively the already articulated message of another."[16] The herald chooses plain speaking over eloquent oratory. The herald targets being clear over being clever. The herald would recoil from the contemporary marketing impulse which attempts to massage the message by "accentuating the positive and

---

13. Ibid., 76.

14. Ciampa and Rosner, *The First Letter to the Corinthians*, 103. See also the headings which Gordon Fee uses for this section: "God's Folly—A Crucified Messiah (1:18–25); God's Folly—The Corinthian Believers (1:26–31); God's Folly—Paul's Preaching (2:1–5)" (see Fee, *The First Epistle to the Corinthians*, 67–97).

15. Garland, *1 Corinthians*, 82.

16. Litfin, as quoted in Garland, *1 Corinthians*, 68.

eliminating the negative." Not so with Paul. "Paul trusts the power of the cross to convict the audience rather than the power of his eloquence."[17]

Not surprisingly, in this description of his calling to be a herald we overhear something of his character as well. "He did not come as one who was self-important, competitive, or proud-hearted."[18] In this handful of verses, there is humility, authenticity, urgency, and love that can be overheard as he addresses them as "brothers and sisters," (1:26; 2:1, NRSV) and as one who had lived among them.

The Christ (1:18–2:5)

So what does this passage reveal to us about the ingredients that comprise Paul's philosophy of preaching? Generally speaking, the world (1:20–25), the believer (1:26–31), and the preacher (2:1–5) each receive a paragraph of attention, while the Scriptures appear at crucial points, near the beginning and the end, to provide a basis for his philosophy.

However, when it comes to the Christ—or, more specifically, the cross, the Christ, and Christ crucified—we discover that he seeps into the entire passage. He is the focus of it all. The *cross* features in the opening summarizing statement (1:18). *Christ* is identified as the "power of God" (1:24), and the "wisdom of God" (1:24). For those "in Christ Jesus," or believers, he becomes "wisdom from God . . . righteousness and sanctification and redemption" (1:30).[19] Then the phrase "Christ crucified" occurs twice—firstly, as a stumbling block for Jews asking for signs and as foolishness for Greeks searching for wisdom (1:23); and secondly, as the focus of Paul's preaching (2:2). For Paul it is about "preaching the Christ, the whole Christ, and nothing but the Christ."[20] A weak and foolish gospel for a weak and foolish

---

17. Garland, 1 *Corinthians*, 62. It is important to temper this with Paul's own practice while he was in Corinth in Acts 18. The verbs associated with his preaching suggest a greater diversity: "reasoned" (18:4); "persuade" (18:4); "preaching" (18:5); "testifying" (18:5); "speaking" (18:9); "teaching" (18:11); "persuading" (18:13); and "speak" (18:14). Drawing more widely from the New Testament, Peter Adam classifies more than forty words into five groups as he argues for "many different ministries of the Word" (see Adam, *Speaking God's Words*, 75).

18. Garland, 1 *Corinthians*, 86.

19. "It is not that Christ *is* these things but that believers *have* these things in Christ." (Garland, 1 *Corinthians*, 79). "The three nouns *righteousness, holiness,* and *redemption* explicate God's *wisdom*. Although all four qualities both characterize Christ and are imparted by Christ, the emphasis is on the fact that believers have them by virtue of being in union with Christ." (Ciampa and Rosner, *The First Letter to the Corinthians*, 109).

20. Vanhoozer, *The Pastor as Public Theologian*, 129.

people is delivered by a weak and foolish preacher. Why? So that it can be God's power and Christ's cross that is magnified.

The master chef has been at work. The five ingredients that mix together in 1 Corinthians 1:18—2:5 to form Paul's philosophy of preaching are the Scriptures, the Society, the Believer, the Preacher—and the Christ. Let's return now to the classroom with which we commenced and to the contemporary practitioners of preaching and their teachers. Can this passage provide a template over which they trace a fuller description of preaching? To explore this possibility is the purpose of this chapter and to do so we suggest a change in metaphor. Rather than the mixing of ingredients, let's imagine a journey through the corners of a room:

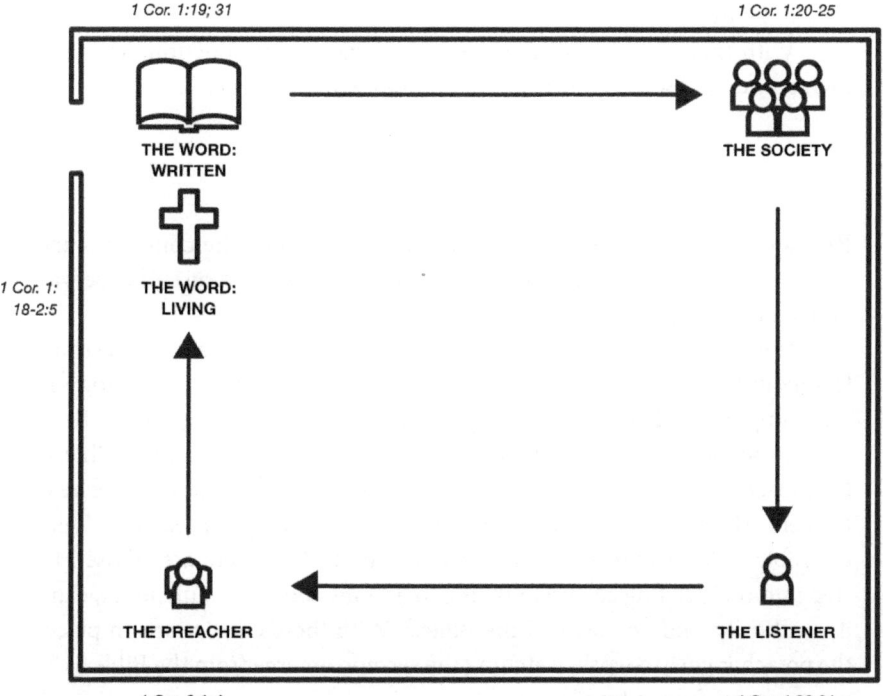

2. The Five Corners

Keeping the 1 Corinthians passage as a template, let us trace the journey through the corners on the way to a fuller description of preaching. It commences with the written word of God. The content and purpose of the text determines the content and purpose of the sermon. Then the preacher moves across to the world beyond the Christian community in the wider society. Where and how does the meaning of this text engage with cultural issues—and how and where can these issues shed light on the text? Building this bridge "between two worlds" is the preoccupation in the second corner. The journey continues on to the listener—mostly, but not exclusively, believers in this model—as the preacher reflects on the way rapport occurs as the connection between the text and the listener is made. Having visited this third corner the journey moves across to the preacher with the earlier "truth through personality" ringing in the ears. The matters of the heart and character are elevated, as preachers express their unique voice in the sermon. Finally, the christotelicity of the sermon becomes clear as the journey finds its destination in Christ, as the preacher heads back to the word corner to find the living word.[21]

With this summary of the journey by way of introduction, let's visit each corner and investigate briefly the issues which emerge.

The Word (written)

Paul took his written Scriptures seriously and so must the contemporary preacher as they commit themselves to a robust theology, a careful observation, and an accurate exegesis.

With preaching, "the essential secret is found not in mastering certain techniques, but in being mastered by certain convictions . . . theology is more important than methodology."[22] This theology must be robust. Be it convictions about God, Christ, the Spirit, the church, history, or the Bible—the preacher does not so much hold on *to* these convictions, as they are held *by* them. The teaching of preaching starts with a theology of preaching. Take the Bible as an example. What is required here? Preachers are advised to step into their calling secure in their convictions about the sufficiency, clarity, authority, and necessity of the Bible.[23] With these convictions in place, the preacher goes to work, watching the sermon emerge from the Bible as "a rose emerges from a bud."[24]

---

21. The sermon's christotelicity is based on the christotelic nature of Scripture: Christ is the goal, the purpose, the *telos*, of all Scripture.

22. Stott, *Between Two Worlds*, 92.

23. Kevin DeYoung uses the acronym SCAN and locates each feature in specific biblical passages (see DeYoung, *Taking God at His Word*). He asserts that "If authority is the liberal problem, clarity the postmodern problem, and necessity the problem for atheists and agnostics, then sufficiency is the attribute most quickly doubted by rank-and-file churchgoing Christians" (45).

24. Source unknown, but attributed to Archbishop Donald Coggan.

Careful observation is a second way in which the Bible is taken seriously. The preacher demonstrates what they think of the Bible by looking at it carefully and fully. "The more firmly we believe the Bible to be the inspired Word of God, the more lovingly and carefully we will pause over individual words."[25] Practices as diverse as inductive Bible study and *lectio divina* are known to serve this purpose well.[26]

After careful observation comes accurate exegesis. The best commentaries will help, but the best preachers demonstrate a commitment to developing exegetical skills themselves. With exegesis certain skills operate *wherever* you are in the Bible (for example, grammatical-syntactical analysis; word studies; historical, literary and theological context); while other principles operate depending on *where* you are in the Bible (for example, genre).[27] In this pursuit of accuracy the greatest determinant of meaning is "the restraining influence of context."[28]

The Society

The 1 Corinthians 1:20 trio of "the wise . . . the scholar . . . the philosopher" can be translated into every culture. Every society cultivates its "professional experts," be they celebrities, academics, politicians, counselors, movie directors, or journalists. Likewise the Jeremiah 9:23 trio of "wisdom . . . strength . . . riches," sitting as they are behind Paul's conclusion in 1 Corinthians 1:31, incarnate themselves in every culture. Paul took these experts and this boasting seriously and so must the contemporary preacher.

It helps to commence by imaging a society as a tree with roots and fruits. The experts and the boasting, at both these levels in the tree, need to be engaged. The contemporary preacher is as interested in the behavior, or the fruits, that are spoken and seen, as they are in the worldviews, or the roots, which usually remain unspoken and unseen. Being equally alert to fruit and root in this way and being able to trace the fruit to its root becomes an exercise in cultural exegesis.[29]

25. Motyer, *Preaching?*, 59. Similarly, "Analysis forces us to ponder detail; in the detail lies the mind of God" (60).

26. For assistance with inductive Bible study, consider Hendricks and Hendricks, *Living By the Book*, and Wald, *The New Joy of Discovery in Bible Study*. For the use of *lectio divina* in preaching, see New, *Live, Listen, Tell*.

27. Fine samples of accurate exegesis, incorporating these skills, can be found in Osborne, *The Hermeneutical Spiral*, 112–17. See also Beynon and Sach, *Dig Deeper*.

28. Carson, *Exegetical Fallacies*, 66.

29. Consider suicide as an example. The root issues underneath youth suicide in New Zealand and farmer suicide in India are likely to be different, but speaking these

In this way every preacher becomes an amateur sociologist committed to preaching worldviewishly. Timothy Keller refers to these worldviews as the "baseline cultural narratives" that are "so pervasive, and felt to be so self-evident, that they are not visible as beliefs to those who hold them."[30] Thus preaching worldviewishly becomes one way by which the subversion and the conversion provided by the gospel, overheard in this Corinthian passage, can be sparked in the contemporary sermon.

Other concerns live in this corner. Using simple, colloquial language that is free of Christian cliché and theological jargon. Using the logic of induction in which the preacher lingers in society, delaying the entrance into the word of the gospel.[31] Given that the secret of illustration is found in the juxtaposing eye, placing the spiritually significant alongside the utterly ordinary, the selection of illustrative material is yet another way for the preacher to linger in this corner.

Having visited these first two corners it is time to bury the "Bible in one hand; newspaper in the other" cliché. It is weary and old, suggesting that the engagement with society belongs in some bygone era. Far better is John Stott's "double listening,"[32] alongside the "between two worlds," and better still is "using *logos* helps me understand the text; using Google helps me understand the context."[33]

The Listener

In this Corinthian passage Paul takes believers seriously by speaking directly to them as a herald. However, further afield in the New Testament, Paul is more than a herald and there are more than believers who are listening.[34]

---

issues into the sermon deepens cultural understanding and enhances the possibility of the sermon traveling "between two worlds."

30. Keller, *Preaching*, 127.

31. Contrasting Paul's message at Athens in Acts 17 with his one at Pisidian Antioch in Acts 13 provides an illustration of this logic. The former is inductive, while the latter is more classically expository, or deductive, in its logic.

32. As I travel with Langham Partnership, a ministry founded by John Stott, this is the phrase which I hear attributed to him the most frequently. It is associated with his *The Contemporary Christian*.

33. I owe this phrase to Dr. Yohanna Katanacho (Bethlehem Bible College).

34. The diversity in Paul's own speaking ministry in Corinth in Acts 18 has already been noted. Thessalonica is another example. Here six different verbs are used to describe the Apostle's speaking—in just three verses: "reasoned . . . explaining and proving . . . proclaiming . . . said . . . persuaded" (Acts 17:2–4, NASB).

As one example, consider *dialegomai*.³⁵ This verb is used in such diverse settings as the synagogues of Thessalonica and Corinth, the marketplace of Athens, the hall of Tyrannus in Ephesus, and on the third story of a home in Troas. Its semantic range of meaning includes reasoning, arguing, debating, and discussing. There is an active involvement from the listener and a higher level of interactivity in the communication. So in any fuller description of preaching, the Corinthian herald provides the starting point for a journey into a more spacious vocabulary which recognizes that a variety of listeners are to be engaged in a variety of ways.

With this in mind the key word in the listener's corner is rapport. What builds rapport? This is the concern that lies behind questions like "Are you with me?" or "Are we on the same page?"—or, the phrase with which my Zambian friend, Albert, punctuated his sermons: "Are we together?" It is the issue of connection. While the issues are many, some of which can be found in other corners, three stand out for us here: clarity, application, and delivery.

Clarity is critical. As my Pakistani colleagues describe it, the journey from the text to the sermon is like moving from the mess in the kitchen to the meal on the table.³⁶ Complexity makes way for clarity—and simplicity. The burden lies not with being clever in some display of knowledge, but in being clear as the word begins to feel accessible to listeners.

With application, the goal of the sermon is to "land the plane"³⁷ in the lives of listeners. "The heart is the target."³⁸ Interestingly, this is where Paul travels in the rest of 1 Corinthians. In being an applicatory document, it is an example of what the contemporary sermon needs to accomplish as it keeps the full diversity of listeners in mind and the issues which they face.

With their focus on how the preacher speaks, rather than what is spoken, issues related to delivering the sermon are also integral to making a connection. This is more the music, rather than the lyrics, which comes from a preacher. While being natural is the key, this does not override the need, periodically, to audit all aspects of delivery for anything that might

---

35. Eight of this verb's ten occurrences in the New Testament are located in the book of Acts—in four consecutive chapters, with two occurrences in each (17:2, 17; 18:4, 19; 19:8, 9; 20:7, 9).

36. Assisting this transition, the use of the metaphor of the body is commonplace. See Bewes, *Speaking in Public Effectively*, and Richard, *Preparing Expository Sermons*. My own preference is to use the metaphor of a map (see, for example, http://paulwindsor.blogspot.in/2013/02/from-text-to-sermon.html).

37. This is the imagery used by Craig Bartholomew in *Excellent Preaching: Proclaiming the Gospel in its Context and Ours*. Darrell Johnson argues that the goal is to uncover the implication of the text, rather than its application (see Johnson, *The Glory of Preaching*, 158–71).

38. See Capill, *The Heart is the Target*. Also helpful is Green, *Cutting to the Heart*.

prove to be an obstacle to making an effective connection with listeners—be it gesture, face, eyes, voice, appearance, or manner.

The Preacher

This Corinthian passage brings the preacher into focus. The humility, the authenticity, the urgency, and the love, which have already been noted, travel easily across the cultures and down the centuries into the life of the contemporary preacher. There is no change. Each of these qualities are still essential.

Humility begins in the knowledge that the preacher does not choose to preach, but is chosen to preach—by God. It is his initiative. It is his work. This God is known to place the preacher in hidden and hard places, so that this humility can grow. Calvin Miller describes the dynamic well:

> Humility is not a state to be struggled for and achieved; it is a naturalness that occurs when you achieve spiritual perspective . . . it is not so much diminishing our self-importance as simply *standing next to Jesus* . . . This towering Jesus, by sheer contrast, will always displace our self-importance.[39]

Authenticity reminds the preacher of the need to be who they really are: genuine, real, and even, at times, vulnerable and transparent. "Let earnestness be your eloquence."[40] Along the way a preacher discovers their own preaching voice, like a signature.[41] This authenticity finds expression in a willingness to bear witness to the truth being proclaimed from the story of their own lives, just as happened with Paul in the book of Acts, where the story of his testimony is recorded on three different occasions.[42]

The prophets and the apostles felt owned by the messages they preached. "The lion has roared—who can but prophesy?" (Amos 3:8). It was as if the message held *them* more than they held the message. In the contemporary preacher this translates into an urgency. That old seventeenth-century Baxterian attitude needs remixing:

---

39. Miller, *The Empowered Communicator*, 53–54.

40. Chapell, *Christ-Centered Preaching*, 338.

41. This is similar to the observation about how effective TED talk presenters "stay in their own lane" (see Gallo, *Talk Like TED*, 239–46).

42. Acts 9:1–19; 22:1–21; 26:1–23. On this matter Craig Blomberg's testimony is a helpful guideline: "I like to disclose something of my own life in most of my messages" (in Blomberg, *Preaching the Parables*, 43).

Still thinking I had little time to live; my fervent heart to win men's souls did strive. I preach'd as never sure to preach again, and as a dying man to dying men.[43]

It is as if Baxter is saying, "Stand up to preach with two things on your mind: this could be the last sermon you preach, or this could be the last sermon a listener hears. Now—how are you going to preach?" It is a no-brainer. You will preach with passion, conviction, and intensity.

And let's not forget love. Although I've never seen it in a published form, I was shaped by a D. A. Carson comment, emerging offhandedly in the classroom one day: "to love to preach is one thing—to love those to whom you preach is quite another; there are gifted preachers who craft their sermons as artists not as lovers. Listeners will forgive almost anything if they are convinced you love them—they will forgive almost nothing if they think you do not."

The Word (Living)

Knowing that four corners is the reality in a room, to speak of *five* corners is deliberately provocative. Most rooms don't have five corners. The idea, however, is that preaching starts and finishes in the same corner with the word. In so doing the preacher guards against two dangers. One is bringing the exegetical harvest from each corner and depositing it in the middle of the room, where the sermon is then crafted. No! We bring the harvest from the Society, Listener, and Preacher corners back to the Word corner because this is where the content and purpose of the sermon is shaped. The second danger is the one that attempts to drive a wedge between the Bible and the Christ, as if they are to be pitted against each other. No! The Bible is the basis of the sermon and Christ is the focus.[44]

It is no coincidence that influential preachers from the nineteenth century (Charles Simeon) and twentieth century (John Stott) both chose 1 Corinthians 2:2 for their tombstone. In their preaching and their lives, as with the Apostle, this verse speaks not just of christocentricity, but also of christotelicity. For the contemporary preacher, Christ is to be the center, but he is also to be the end, the destination, of every sermon—as the fifth corner.

It is not within the purpose of this essay to canvas the arguments on whether every sermon, particularly from the Old Testament, must reach

---

43. Baxter, "Love Breathing Thanks and Praise," 40.

44. This is depicted so simply in the sixteenth-century Lucas Cranach painting, *The Reformation Altar*, where Martin Luther preaches with one hand on the Bible and the other hand pointing to the crucified Christ.

a destination in Christ. Maybe the cautious can be left to consider a set of simple questions hidden away at the end of a chapter in one of the most basic books on preaching that is available. When preaching from any passage of Scripture the authors urge the preacher to ask the following questions:

> What aspects of the character of God does this passage reveal, and how does Christ exemplify them? What aspects of the identity of humanity does the passage reveal, and how does Christ fulfil them? What aspects of the promises of God does the passage reveal, and how does Christ complete them? What aspects of the need of humanity does the passage reveal, and how does Christ meet them?[45]

Postscript

Just as the contemporary preacher is on guard against driving a wedge between the Bible and the Christ, so also must they be on guard against a similar division between the Bible and the Spirit. After all, "in biblical thought the Spirit of God is as closely connected to the word of God as breath is connected to speech."[46]

It is interesting to note that this is where the Apostle is now headed, with the very next Corinthian passage alerting the preacher of the need to keep Spirit and word together—a Spirit that is active in each corner. Echoes of the Spirit's work of inspiration in the word's corner can be overheard in 1 Corinthians 2:10–12. Echoes of the Spirit's work of anointing in the preacher's corner can be overheard in 1 Corinthians 2:13. And echoes of the Spirit's work of illumination in the listener's corner can be overheard in 1 Corinthians 2:14–15. While the Society corner is left unmentioned, in the Spirit's sovereignty, blowing like a wind where e wills, the illumination can extend to the unbeliever at those times when the inner witness of the Spirit authenticates the Word to them, convincing them that it is true.

---

45. Chester and Honeysett, *Gospel-Centred Preaching*, 76.
46. Woodhouse, "The Preacher and the Living Word," 55.

THE WORD: WRITTEN
the Spirit who inspires

THE SOCIETY
the Spirit who authenticates

THE WORD: LIVING
the Spirit who leads (to Christ)

THE PREACHER
the Spirit who anoints

THE LISTENER
the Spirit who illuminates

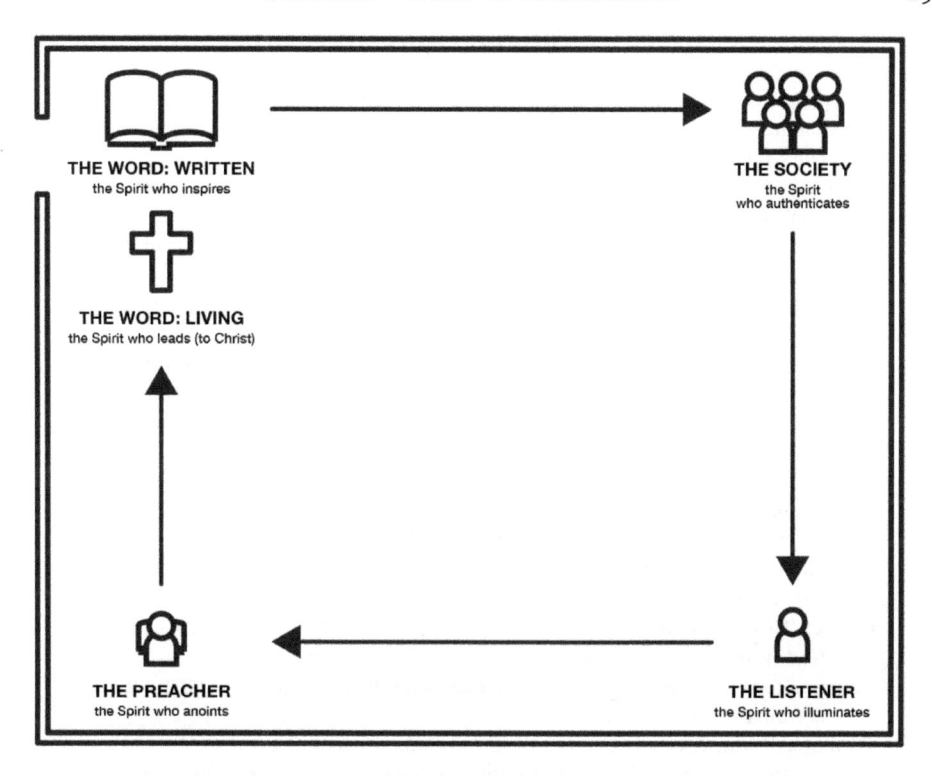

This essay has been about the search for a fuller description of preaching. It is more of a glimpse at—than a gaze on—what is needed in the training of preachers today. Sparked by a passage central to the Apostle Paul's philosophy of preaching (1 Cor 1:18–2:5), it introduces a "five corners" model. The journey to the sermon starts with the written word and finds its destination in the living Word. Along the way it rests awhile with the listener, the society and the preacher. Preaching *is* about taking the stories of the listeners, the society, and the preacher and weaving them around the central biblical story with its focus on Christ. Furthermore such preaching is pursued in overt and vocal dependence upon the Spirit of God who can be relied upon to superintend the entire process because it acknowledges his inspiring, illuminating, authenticating, and anointing work—as he leads people to Jesus.

Bibliography

Adam, Peter. *Speaking God's Words*. Leicester, UK: InterVarsity, 1996.
Bartholomew, Craig. *Excellent Preaching: Proclaiming the Gospel in its Context and Ours*. Bellingham, WA: Lexham, 2015.
Baxter, Richard. "Love Breathing Thanks and Praise." In *Poetical Fragments*, 1–50. London: T. Snowden, 1681.
Beale, G. K., and D. A. Carson, eds. *Commentary on the New Testament Use of the Old Testament*. Grand Rapids: Baker, 2007.
Bewes, Richard. *Speaking in Public Effectively*. Fearn, UK: Christian Focus, 1998.
Beynon, Nigel, and Andrew Sach. *Dig Deeper*. Nottingham, UK: InterVarsity, 2005.
Blomberg, Craig. *Preaching the Parables: From Responsible Interpretation to Powerful Proclamation*. Grand Rapids: Baker, 2004.
Brooks, Phillips. *Lectures on Preaching: The 1877 Yale Lectures*. Grand Rapids: Baker, 1969.
Capill, Murray. *The Heart is the Target: Preaching Practical Application from Every Text*. Phillipsburg, NJ: P & R, 2014.
Carson, D. A. *Exegetical Fallacies*. Grand Rapids: Baker, 1984.
Chapell, Bryan. *Christ-Centered Preaching: Redeeming the Expository Sermon*. 2nd ed. Grand Rapids: Baker, 2005.
Chester, Tim, and Marcus Honeysett. *Gospel-Centred Preaching: Becoming the Preacher God Wants You to Be*. Epsom, UK: The Good Book Company, 2014.
Ciampa, Roy E., and Brian S. Rosner. *The First Letter to the Corinthians*. Grand Rapids: Eerdmans, 2010.
DeYoung, Kevin. *Taking God at His Word*. Wheaton: Crossway, 2014.
Fee, Gordon. *The First Epistle to the Corinthians*. Grand Rapids: Eerdmans, 1987.
Gallo, Carmine. *Talk Like TED*. New York: Macmillan, 2014.
Garland, David E. *1 Corinthians*. Grand Rapids: Baker, 2003.
Green, Chris. *Cutting to the Heart: Applying the Bible in Teaching and Preaching*. Nottingham, UK: InterVarsity, 2015.
Hendricks, Howard G., and William D. Hendricks. *Living By the Book*. Chicago: Moody, 1991.
Johnson, Darrell. *The Glory of Preaching*. Downers Grove, IL: InterVarsity, 2009.
Keller, Timothy. *Preaching: Communicating Faith in an Age of Skepticism*. New York: Viking, 2015.
Litfin, Duane. *Paul's Theology of Preaching: The Apostle's Challenge to the Art of Persuasion in Ancient Corinth*. Downers Grove, IL: InterVarsity, 2015.
Miller, Calvin. *The Empowered Communicator: Keys to Unlocking an Audience*. Nashville: Broadman & Holman, 1994.
Motyer, Alec. *Preaching? Simple Teaching on Simply Preaching*. Tain, UK: Christian Focus, 2013.
New, Geoff. *Live, Listen, Tell: the Art of Preaching*. Carlisle, UK: Langham Preaching Resources, 2017.
Osborne, Grant. *The Hermeneutical Spiral*. Downers Grove, IL: InterVarsity, 2004.
Perkins, Pheme. *First Corinthians*. Grand Rapids: Baker, 2012.
Richard, Ramesh. *Preparing Expository Sermons*. Grand Rapids: Baker, 2001.
Stott, John. *Between Two Worlds: The Art of Preaching in the Twentieth Century*. Grand Rapids: Eerdmans, 1982.

———. *The Contemporary Christian: An Urgent Plea for Double Listening.* Nottingham, UK: InterVarsity, 1992.
Thiselton, Anthony C. *The First Epistle to the Corinthians.* Grand Rapids: Eerdmans, 2000.
Vanhoozer, Kevin. *The Pastor as Public Theologian.* Grand Rapids: Baker, 2015.
Wald, Oletta. *The New Joy of Discovery in Bible Study.* Minneapolis: Augsburg, 2002.
Woodhouse, John. "The Preacher and the Living Word." In *When God's Voice is Heard: The Power of Preaching,* edited by Christopher Green and David Jackman, 43–61. Leicester, UK: InterVarsity, 2003.

PART I
Text

PART I

The Transforming Power of Text

Seven Discoveries

DARRELL W. JOHNSON

ONE OF MY MOST precious treasures is a book by twentieth-century New Testament scholar W. Robertson Nicoll, entitled *Princes of the Church*.[1] In the book, Nicoll writes what he calls "tributes to notable figures in the Christian world,"[2] eulogizing colleagues and friends who, having served Jesus Christ in this world, mostly as teachers and preachers of the word, passed through to the next world ahead of him. He speaks gratefully and fondly of people whom preachers in our time still consult, most notable among them Horatius Bonar, J. B. Lightfoot, John Henry Newman, Charles Haddon Spurgeon, Alexander M'Laren, and Alexander Whyte. I try to read four or five of the entries every year.

A number of the tributes have especially spoken to me. Nicoll writes fondly of one Principal Charles Edwards (1837–1900), whose "passionate personal love for our Lord burned like a hidden flame at the heart of all his thought and speech and action."[3] It is what I trust someone will say of me when I pass through to the other side! According to Nicoll, Edwards said on many occasions, "A great preacher is Christ's last resource."[4] A bold claim in any era! By this he meant that when the church was "cooling," as he

---

1. The book was commended by Dr. Robert Meye, Emeritus Professor of New Testament, Fuller Theological Seminary as I took up the post of Associate Professor of Pastoral Theology, Regent College, in the fall of 2000.
2. Nicoll, *Princes of the Church*, v.
3. Ibid., 121.
4. Ibid., 129.

put it, the hope was for "the sudden appearance" of an anointed preacher. Why? Here is the line that has encouraged me many times: preaching would continue "to the ages of ages," for "Christ would not leave his people to die."[5]

And he has not, for in every era he has raised up great preachers. Jesus Christ loves his church, and the world in which his church is sent to bear him witness. And he so loves his church, and thus, his world, that he will never leave us to die; he will raise up and send preachers in our era to speak the word that is life and light and truth and healing. To put it more simply: we "do not live by bread alone, but by every word that proceeds from the mouth of God. (Matt 4:4)" And Jesus Christ, the Bread of Life himself, will make sure we are fed the only food that finally satisfies. Blessed be his name!

As of the writing of this chapter, the present world could be characterized as an iPhone world. But given the speed at which technology is advancing, that could change into a whole other kind of world! And, as of the writing of this chapter, the major way human beings communicate is via text messaging. Or is it by tweeting? Or is it by chat-rooming? Regardless of the form of communication, Jesus Christ will make sure people hear, receive, and be fed by his word. And although the mode of his speaking his word may change, the mode will always involve a text, a biblical text. Text messaging the word will always involve a biblical text . . . as the source of the message being texted, as the focus of the message being texted, as the content of the message being texted.

Why? Because the call to preach is the call to preach the word of another. Preachers are not sent to the church and into the world with a word of their own. We are sent with the word of another, the word of the Living Word himself. And the only way to be sure we are speaking his word is to speak texts, texts from his word, biblical texts, his texts.

Preachers in any era take their stand on and in a text. Where else are we going to stand? On our own insights and imagination? On our own Christianized insights and imagination? Commenting on the latest news? Reflecting on the latest cultural trends? Where has that gotten the mission of the church? Our responsibility is to say what the biblical text says. Nothing less and nothing more. To say what the text says in the language, imagery, and thought-forms of the people to whom we speak, so that they hear for themselves what the text says. As Lesslie Newbigin (who spent most of his life in India) puts it in the introduction to his theological commentary on the Gospel of John: "My task is to make clear to myself and (if possible) to others the word which is spoken in the Gospel in such a way that it may be

---

5. Ibid.

heard in the language of this culture of which I am a part with all its power to question that culture."⁶ It is my task. It is your task. Text message texts!

I learned this from John R. W. Stott, whom I consider to be the most faithful, purest expository preacher in world history. I mean the claim in all seriousness. Stott never spoke anywhere for any reason without speaking from a biblical text. He practiced what he advocated in his now classic definition of expository preaching:

> Whether it (the text) is long or short, our responsibilities as expositors is to open it up in such a way that it speaks its message clearly, plainly, accurately, relevantly, without addition, subtraction, or falsification. In expository preaching, the biblical text is neither a conventional introduction to a sermon on a largely different theme, nor a convenient peg on which to hand a rag-bag of miscellaneous thoughts, but a master which dictates and controls what is said.⁷

This conviction both constrains us and liberates us. It constrains us to what the great preacher, Jesus Christ, through the Holy Spirit, is saying in the text. It liberates us because we have to have it altogether in order to say what the text says. The text is the authority in the moment, not the preacher. We are constrained and liberated to say what the text says even if we do not yet fully understand it (see 1 Corinthians 13:12), and even if we do not yet fully believe it yet! We simply do our best to say what is being said in the text. Nothing less and nothing more.

Two mentors shaped me most as I began to preach: James Daane and Daniel Fuller, both of whom were on the faculty at Fuller Theological Seminary when I was preparing for ministry (1969–1972).⁸ Daane, fiercely reformed, pushed us hard to take our stand on the text. And Fuller, fiercely biblical, pushed us hard to get to the fundamental affirmation of the text. Since being tutored by them, nearly every Saturday afternoon or evening, the two of them are, so to speak, sitting on my shoulders. Fuller on my right, asking me, "Do you have the message of the text?" Daane on my left, asking me, "Are you trusting the text? Or are you trusting your own cleaverness or personality?" Both mentors keep driving me deep into the text. To the text! To the text!

---

6. Newbigin, *The Light Has Come*, ix.
7. Stott, *Between Two Worlds*, 26.
8. Other mentors at a distance include: Charles Swindoll, G. Campbell-Morgan, James S. Stewart, E. Stanley Jones, and through personal friendship, Earl F. Palmer and F. Dale Bruner.

I submit that therein lies the crisis of preaching in this era in which I am writing this chapter. Preachers are tempted to do everything but deal with a text! But to repeat (an instinctive move of preachers!), we are called and sent to speak the word of another, not our own word. And to repeat (repeat, repeat, repeat) the only way to be sure we are in fact speaking his word is to speak texts of his word. And as a result of messaging text after text after text, week after week after week, individuals and congregations are transformed into the image of the Word himself, and through the church, the world hears the only word that gives us life.

As of the writing of this chapter, I have been preaching Jesus and his word, Jesus and his gospel, for forty-six years. I preached my first official sermon in June of 1971, as a seminary intern. It was an overly ambitious, clumsy attempt to preach the gospel of Ephesians 1:3–14 . . . in twenty-five minutes. The night before, as I read my manuscript out loud, it took me forty minutes! So the next morning I just spoke really fast! I am embarrassed just thinking about it! Yet, many people afterwards spoke of being blessed, of being fed, of having their hearts warmed and minds stretched, and of wanting to know more. The text got a hearing, even through my woefully inadequate messaging of it. Since that Lord's Day in 1971, I have had the privilege of preaching in over 150 cities of the world, in 16 different countries, in nearly every denominational tradition of the church.

And through it all I have made a number of discoveries about the preaching of texts (I anticipate making many more!). Seven of the discoveries have become deeply held convictions about the preaching ministry.

1. The Preaching of the Word is the Word

This, of course, is one of the fundamental convictions of the Protestant tradition shaped by Martin Luther and John Calvin. The term "word of God" refers to three realities. First of all, it refers to Jesus Christ, whom the Apostle John calls the Word, the *Logos*. Jesus is the Word of God, God's eternal self-disclosure "made flesh" (John 1:1, 14). Secondly, the term refers to the Scriptures, the collection of God's speaking in and through many authors over many centuries, and centrally, the collection of the speaking of the Word-made-flesh, the definitive speech of God. And third—amazingly—the term refers to the preaching of the word by those called by the Living Word to speak the word. My longtime friend, Gordon Smith[9], when

---

9. Gordon is presently President of Ambrose University and Seminary in Calgary, Alberta, Canada, where he also serves as Professor of Spiritual Theology. He is also a prolific author.

preaching on the Lord's Day, will read the biblical text to be exposited, and then say, "Thus far God's word," implying that what is to come in the act of exposition *is also* the word of God.

Not that every word a preacher speaks is God's word! Preachers can say things they think are God's word but are not; they are just our word, a word God may or may not use to speak to his people. But any word we preachers speak that points to the Word himself and that emerges from and is faithful to the text of the word being exposited, *is the living word of the Living Word*. Mercy! What a privilege!

"Any word that points to the Word." I have discovered that the preaching that most transforms is preaching that is all about the Word himself. For, after all, the written word is radically christocentric.[10]

2. Preaching that is the Word of God Consistently, Relentlessly, Focuses on the Word of God Himself

I first discovered this in that moving experience recorded in Luke 24, a text I have subsequently come to lean on many times. On the first Easter, on Resurrection Sunday, in the afternoon, Jesus saddles up alongside two downcast disciples, who had not yet realized what had happened in Jerusalem that morning. They do not initially know that it is Jesus who is walking beside them. That is because they had not yet realized that Jesus, whom they knew to have been crucified, and whom they assumed was gone, had gone through the grave, and was alive, never to die! Luke tells us that after having asked them, "Was it not necessary for the Messiah to suffer these things and to enter into his glory?" (Luke 24:26), Jesus then, "beginning with Moses and all the prophets, explained to them the things concerning himself in all the Scriptures" (24:27). How I wish one of the two had taken notes that afternoon! Jesus shows them how every text of the word somehow points to him; every text is somehow finally about him. Which is why preaching of texts is somehow all about him!

The preacher who has most formed this conviction in me is John the Baptist. Listen to him preach, and we hear and see how radically christocentric he is. "I am a voice of one crying in the wilderness, 'Make straight the way of the LORD'" (John 1:23). "Look! The Lamb of God Who takes away the sin of the world!" (John 1:29). John consistently pointed to Jesus.

---

10. Keller, *Preaching,* 70–92, 256–64. Also see Clowney, *Preaching Christ in All of Scripture,* and *The Unfolding Mystery: Discovering Christ in the Old Testament;* Goldsworthy, *Preaching the Whole Bible as Christian Scripture;* and Greidanus, *Preaching Christ from the Old Testament.*

I have on my study wall a small reprint of the painting by Matthias Grünewald on the Isenheim Altarpiece.[11] And, famously, a large reproduction hung on the wall of Karl Barth's study, right in front of his desk, for all fifty years of his ministry. In the painting, people in desperation and longing are gathered around Jesus being crucified. John the Baptist is off to the side, holding an open Bible in his left hand. With his withered, bony right hand he is pointing to Jesus hanging on a cross, blood flowing from his side. John is saying that the texts of the Bible are all pointing to the crucified. In a lecture in 1920, Karl Barth says, "We think of John the Baptist in Grünewald's painting of the crucifixion, with his strangely pointing hand. It is the hand which is in evidence in the Bible."[12] Barth later asks, "Shall we dare turn our eyes in the direction of the pointing hand of Grünewald's John? We know whither it points. It points to Christ. But to Christ the crucified, we must immediately add. That is your direction, says the hand."[13]

Do we believe with John the Baptist that it all points to Jesus? We all have those times when we painfully, agonizingly, ask ourselves, "Is Jesus of Nazareth the 'one word in which we are to trust'?[14] Can I really believe this

---

11. This painting, produced between 1512 and 1516, is on display at the Unterlinden Museum at Colmar, Alsace, in France.

12. Barth, *The Word of God and the Word of Man*, 65.

13. Ibid., 76.

14. The Theological Declaration of Barmen.

in our time? Can I really say this with integrity in our massively pluralistic societies? Is Jesus who John and the rest of the New Testament says he is? Can I trust the New Testament (and First Testament) witness to him? Will he speak for himself as I name his name in the present arena of conflicting claims about truth?"

I like how Michael Reeves of England puts it for us preachers. In our preaching, teaching, thinking, ministry:

> we naturally gravitate, it seems, toward *anything* but Jesus—and Christians almost as much as anyone—whether it's "the Christian worldview," "grace," "the Bible," or "the gospel," as if they were things *in themselves* that could save us. Even "the cross" can get abstracted from Jesus, as if the wood had some power of its own. Other things, wonderful things, vital concepts, beautiful discoveries so easily edge *Jesus* aside. Precious theological concepts meant to describe *him* and *his* work get treated as things in their own right. He becomes just another brick in the wall. But the center, the cornerstone, the jewel in the crown of Christianity is not an idea, a system, or a thing; it is not even "the gospel" as such. It is Jesus Christ.
>
> He is not a mere topic, a subject we can pick out from a menu of options. Without him, our gospel or our system—however coherent, grace-filled, or Bible-based—simply is not Christian. It will only be Christian to the extent that it is about *him*, and then what we make of him will govern what we mean by the word *gospel*."[15]

He nailed it!

Now, as we "consistently, relentlessly focus on the Word of God himself," we sooner or later have to grapple with what is called "the scandal of particularity," the seemingly audacious claim that Jesus is the Creator of all things come into the world as one of us; who is at once the final and perfect revelation of the Living God ("They who see me have seen my Father" [John 14:9]) and the perfect revelation of what it means to be human; who by his death on the cross has done everything that needs to be done for us imperfect humans to have an intimate, life-giving relationship with the Living God; who has defeated the powers of death and evil; who now reigns as sovereign above all sovereigns; who is soon to come and bring about a whole new creation. Can we really take our stand on this "scandal?" Can we get up before our contemporaries, and say with the Apostle Peter, "And there is

---

15. Reeves, *Rejoicing in Christ,* 10; see also his *Delighting in the Trinity.*

salvation in no one else; for there is no other name under heaven that has been given among humans, by which we must be saved" (Acts 4:12)?

Phrases like "no other" and "no one else" quickly ruffle feathers in our time. They are not politically correct. They offend our inclusive, egalitarian sensibilities. I have often had people say, "What do you mean, only Jesus? How can you, a mere human being, in one little corner of the globe, say that there is no other name under heaven by which we must be saved? What about Buddha and Muhammad and the Dalai Lama? What about Eckankar and Scientology?"

What helps is remembering that pluralism, and thus "the scandal of particularity," is not new to our time. For the fact of the matter is, the scandalous gospel emerged in the context of pluralism! Mark tells us that Jesus was walking through the villages of Caesarea Philippi (8:27). As they traveled, Jesus asked them, "Who do people say that I am?" The disciples gave a number of answers; we can give even more. Then Jesus asked, "And who do you say that I am?" Peter, responding for the whole group, said, "You are the Messiah."

Caesarea Philippi was an amazingly pluralistic setting. A kind of religious "Mount Rushmore," as a number of scholars have described it. It was established as a place of worship of Baal, the fertility god,[16] and thus first called Balinas. When the Greeks moved in they changed the name to Panias, in honor of the god Pan, "The All." When the Romans moved in they changed the name to Caesarea Philippi in honor of Caesar, who by that time was beginning to be worshipped as divine. And in that place, of all places, Jesus asks, "Who do people say that I am?" Disciples of Jesus have faced the challenge of pluralism from the beginning.

What further helps me as I prepare to preach the scandal is to be clear about what the scandal is not saying. First, when we say, "there is no other name," we are not saying, "there is no truth in other names." In preaching salvation in no one else, Peter was not thereby canceling out all the claims of the Judaism in which he was raised. All truth is God's truth, and points to Jesus Christ, no matter where it is found. As Paul said in the city of Lystra, "God did not leave himself without witnesses" in any part of the world (Acts 14:17). Every culture, and every religion (or, most religions) expresses something of God's truth, or it would not win human hearts. Second, when we say, "there is no other name," we are not saying that the disciples of Jesus

---

16. I like to refer to Baal as "the god of the way things are," versus Yahweh as "the God of the ways things were supposed to be and one day will be." Baal-worshippers base their ethics on "this is the way I am," Yahweh-worshippers on "this is the way we were supposed to be and one day will be." Baal-worship, sadly, is still very much alive. And, gladly, so is Yahweh-worship!

Christ cannot learn from other names. We Christians in the West, and especially in North America, can learn a great deal from other people of the world. The intensity with which some Hindus seek union with the divine makes me feel very lazy in my pursuit of God. The discipline of some Muslims makes me feel like a hypocrite. I am often shamed by the peace I sense in the Buddhist monks of the city where I live. We who name the name of Jesus have much to learn from other faiths and worldviews. Dialogue can actually enlarge our view of Jesus: we see him through others' glasses than those shaped by our traditions and cultures. Third, when we say, "there is no other name," we are not saying that Christianity is the one true religion. Peter was not making any claim for a religion. He was making a claim about a person. Christianity does not save; Jesus saves. Indeed, sadly so, much of what is called "Christianity" has not even begun to grasp the message of Jesus, and the world-transforming consequences of his death, resurrection, and subsequent exaltation. A person is the scandal. A beautiful scandal. A life-giving scandal.

Let us linger here a while since this is such a critical issue for preaching in this pluralistic world.

As I have grappled with all of this over the years, I keep coming back to a simple answer to "Why no other name?" It is a two-fold answer. One, *no one said the things Jesus of Nazareth said*. And, two, *no one did the things Jesus of Nazareth did*. No one said, no one did. Objective facts.

No one said the things Jesus said.

You have, no doubt, had people say to you, "Look, all the great religious figures are basically saying the same thing." But that simply does not fit the facts. And on this point one could write a very big book!

For instance, no one spoke or speaks with the authority with which Jesus speaks. That is what struck the crowds who heard Jesus preach his Sermon on the Mount. Matthew tells us that, "When Jesus finished, the crowds were amazed because he taught as one who had authority, and not as their teachers of the law" (7:29). "Other teachers spoke by authority . . . Jesus spoke with authority."[17] Jesus simply says, "Amen, Amen, I say to you." I agree with the scholars, who after reading as widely as possible in the works of Jesus' Jewish contemporaries, conclude that no one else ever introduced their sayings with the solemn, "Amen, Amen." No appeal to any higher authority. Jesus even dared to set his words over against the words of religious authorities who came before him. Six times in the Sermon on the Mount he says, "You have heard it was said . . . but I say unto you." After he hears

---

17. Bruce, *The Training of the Twelve*, 42.

Jesus speak this way, Rabbi Jacob Neusner's incredulous response is to write an entire book in rebuttal as if to say, "Who do you think you are—God?"[18]

This note of authority is sounded in other ways. Some men bring their paralyzed friend to Jesus seeking healing. Jesus says to the man, "Your sins are forgiven." What? The teachers of the Law ask themselves, "Why does this fellow speak like that? He is blaspheming! Who can forgive sins but God alone?" (Mark 2:7). Mark tells us that Jesus spoke to demonic powers that had a hold on people. No weird incantations. No waving of magic wands. Just a word—"Be gone!"—and the powers obey! And the people who witness the event ask each other, "What is this? A new teaching—and with authority! He even gives orders to evil spirits and they obey Him" (Mark 1:25–27). Mark tells us of that evening when the disciples are caught in a violent storm on the Sea of Galilee. Waves are breaking over the sides of the boat. Jesus is on board, fast asleep on a cushion in the stern. The disciples wake him up: "Master, we are perishing!" Jesus stands up, and speaks to the environmental forces. "Be still!" No appeal to a Higher Power. No prayer. Just his own word: "Hush!" The winds die down, the sea becomes perfectly calm, and the disciples ask, "Who is this that even winds and waves obey Him?" (Mark 4:41). Who indeed?

No one else made himself the issue of his preaching and teaching the way Jesus of Nazareth did. While others said things like, "follow the Law," or, "follow the way of love," or, "follow the Eightfold Path to Enlightenment," or, "obey the karma," Jesus said, and says, "follow me" (Matt 4:19), "attach yourself to me" (John 15:4), "drink of me" (John 6:53), "eat of me" (John 6:56), "abide in me" (John 15:4), "be yoked to me" (Matt 11:29). Moses never made himself the issue of Judaism. Muhammad never made himself the issue of Islam. Buddha never made himself the issue of Buddhism. In fact, Buddha told his disciples that he could do nothing for them; they had to find their own way to enlightenment. Rabbi Solomon B. Frehoff once observed that no Muslim ever sings, "Muhammad, lover of my soul," nor does any Jew sing to Moses, "I need thee every hour."[19] Disciples of Jesus—especially preachers—sing both.

No one else made the kinds of claims about himself that Jesus made and makes. One might choose to conclude he is wrong, but one has to admit no one ever said what Jesus says about himself: "I Am the Bread of Life" (John 6:35). I am that without which you cannot live. You need me more than you need your next meal, as Earl Palmer likes to paraphrase it. "If you are thirsty, come to me and drink, and out of your innermost being will flow

---

18. Neusner, *A Rabbi Talks with Jesus*.
19. Quoted by Speer, *The Finality of Jesus Christ*.

rivers of living water" (John 7:37-38). "I am the light of the world; follow me and you will not walk in darkness" (John 8:12). "I am the resurrection and the life; whoever believes in me will live even if they die" (John 11:25). On it goes. John tells us that guards sent to arrest Jesus return to the Temple without him, excusing their disobeying of orders by saying, "Never did a man speak the way this man speaks" (John 7:46). No one—except Yahweh, the God of the Hebrews—made the kinds of claims about himself that Jesus makes about himself.

Heighten the scandal. Other teachers and prophets claimed to be sent *from* God. Jesus claims to be sent *out of* God. The Greek preposition is not just *para*, "alongside," but *ek*, "out of the center of." Others claimed to be representing God; Jesus claims that in him we are actually meeting God.

No one said the things Jesus said. No one. C.S. Lewis makes the point best:

> If you had gone to Buddha and asked him: "Are you the Son of Brahma?" he would have said, "My son, you are still in the vale of illusion." If you had gone to Socrates and asked, "Are you Zeus?" he would have laughed at you. If you had gone to Mohammed and asked, "Are you Allah?" he would first have rent his clothes and then cut your head off. If you had asked Confucius, "Are you Heaven?" I think he would have probably replied, "Remarks which are not in accordance with nature are in bad taste."[20]

But get this. In October of AD 32, when the religious authorities went to Jesus of Nazareth during the Jewish Feast of Tabernacles, and asked him, "Whom do you make yourself out to be?" Jesus answered, "Unless you believe that I AM, you shall die in your sins" (John 8:24); "When you lift up the Son of Man [Jesus' favorite self-designation] then you will know that I AM" (8:28); "Before Abraham was, I AM" (8:58). And John tells us that the authorities took up stones to throw at Jesus. They concluded he was wrong about what he was claiming about himself. But they could not deny that no one else ever spoke the way Jesus spoke. It is a fact of history: Jesus of Nazareth was crucified because he spoke of himself in ways no one ever dared to speak.

"No other name" because no one said the things Jesus said. And because no one did the things Jesus did.

I am not here thinking of his miracles, the likes of which others have done, especially in his name. I am here thinking of the kind of salvation Jesus said he was accomplishing. What Jesus claimed to be doing in coming down and going to the cross, no one else ever remotely claimed to do.

20. Lewis, "What are We to Make of Jesus Christ?," 157.

Every religious and philosophical system acknowledges that we humans are caught in some sort of bondage, right? Something is off; terribly off. Something keeps us from being what deep down inside us we feel we were meant to be, right? Some say we are in bondage because of a lack of education; others because we have not yet mastered some special techniques; others because we need to transcend our creatureliness. Jesus of Nazareth, the Word made flesh, understands our bondage in very different terms. In a way no one else understands it. He sees us as hostages, held by the powers of sin, evil, and death. He sees us as prisoners, held by an all-pervading infection, under an all-pervading spell, resulting in death. And he says that, try as we might, we cannot free ourselves from this bondage. Other would-be saviors think we can free ourselves, and offer us steps to liberation. Jesus says there are no steps. So he comes to do for us what we could not do for ourselves. He comes to get rid of the infection, break the spell, and overcome the reign of death.

No one did the things Jesus did.

And the surprising thing—the scandal of scandals—is he looked to the cross, to the weakness and foolishness of the cross, as the means by which he would deal with the forces that held us captive. He went to the cross to engage the powers. At the cross, Jesus entered into hand-to-hand combat with the powers that threaten to destroy us.

No one did the things Jesus did.

For three days it appeared that the powers, especially death, had beaten him. It appeared that the darkness of death had snuffed out the one who claimed to be the light. But appearance is not always reality! On Sunday morning, the women went to the tomb to anoint his body, his dead body. And to their utter surprise, the tomb was open and the body was gone. Not stolen, but transformed. Not resuscitated, but resurrected. Taken through death into a whole new order of existence. Death had not won!

No one did the things Jesus did. Lesslie Newbigin puts it so powerfully: "I know of no place in the public history of the world where the dark mystery of human life is illumined, and the dark power of all that denies human well-being is met and measured and mastered, except in those events that have their focus in what happened 'under Pontius Pilate.'"[21]

That is finally why "there is salvation in no other name." No other name even comes close to claiming to do what Jesus was claiming to do. So Lutheran theologian Carl Braaten, working at the forefront of pluralism, can write:

---

21. Newbigin, "Religious Pluralism and the Uniqueness of Jesus Christ," 50–52, 54.

> If salvation is the experience of "illumination," then perhaps Buddha "saves." If salvation is "the experience of union with the cosmic All," then perhaps Hinduism "saves." If salvation consists in "being faithful to one's ancestors," then perhaps Shintoism "saves." If salvation is "being freed from the oppression of the bourgeoisie," then perhaps Marxism "saves." If salvation is "material well-being," then perhaps Capitalism "saves." If salvation means "feeling good," then perhaps there is salvation not only outside of Christ but outside of religion in general. But if salvation is "liberation from the powers of sin and death," then only Jesus saves.[22]

No one said the things the great preacher said, and no one did the things the great preacher did. Oh blessed scandal of particularity! May we be given grace to proclaim it graciously, and courage to take the flak.

The preaching of the word of God is the Word of God, is preaching which joyfully, winsomely, keeps pointing to the Word of God. Always pointing to the Word-made-flesh for us and for our salvation. Always pointing to Jesus. To whom else should we point?

This is, after all, the passion of the Holy Spirit. "He will bear witness of me," says Jesus (John 15:26). "He shall glorify me; for he shall take of mine, and shall disclose it to you," Jesus goes on to say (John 16:14). Is it any wonder then that all Spirit-breathed texts somehow speak of Jesus? And is it any wonder then that all Spirit-empowered preaching of Spirit-breathed texts somehow speaks of Jesus?

I thank God for the way Sally Lloyd-Jones introduces her *The Jesus Storybook Bible*. For it is possible that a whole new generation will keep the focus where it is supposed to be. She says to the children reading her book:

> Now, some people think the Bible is a book of rules, telling you what you should and shouldn't do. The Bible does certainly have some rules in it. They show you how life works best. But the Bible isn't mainly about you and what you should be doing. It's about God and what he has done.
>
> Other people think the Bible is a book of heroes, showing you people you should copy. The Bible does have some heroes in it, but (as you'll soon find out) most of the people in the Bible aren't heroes at all. They make some big mistakes (sometimes on purpose). They get afraid and run away. At times they are downright mean.
>
> No, the Bible isn't a book of rules, or a book of heroes. The Bible is most of all a Story. It's an adventure story about a young

---

22. Braaten, "The Uniqueness and Universality of Jesus Christ," 82–83.

Hero who comes from a far country to win back his lost treasure. It's a love story about a brave Prince who leaves his palace, his throne—everything—to rescue the one he loves. It's like the most wonderful of fairy tales that has come true in real life!

You see, the best thing about this Story is—it's true.... And at the center of the Story, there is a baby. Every Story in the Bible whispers his name.[23]

And so does every text message of every text!

The preaching of the word *is* the Word when it points to and is all about the Word himself.

3. The Preaching of the Word of God Participates in the Preaching of the Word of God by the Word of God

This discovery has been the most liberating and empowering one thus far!

I learned it from the Apostle Paul, in his letter to the Romans. He asks a series of questions and then makes a declaration about the mystery of preaching:

> How then will they call on him in whom they have not believed? How will they believe in him whom they have not heard? And how will they hear without a preacher? How will they preach unless they are sent? Just as it is written, "How beautiful are the feet of those who bring good news of good things?" (Rom 10:14–15).

Notice that Paul has changed a biblical text. He is quoting the prophet Isaiah: "How beautiful are the feet of him who brings good news." Of *him*. Singular. Isaiah is thinking of an individual who comes with good news. The individual turns out to be the suffering servant, whose person and work Isaiah describes in that central text of the whole Bible, Isaiah 53 (more exactly, Isa 52:13—53:12). How beautiful are his feet indeed! But when Paul quotes Isaiah's text, he changes it! If you know Paul's respect and reverence for sacred texts, you realize what a huge move that is; he does not easily alter texts, especially one as central to the Grand Story as the one he quotes. How does he alter it? He changes the pronoun from the singular to the plural! From "him" to "those." From Jesus the servant to others he calls and sends to preach. "How beautiful" are those feet, your feet, my feet. Amazing.

Why the change? Why alter the pronoun from "him" to "those?"

---

23. Lloyd-Jones, *The Jesus Storybook Bible*, 14–16.

For many years I took Paul to mean that now Jesus has passed the baton to us, so to speak. Jesus has finished his preaching ministry, his earthly preaching ministry, and has now called and sent us to carry on the task. I was wrong. For the fact is Jesus the Word has not stopped being the Word, he has not stopped speaking the word. As he continues to be the healer, the bringer, and bearer of the kingdom of God, the Good Shepherd, the Bread of Life—the list goes on—so he continues to be the preacher, *the* preacher, the *great* preacher. As the writer of Hebrews has it: Jesus says, now, in the present, to his Father, "I will declare your name to my brothers and sisters; in the presence of the congregation I will sing your praise" (Heb 2:12, quoting Ps 22:22). Jesus *the* preacher continues to preach, and draws others into his preaching. He invites us to join him in his preaching. "How beautiful are the feet of those . . . " because they are participating in the preaching of him whose feet are exquisitely beautiful. Paul is declaring a wonderful mystery: we preachers are participating in the preaching of another. We not only speak the word of another; we join the another in his speaking his word!

Do you see what this means on a practical level? When you and I walk up to a pulpit or music stand, and dare to speak Jesus' word, Jesus himself is there in the pulpit with us! We are never alone. I should say it more accurately, not that he is there with us, but we are there with him. He is there in the pulpit before we stand there, and is inviting us to join him. He is *the* preacher in every preaching moment.

Which is why the things that happen in preaching happen. We cannot make them happen, but he can and does, and he calls us to partner with him, as he does in other ministries, especially the healing ministry. He is *the* healer. We are not. We can heal no one by ourselves (as thoughtful doctors will tell us). He is the one doing the healing, inviting us to join him with our prayers and laying on of hands and employing the medical gifts he has worked in the world. He is *the* preacher in any preaching moment. And he invites us to join him in his work.

What a relief to know! What a burden is lifted! Jesus *the* preacher makes the preaching moment his moment! And the glory of preaching is we get to witness it firsthand by standing with him, in him, serving as the audible voice of his voice.

4. Preaching the Word with the Word is Hard Work

This is important to emphasize after discovery three. Even though we are participating in the work of another, it is still hard work.

For one thing, preaching involves the whole self. Head, heart, eyes, and ears, both literally and metaphorically. Diaphragm, lungs, stomach, hands, feet, spirit, and soul, which is why we are often so tired afterwards; we have employed every dimension of our humanity in the work! The full self: thinking, feeling, breathing, intuiting.

Preaching is hard work because it involves the full range of human skill. Devotion, prayer, research, exegesis, hermeneutics, rhetoric, writing, prayer—again and again.

Preaching is hard work because of the many obstacles encountered, both in the moment and in preparation for the moment. Distracted hearts and minds. Overloaded hearts and minds, bombarded by all kinds of visual and audio media. Fear. Philosophical pre-suppositions. Spiritual powers that do not want the word spoken or heard (they do not want to "fall like lightning"). And the inadequacy of language, of human words. All of it making for very hard work.

Which is why discovery three is so crucial to grasp: we are not alone in the hard work. The Word himself is at work, and—thanks be to his name—he is able to overcome any and every obstacle. "How lovely are the feet of him" who does not get weary, who is unmatched by any person, power, ideology raised against him, whose word out-performs any other word.

5. The Word "Deliver" is Exactly the Right Word to Use for Preaching

For two reasons.

First, we are "delivering" a message of another, from another, about another. We are not speaking our own message. We are ambassadors of another (2 Cor 5:20). We are not passing on what we have thought up or dreamed up or imagined up. We are simply the "delivery woman," the "delivery man," which, if we are faithful to this fact, gives us great freedom—especially when the word is a hard word to speak and hear; we can say to ourselves and to our listeners, "I am only saying what I have been told to say. Don't shoot the messenger!"

Second, "deliver" is the right word because of the dynamics of the preaching moment. The word comes from the realm of childbirth; a woman "delivers" a child. The process involves conception, gestation, birth pangs, delivery, and post-partum blues. Is that not how it works? Conception—we are drawn to a text, we get a great idea about how to preach it. Gestation—the text and idea begin to work on us, and often we, like a pregnant mother, say, "what possessed me to do this?" Birth pangs—mostly on Saturdays. Then the actual delivery—hopefully at the appointed hour! And then post-partum blues—when we have given our all and feel we can never do it again. (I do not like Sunday afternoons. Neither does my family. Sorry about that. And I do not like Monday mornings. So be it. It all comes with the call).

6. The Preaching of the Word Takes Place in Many Different Modes

There is no "one way" to preach. Review the New Testament story of preaching and we see there are many different verbs used for preaching.[24]

Sometimes the text calls the preacher to evangelize, to simply announce good news. Sometimes the text calls the preacher to herald, to simply declare, "Hear ye, Hear ye." I love those times! Sometimes the text calls the preacher to teach, to simply outline the truth of the gospel as it is unfolded in the particular portion of Scripture for that day. Other times the text calls the preacher to exhort, to call for action; to, in the words of the old saying, comfort those who are disturbed and to disturb those who are too comfortable. When exhorting, one needs to always be careful to ground any exhortation in the prior action of God, to make sure any good advice is grounded in good news, because without good news it is not even possible to offer good advice. Other times the text calls the preacher to witness, to simply say what we ourselves know to be true at this particular time in history in light of the text of the day. Other times the text calls the preacher to speak apocalyptically, to pull back the curtain and simply let people see the dimensions of reality all around us of which they are ordinarily not aware. It is my favorite kind of preaching. I think it automatically takes place in every other kind of preaching.

Different preaching moments happen in different preaching modes. The mode is a function of the text. What a privilege, over a span of years, to operate in all these different modes.

---

24. I develop this in greater depth in my *The Glory of Preaching: Participating in God's Transformation of the World*, 76–100.

7. Preaching that Participates in the Preaching of the Word Himself has the Transforming Power it does Because of what the Word Himself Designed Texts to do

The Spirit-breathed texts of the Bible bring us into another reality. The texts give us what Walter Brueggemann calls "an alternative reading of reality."[25] But more than "a reading" of that other reality, the text, by the power of the Spirit, actually takes us into the other reality itself. This is the great wonder of preaching texts.

Any given text of Scripture is describing something of the whole of reality as it in relationship with the living God. Would you agree? No one text describes the whole of reality as it is in relationship with the Creator and Redeemer. That would not be possible. Any given text—Old Testament, New Testament, Psalm, Prophet, Gospel, Epistle—is describing a particular dimension of the larger alternative reality. And any given text brings us into that particular dimension of the larger reality.

Think of it this way. Any given text is taking us into and describing a room, a space, within the whole of reality.

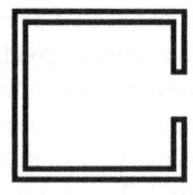

Not hard to imagine, is it? Is this not what a good novel does? Or a good film? Takes us into and opens up for us another room to inhabit and explore? Thus we speak of getting lost in a book, or of being transported by the cinematography into another world. Any given text inspired by the Spirit of the great preacher is opening up for us another room in God's big house, another space in God's big space.

But more than simply opening up, any given text is inviting us into its space. Any given text, by the work of the Spirit, brings us into the actual alternative reality it is describing. It is thrilling to contemplate and experience!

The task of preaching is to help people enter the room. (The introduction is answering the implicit question, "Why would I want to enter this room?" or "What is going to happen to me if I do enter this room?"). To help people begin to make some sense of the room, to help people begin to navigate their way around the room. (This is what the work of exegesis

---

25. A major theme of his! See, for example, *The Prophetic Imagination*.

is finally all about, and what the various homiletical moves are seeking to accomplish). And ultimately, the task of preaching is to help people *want to go on living in* the room.

This all suggests that a sermon is all about getting people in the room, that is, it is not so much that we get a message out of the text, as much as we help people get into the text.

Now this is what I want to especially emphasize. The goal of preaching any text is to so help people enter the new space to such a degree that they do not want to leave it! The goal is to preach the text in such a way that people so experience the reality of the text that they do not want to go back to life as they knew it before the text and its alternative reading of reality got a hold of them. Not as in the diagram: leave old reality, enter new reality for 25–30 minutes, and return to old reality. Which is what I think most people are doing: just getting a little pick-me-up to keep me going.

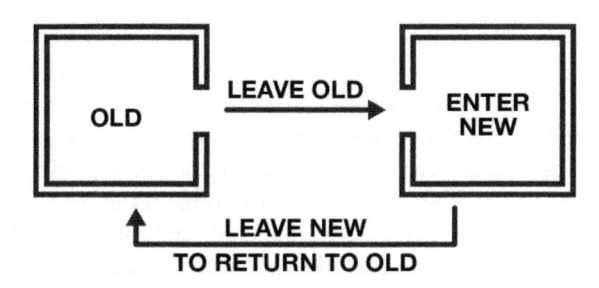

```
┌──────┐  LEAVE OLD   ┌──────┐
│ OLD  │ ──────────▶  │ ENTER│
│      │              │ NEW  │
└──┐ ┌─┘              └─┐ ┌──┘
   │ │    LEAVE NEW     │ │
   └─┴──TO RETURN TO OLD┘ │
     ▲──────────────────────
```

Not even bringing the new reality into the old reality; applying the text to my life, meaning "my life" is the main thing, not the "new life."

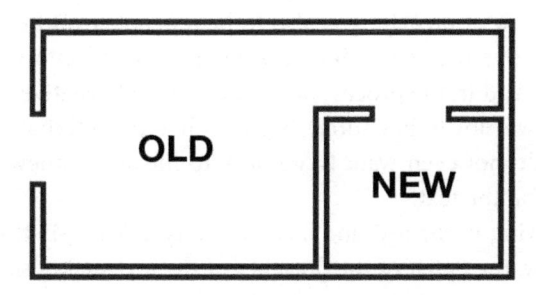

```
┌────────────────────────────┐
│                            │
│   OLD                      │
│              NEW           │
│                            │
└──────┐ ┌───────────────────┘
       │ │
```

But having the old reality brought into and transformed by the new reality.

```
┌─────────────────────────────┐
│   ┌──────┐ ┌──────────┐    │
│   │ NEW  │ │   OLD    │    │
│   └──────┘ └──────────┘    │
└─────────────────────────────┘
```

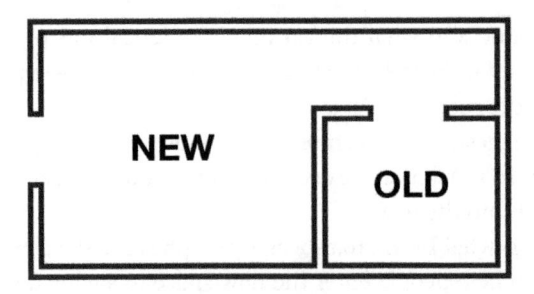

The old reality is taken up into the new; the old reality is transformed by the new. The new reality takes over the old; the new reality engulfs the old. So that any problem folks bring to the text is now seen in a new light. Any challenge is now seen in a new light. Any relationship is now seen—and experienced—in a new light.

Jeromey Q. Martini has put it this way, the Bible is:

> a collection of words but of words that have been breathed from Beyond and carry with them the weight and authority of that Breath. These are words with power to penetrate and interrupt lives and to alter people for Eternity. . . . The Bible is a gateway to another realm . . . a portal that seeks to transport people from this world to another and to point from this reality to a better Reality—a Reality that is Way and Truth and Life. And when that portal has been opened the power of that world is loosed onto this one so that it begins to effect its influence within it.[26]

The task of preaching is to help people enter the space the text is describing, and help them then begin to understand the reality they have entered. The task of preaching is also to help people explore and begin to live the alternative reality to which the text points and into which the text is inviting us. And in the process of exploring the alternative reality we are changed; for we slowly but surely begin to live the alternative reality. So much so we do not even want to go back to life as we knew it before we began to inhabit the text.

While living in the text and its new reality, at least six things happen. More precisely, the Spirit of the preacher of the text makes six things happen.[27] They are: engendering an encounter, announcing news, affecting a worldview shift, awakening new desire, calling for the obedience of faith, and enabling the living of the desire and acting in obedience.

---

26. Jersak, *Can You Hear Me?*, 40.

27. I develop five of these things more fully in *The Glory of Preaching*, 59–75. I develop the first one in a new way in this chapter.

Through the text, the Spirit of the preacher engenders an encounter with the subject of the text, with the Jesus of the text. I have witnessed this again and again—and it is a wonder to behold! Somehow the Holy Spirit works a living encounter with the living Savior and Lord. How? I do not know. But it is the Spirit's passion to make it happen.

In his very helpful book, *Meditation and Communion with God: Contemplating Scripture in an Age of Distraction*, theologian John Jefferson Davis (of Gordon-Conwell Seminary in Boston, Massachusetts) works with the philosophical concept of the extended self. Without going into great detail here,[28] the point Davis is making is that we as humans, although remaining in one fixed spot, can extend ourselves beyond that spot to other human beings in other spots. As I read Davis, I think back to how I was able to relate to my grandmother—the most important person in my life as I was growing up—through letters. As I wrote her I had the sense that I was extending myself to her; when I received a letter from her, I had the sense that she had extended herself to me. Which is why I kept her letters close by: there was a sense in which holding the letter was holding her. Then there were those phone calls! Oh mercy, as we talked it seemed as if she were really close at hand. She did not live long enough to see the advent of FaceTime or Skype! As Davis puts it:

> when we use Skype, we are extending ourselves into cyberspace and representing ourselves in real time into the two-dimensional reception space of our friends' computer screens: our molecular selves are definitively and circumscriptively present within our bodies and a particular geographic location; our extended/Skyped selves can be repletively (and digitally) present in many locations simultaneously.[29]

So, if we mere mortals are able to so extend ourselves, think how much more our Creator! The risen and ascended Jesus, through the agency and creativity of the Holy Spirit, can extend himself to us. Which is what he does through any Spirit-breathed text of his word. Davis again:

> The heavenly Christ Skypes his extended self into my heart by the Holy Spirit, his real-time broadband connection. In this case, however, the Skype analogy of course has its limitations, because in Christ my connection with Christ is *more real*, not less real, than a Skype connection; the *Holy Spirit* is surprisingly

---

28. Davis, *Meditation and Communion with God*, 55–62.
29. Ibid., 58, see n. 55.

more real and weighty than any mere points of light on a computer screen.[30]

In any Spirit-breathed text the Spirit is engendering an encounter with the Jesus of the text.

In this encounter, the Spirit of the preacher speaks news, his good news. Not just good advice; but good news. News about what God has done, is doing, and will do in Jesus.

This news then causes a shift in worldview; we see things differently. Our minds are renewed (Rom 12:2).[31] Or to put it more simply, through the text the Spirit of the preacher gives us a new set of glasses, and we see our lives differently than before we heard the text.

This shift then awakens new desire(s). Our hearts are moved; "Were not our hearts burning within us while he was speaking to us on the road?" ask the two disciples on the first Easter (Luke 24:32). As James K. Smith is teaching us, "we are what we desire," and "what defines us is what we love," or desire.[32] What Smith says about Christian education in general is all the more true of preaching the word, it "shapes us, forms us, molds us to be a certain kind of people whose hearts and passions and desires are aimed at the kingdom of God."[33] Or as Timothy Keller emphasizes:

> What the heart most wants the mind finds reasonable, the emotions find valuable, and the will finds doable. It is all-important then that preaching move the heart to stop trusting and loving other things more than God. . . . People, therefore, change not by merely changing their thinking, but by changing what they love most."[34]

Texts touch the heart as well as the mind.

The shift in thinking and the awakening of new desire then calls for a new step of faith, a new expression of what the Apostle Paul calls "the obedience of faith" (Rom 1:5; 16:26). A step that always involves repentance (turning around), and faith (placing our weight on).

And then the Spirit of the preacher empowers that new step. No text of the Bible ever leaves us in our own power; every text in one way or another takes the burden off our inadequate selves and places it on the subject of the

---

30. Ibid., 61.

31. This is so clearly developed by Os Guinness in *Fool's Talk: Recovering The Art of Christian Persuasion*. See also my *The Glory of Preaching*, 65–71.

32. Smith, *Desiring the Kingdom*, 25.

33. Ibid., 18.

34. Keller, *Preaching*, 159.

text who gives us the power to live a new way, even if we are not immediately aware that such empowerment is happening.[35] After all, we are not changed by our realization (a kind of salvation by knowing) but by the work of the great preacher. Which suggests to me that we best prepare to preach a text by living in the text until we have met the Jesus of the text, until we have heard his good news for ourselves, until we have had our worldview corrected, until new desire is awakened in us, until we begin to take a new step of faith, until we are ourselves empowered to walk in newness of life.

I said at the beginning that I have made seven discoveries about preaching. In the spirit of the author of Proverbs—"There are three things which are too wonderful for me, four which I do not understand" (30:18)—there is an eighth.

8. The Person Most Transformed by the Preaching of the Word is the Preacher

I am profoundly grateful that the Lord Jesus called me to join him in preaching his word, for I do not think I would be where I am in the journey of discipleship had he not. In order to preach I have had to be disciplined to read over, pray over, research, agonize with, and be shaped by the text. Week after week, decade after decade, Jesus has met me, and with his sharp two-edged sword (Rev 1:16), he has "judged the thoughts and intentions" of my heart, slowly, but surely, cutting away all that is not of him, moving me slowly but surely further and further into conformity with his nature and character (2 Cor 3:18). Others have been changed; I know, because they have told me so. But the person most transformed by forty-five years of preaching is me.

In that precious treasure on my bookshelf in my study which I mentioned at the beginning of this chapter, in *The Princes of the Church*, W. Robertson Nicoll speaks most fondly of Alexander M'Laren of Scotland (1826–1910). What he writes about his friend is what I want someone to be able to say of me when I pass to the other world.

> If ever any one was apprehended of Christ Jesus in early years, it was Alexander M'Laren. . . . Never was any one more profoundly loyal to the lessons of the morning. He desired no other and no better thing than that the end of his life should circle around the

---

35. This is what Jonathan Edwards stressed. "The main benefit that is obtained by preaching is by the impression made upon the mind in the time of it, and not by the effect that arises afterwards by a remembrance of what was delivered." Quoted by Marsden, *Jonathan Edwards*, 282.

beginning, only with a deeper conviction and a stronger love at last.[36]

And then this: "Those who observed him recognized that he drank from fountains older than the world, and for him they were always running fresh."[37]

It is what happens to those who live in texts—text after text after text—going deeper into the life and love of the great preacher.

---

36. Nicoll, *Princes of the Church*, 245.
37. Ibid., 246.

Bibliography

Barth, Karl. *The Word of God and the Word of Man*. Translated by Douglas Horton. New York: Harper Torchbooks, 1957.

Braaten, Carl E. "The Uniqueness and Universality of Jesus Christ." In *Mission Trends, No. 5: Faith Meets God*, edited by Gerald H. Anderson and Thomas F. Stransky, 82–83. Grand Rapids: Eerdmans, 1981.

Bruce, A. B. *The Training of the Twelve*. Grand Rapids: Kregel, 1971.

Brueggemann, Walter. *The Prophetic Imagination*. Minneapolis: Fortress, 2001.

Clowney, Edmund P. *Preaching Christ in All of Scripture*. Wheaton, IL: Crossway, 2003.

———. *The Unfolding Mystery: Discovering Christ in the Old Testament*. 2nd ed. Phillipsburg, NJ: P&R, 2013.

Davis, John Jefferson. *Meditation and Communion with God: Contemplating Scripture in an Age of Distraction*. Downers Grove, IL: IVP Academic, 2012.

Goldsworthy, Graeme. *Preaching the Whole Bible as Christian Scripture*. Grand Rapids: Eerdmans, 2000.

Greidanus, Sidney. *Preaching Christ from the Old Testament: A Contemporary Hermeneutical Method*. Grand Rapids: Eerdmans, 1999.

Guinness, Os. *Fool's Talk: Recovering the Art of Christian Persuasion*. Downers Grove, IL: InterVarsity, 2015.

Jersak, Brad. *Can You Hear Me? Tuning Into the God Who Speaks*. Abbotsford, BC: Fresh Word, 2003.

Johnson, Darrell. *The Glory of Preaching: Participating in God's Transformation of the World*. Downers Grove, IL: IVP Academic, 2009.

Keller, Timothy. *Preaching: Communicating Faith in an Age of Skepticism*. New York: Viking, 2015.

Lewis, C. S. "What are We to Make of Jesus Christ?" In *God in the Dock*, 156–160. Grand Rapids: Eerdmans, 1970.

Lloyd-Jones, Sally. *The Jesus Storybook Bible*. Grand Rapids: Zonderkidz, 2007.

Marsden, George M. *Jonathan Edwards: A Life*. New Haven, CT: Yale University Press, 2003.

Neusner, Jacob. *A Rabbi Talks with Jesus*. Montreal: McGill-Queen's University Press, 2000.

Newbigin, Lesslie. *The Light Has Come: An Exposition of the Fourth Gospel*. Grand Rapids: William B. Eerdmans, 1982.

———. "Religious Pluralism and the Uniqueness of Jesus Christ." *International Bulletin of Missionary Research* 13:2 (April 1989) 50–52.

Nicoll, W. Robertson. *Princes of the Church*. London: Hodder and Stoughton, 1921.

Reeves, Michael. *Rejoicing in Christ*. Downers Grove, IL: IVP Academic, 2015.

———. *Delighting in the Trinity: An Introduction to the Christian Faith*. Downers Grove, IL: IVP Academic, 2012.

Smith, James K. *Desiring the Kingdom: Worship, Worldview, and Cultural Formation*. Grand Rapids: Baker Academic, 2009.

Speer, Robert. *The Finality of Jesus Christ*. Grand Rapids: Zondervan, 1933.

Stott, John R. W. *Between Two Worlds: The Art of Peaching in the Twentieth Century*. Grand Rapids: Eerdmans, 1982.

Lost for Words

How to Read Scripture in a Smartphone World

GEOFF NEW

WHEN IT STRUCK, IT felt like a perfect storm. A series of seemingly unrelated events conspired to confront me. The first weather event occurred when I commenced as Dean of Studies for a denominational training center after 17 years as a pastor. One day while teaching a preaching class, I asked ministry interns to look up a Bible reference. One of the interns began using her smartphone to find the passage. After a moment she half tossed the phone to one side saying to herself, "Where's a Bible? I need to see more of the text!"

In that moment I wondered, "For all the power and accessibility to Scripture that a smartphone affords, has a 12-centimeter screen abbreviated our engagement and experience of Scripture?"[1]

The second contributing weather event for this perfect storm occurred when I was no longer in a congregational setting as the pastor-preacher. I was able to visit multiple contexts and observe "how it was done elsewhere."[2] I observed the practice of projecting the Scripture passage for the sermon onto a large screen. As I looked around the congregation during worship, I noted few if any had a Bible with them. Yes, maybe some had a smartphone or device, yet there was a sense that people were relying on projection of the

---

1. By way of analogy, maybe it is the difference between an analog watch and a digital watch. One allows the user to see the sweep of time and the other a moment in time. My concern here is whether the way we read allows us to appreciate the sweep of Scripture or glimpse merely a fraction of it.

2. My ministry context is Aotearoa New Zealand.

Scriptures on a screen rather than using their own Bibles and continuing to become familiar with their use.

In that moment I wondered, "In projecting Scripture onto screens, have we inadvertently taken the Scriptures out of people's hands?" Alan Jacobs writes:

> Thus the primary way many millions of Christians today encounter Scripture: seated a hundred feet or more from a screen on which they see displayed fifty or so foot-high letters. (Yes, these Christians know that they're supposed to have their own personal Bibles and study them diligently when at home alone, during their "quiet time." But how many do so?) When you consider how thoroughly such a presentation decontextualizes whatever part of the Bible it is interested in—how completely it severs its chosen verse or two from its textual surroundings—how radically it occludes any sense of sequence within the whole of the Bible—it becomes, I think, difficult to worry about the pernicious effects of iPads and Kindles. And impossible to see all screens as having the same effects.[3]

Allowing for the positive aspect of projectors in contexts where books are difficult to access, Jacobs then comments about the use of cell phones and Scripture:

> Curiously, what these tiny screens do to the Bible is almost identical to what the big screens do: reduce it to chunks of one or two verses. It is true that the cell phone reader looks down, and looks down upon his own screen, as opposed to the upward-turning congregant sharing one big screen with many others, but the same decontextualizing effect is at work.[4]

Such is the prevalence and normality of such use I wonder if the effects are largely imperceptible.

A third weather front collided. I began to notice that the main fare of sermons I was hearing was topical. Rather than a sustained treatment of the biblical passage which had been read prior to the commencement of the sermon, there was only a nodding reference to it at best. The sermons were largely bereft of Scriptural engagement and vocabulary. When I preached in these contexts and endeavored to linger in the text, I had the distinct and unnerving unspoken message from the congregation: "what on earth are

---

3. Jacobs, "Christianity and the Future of the Book," 34.
4. Ibid., 34–35.

you doing?!" In those moments I wondered, "As the people of God, are we now in danger of being lost for words—biblical words?"

The Cost of the Internet

Maybe these are separate and unrelated weather events but there does seem to be a climate of a paucity of sermons which linger in the text. A famine of the word (Amos 8:11). With the advent of search engines, screens, and smartphones, our ability to access Scripture is immediate, convenient, and accessible like never before. Yet is there a hidden cost we are paying? Is our experience and engagement with the text abbreviated? Questions about the impact of reading and writing technology on preaching are not new. Yet as a preacher and a user of such technology I am increasingly aware that I am not aware of some of these implications. For example, whereas I was once able to conduct a word-study using various publications to search out the range of meaning of a biblical word and its usage, I discovered that over time my reliance on Bible software has resulted in a loss of that skill. Now with powerful Bible study software, a few mouse clicks gives me colorful graphics and charts like never before. However, one day my software developed an error which I could not rectify. No problem, I simply reached for my word-study books and tools on my shelf. That was when I realised there *was* a problem; I had literally forgotten how to use them!

I need to confess that, up until very recently, I have not given a lot of thought to the implications of technological advances and the effect on the reading, hearing, and preaching of the Scriptures. Yet I do wonder if smartphones, search engines, and screens are like fire; a good servant but a cruel master. Scripture is now immediately and conveniently there on screen yet not quite in hand. Scripture is in people's hearing but mainly seen rather than heard. The images on screen excite the sight (with colorful background) and make it more visual than aural. Maybe it is a bit harsh but is there some relevance now in Isaiah's warning:

> He said, "Go and tell this people:
> 'Be ever hearing, but never understanding;
> be ever seeing, but never perceiving.'
> Make the heart of this people calloused;
> make their ears dull
> and close their eyes.
> Otherwise they might see with their eyes,
> hear with their ears,

understand with their hearts,
and turn and be healed." (Isa 6:9–10)

The issue can be exhilarating and overwhelming. When I began to explore and examine the landscape of this issue I quipped to some colleagues that "I wish I were Amish! Just give me my horse and cart and no technology."[5] I was overwhelmed by the enormity of the task and the complexities and nuances which make up the history of how technological advancements have both placed the Scriptures in our hands and threatened to slap them out of our hands. And maybe that's the thing: "placed the Scriptures in our hands." There's the issue. How does that sit with the majesty of Deut 30:11–14:

> Now what I am commanding you today is not too difficult for you or beyond your reach. It is not up in heaven, so that you have to ask, "Who will ascend into heaven to get it and proclaim it to us so we may obey it?" Nor is it beyond the sea, so that you have to ask, "Who will cross the sea to get it and proclaim it to us so we may obey it?" No, the word is very near you; it is in your mouth and in your heart so you may obey it.[6]

Maybe the speed of accessibility with which we can now access Scripture and the form by which it is in hand is somehow affecting how it enters the heart and how it is proclaimed. Maybe it is in hand but not taken to heart.

I need a vision to navigate the use of technology with Scripture and preaching and I find the ending of 2 John an unexpected source of such a vision.[7] The ending provides a gentle vision of where to go from here as issues of smartphones and preaching coalesce:

---

5. Ironically, not long after I made that flippant comment, I read the following: "Amish technological practices are directed against two vices above all: vanity and the pursuit of material wealth.... [T]he Amish are on to something when it comes to competition. If you're looking for the single strongest reason why technological determinism works as a model of history—why, in the long term, technological developments seem to determine what happens to us as a species—competition is the decisive factor." Chatfield, "The Art of Amistics," 78.

6. This passage from Deuteronomy is quoted in Rom 10:8 also.

7. 3 John 13–14 is practically identical to 2 John 12. The ending of John's gospel has the same sentiment; writing has its limitations. In John 21:25 the Apostle writes, "Jesus did many other things as well. If every one of them were written down, I suppose that even the whole world would not have room for the books that would be written." Taken together, this constellation of verses advances the idea that the technology of writing and reading needs to lead to something else. Writing and reading is not the end of the matter but only the beginning.

> I have much to write to you, but I do not want to use paper and ink. Instead, I hope to visit you and talk with you face to face, so that our joy may be complete. (2 John 12)

"I have much to write you but I do not want to use paper and ink" recognizes the nature of technological connection. "Paper and ink" provide connection in the absence of the person *and* highlight the absence of the person. Writing and reading facilitate connectivity and disjunction.

"I hope to visit you and we will talk face to face" recognizes the nature of human connection. Ideally technology enhances and leads to people communicating in person. Writing and reading are best supplemented with talking and listening.

"So that our joy may be complete" recognizes the nature of human community in Christ. Ultimately it leads to the joy of being connected together in Christ. Insofar as technology and preaching are concerned; reading, writing, talking, and listening are only means to the ultimate end of deepening joy in Christ and the community he is forming.[8]

It's Not What We're Reading but How

The Apostle John is signaling that reading leads to living. If there is one enduring lesson from the history of writing and reading it is this: how we read affects how we live. The Christian church most certainly has not been immune to this lesson. Eugene Peterson makes the intriguing observation that Jesus' question of the lawyer (Luke 10:26) is "What is written in the Law? *How* do you read it?"[9] Note, "how" not "what." Jesus is responding to the question "What must I do to inherit eternal life?" and his answer leads into the parable of the Good Samaritan. The essence of Jesus' question "How do you read?" calls for participation in what we read. "Live what you read. We read the Bible in order to live the word of God."[10] The technological development of writing and reading has changed *how* we read the Scriptures or rather *how* we hear the Word of God. A historical survey of the ways in which the word of God has been mediated and how people have responded is instructive as we consider our engagement with Scripture in a smartphone world. Such a survey tracks the oral and aural to the literary and read.

---

8. Psalm 45:1 also poetically captures the interplay between spoken and written word: "My heart is stirred by a noble theme / as I recite my verses for the king; / my tongue is the pen of a skillful writer."

9. Peterson, *Eat This Book*, 83–84.

10. Ibid., 84.

God spoke the worlds into existence (Gen 1–2; Prov 8:22–31; John 1:1–3, 10; Col 1:15–17; Heb 1:3), commanding and appealing to humanity in the process. He called the Patriarchs (Gen 12:1–3; 26:24; 28:12–15) and then Moses through the burning bush (Exod 3:1–4). Then the finger of God wrote the Ten Commandments on stone tablets (Exod 31:18; 32:15–16), probably the first instance of the word of God being inscribed. "The tablets were the work of God; the writing was the writing of God, engraved on the tablets" (Exod 32:16). Unfortunately the first edition did not last long as Moses smashed them in anger at the Israelites' rapid descent into idolatry (Exod 32). God published a second edition (Exod 34:1). Throughout the Scriptures various moments describe the words of God being captured in print; Jeremiah and Baruch being a classic example (Jer 36). Again though, a second printing was required given that King Jehoiakim had the scroll read to him only to periodically cut off sections and burn it in the fire. Jeremiah dictated it again to Baruch who once again wrote out the scroll. By Jesus' day the Hebrew Scriptures were captured on scrolls and Luke (4:16–21) describes the moment when Jesus read from the scroll of Isaiah. As Jesus read Scripture aloud he announced his ministry and that the year of the Lord's favor was upon them. Throughout the New Testament editorial notes and instructions make it clear that the writing and reading of the Scriptures was the increasing norm (e.g., John 21:25; Rom 16:22; Gal 6:11; Col 4:16; Rev 1:11).

By AD 100 the development of the codex (or book as we know it) was established and this increased the capacity and transportability of the documents. By the sixth and seventh centuries (and particularly up until the eleventh century) monks in Scotland and Ireland introduced spaces between written words so that the Celts could learn Latin.[11] Up until then writing was without punctuation and grammar and was *scriptio continua*; after all, when people spoke there did not seem to be spaces between words so why write with spaces between words? Hence reading was a community event because it needed to be interpreted in the very act of reading. However, with the advent of spaces between words, reading became increasingly a private and mental exercise. The Scriptures began to be written on pages and beautifully adorned; they were incredibly expensive. Theologians of the thirteenth century were called *magister in sacra pagina* (master of the sacred page) signifying the high value of each page.[12] Then, even though the Chinese had invented the printing press several centuries earlier, Gutenberg's

---

11. Phillips, "Scripture in the Age of Google," 40–41. This relatively short article is extraordinary in its breadth and depth of reflection concerning the historical and contemporary technological issues the church has wrestled with and needs to wrestle with. This particular work has had a significant influence on my thinking.

12. Ibid., 41.

invention of the printing press in the sixteenth century is recognized as being of huge significance in the printing and distribution of the Scriptures to the masses. There was, thereafter, a bit of a lull in the technological development of the written word; after all, how do you better the printing press? But eventually, with the development of photography and cinematography and especially electrographic and electrophonic communications in the late nineteenth and early twentieth centuries, we entered the digital era.[13]

A Culture of Distraction

With the advent of the internet, how we read has changed and if history is anything to go by then our living is being affected too. When we read on the internet, we no longer read left-to-right or even top-to-bottom.[14] We read here and there and click on this and that. We are increasingly living in a culture of distraction:

> Perhaps the best counterpoint to our internet age distractibility is a technology that facilitates just the opposite style of thought: the book. . . . Books shielded the mind from distraction, and the reader's thinking could lean on the scaffold of the text to sustain a single line of thought for longer. Readers developed a capacity for deep attention that had been rare in the history of thinking. . . . If a book's fundamental nature is contemplative and empathetic, the internet's is precisely the opposite. The same hyperlinks that layer related pieces of information into a powerful research tool also erode our ability to absorb that information. In studies of online reading in which subjects read passages with varying numbers of embedded links, the more richly-hyperlinked passages led to lower comprehension, even when subjects did not click on any of the links. Each highlighted link is a tax on working memory. The reader must decide each time whether to venture blindly into another, potentially more diverting webpage.[15]

The culture of distraction has been some time in the making. It is intriguing to consider that the concerns of Socrates in the fifth century BC have unnerving relevance in the twenty-first century:

---

13. Chong, "Exploring Innovations, Impacts, and Implications of New Communications and Media Development," 93–94, drawing on Moran, *Introduction to the History of Communication*, 8.
14. Phillips, "Scripture in the Age of Google," 42.
15. Gamble, "Caught in the Net," 64–65.

Writing, said Socrates, was "an aid not to memory, but to reminiscence," and gave to readers, "not truth, but the semblance of truth; they will be hearers of many things and will have learned nothing; they will appear to be omniscient and will generally know nothing; they will be tiresome company, having the show of wisdom without the reality." . . . [A] study by the University College London that examined the browsing habits of visitors to two popular research sites . . . concluded that it was clear that "users are not reading online in the traditional sense; indeed there are signs that new forms of 'reading' are emerging as users 'power browse' horizontally through titles, contents pages, and abstracts, going for quick wins." The worry is a Socratic one: that this wonderful new technology, like writing itself, will only give us the shadow of knowledge—information. Or, as cognitive neuroscientist Maryanne Wolf has put it, the advent of the internet means that people are destined to become mere "decoders of information who have neither the time nor the motivation to think beneath or beyond their googled universes."[16]

This Socratic "worry" has particular relevance for the preacher whose primary skill rests on sound appreciation, adeptness, and agility with the Scriptures and yet seeks to minister in the midst of a culture of distraction:

> Popular interpreters often take Scripture out of context, and as our culture moves increasingly further toward communicating in sound bites and concise tweets the ability to follow an entire argument, relevant to some genres in Scripture, will become increasingly scarce.[17]

The Death of Distance

Combined with this culture of distraction there is a curious paradox: the death of distance *and* an increase in a sense of isolation.

> Electronic culture disembodies and separates us from those closest to us. Most of us are quite unaware of this phenomenon and, in fact, believe our technology is bringing us closer. . . . The near has become far, and the far are brought near. . . . This is the paradox of the electronic age. In this sense it retrieves and combines the characteristics of two previous media eras. If oral

---

16. Dao, "The End of the World," 55–56.
17. Keener, *Spirit Hermeneutics*, 24.

culture is tribal and literate culture is individual the electronic age is essentially a tribe of individuals.[18]

The phrase the "death of distance" has been applied to the advent of technology such as the smartphone and the like.[19] But in the context of worship and the engagement of Scriptures, has it "birthed distance?" Does it bring in another level of distraction and isolation? Once, when speaking to a group of twenty-something Christian professionals, my main takeaway was their observation that when they use their smartphone in worship they feel isolated. They spoke of a sense of disconnect with the rest of the community in the moment they used their smartphone to look up Scripture. They also spoke of a desire for authenticity in it all. I did wonder what the difference was between reading a screen held in your hand and sitting reading with a Bible in your lap. But as a friend pointed out, a smartphone tends to cultivate a degree of self-absorption and distraction, which can lead to a sense of isolation. After all, when was the last time someone pulled out their pocket Bible and began leafing through the pages as they continued their conversation with you? As you think about that, when was the last time someone pulled out their smartphone to read a text message in the middle of a conversation with you? Hence we have a troubling constellation of the effect of the medium of reading affecting our living, a culture of distraction, death of distance, and a new sense of isolation. What does that look like? A rather unnerving example provides a bleak vision.

A person once could pick up a hard copy of the Bible and say "This is a sacred book" and then pick up a pornographic magazine and say "This is a dirty magazine." Now that same person can possess the one device (medium) which can access either.[20] What does that do to a person's approach to the word of God? This is no hypothetical doomsday scenario. As a pastor the most common addiction I encountered in people's lives was an addiction to online pornography. In talking to colleagues in ministry I have discovered that my experience is not an aberration.

Let me put it another way: what difference does smartphone technology make to the question "How do you read?" The oft-quoted saying (by Karl Barth) that "We must hold the Bible in one hand and the newspaper in the other" takes on a different complexion if we consider that literally. By virtue of smartphone technology what does it now mean to have the Bible and newspaper in the one hand?[21] I find Marshall McLuhan's contention that

---

18. Hipps, *Flickering Pixels*, 107.
19. Stafford, "The Face-to-Face Gospel and the Death of Distance," 30–33.
20. Phillips, "Scripture in the Age of Google," 43.
21. Karl Barth is reputed to have said: "We must hold the Bible in one hand and

technologies are both an extension of human abilities and an amputation of human capacities compelling:

> The question "What does technology do *for* me?" must also be accompanied by another question, "What does technology do *to* me?" Otherwise, under the illusion of human advancement, uncritical users will glory in countless extensions while remaining ignorant of the severe amputations that erode critical aspects of their humanity.[22]

For instance, the eye can view a microscopic organism through a microscope (extension) yet in that moment is totally blind (amputation) to a person approaching them. Consider the context of worship and preaching. By virtue of being able to powerfully project images on screen people can see so much more (extension) but at times hear less (amputation). Once I took a group of ministers-in-training to a funeral home to meet with staff and talk through the finer points of death and funerals. I invited the funeral director to have a "free shot"; he had a captive audience of ministers-in-training, what did he want to tell them? In response he spoke about the practice of having images of the deceased projected on screen as the funeral took place. He described how during the eulogies someone would be speaking but the images on screen behind them would detract and distract. He talked about occasions when the congregation would break out in laughter at a humorous photo on screen while the person delivering the eulogy was emotional. Hence seeing was extended and hearing was amputated.

---

the newspaper in the other." Actually, the Center for Barth Studies at Princeton Theological Seminary has not been able to pin down exactly from whence that quote emanated. However, it is widely known that Barth made the Bible/newspaper connection frequently throughout his illustrious career. In an interview from 1966, for example, he stated: "The Pastor and the Faithful should not deceive themselves into thinking that they are a religious society, which has to do with certain themes; they live in the world. We still need—according to my old formulation—the Bible and the Newspaper." Perhaps the source that is most consistent with the alleged quote comes from a *Time* magazine article published on Friday, May 31, 1963, which states: "[Barth] recalls that 40 years ago he advised young theologians 'to take your Bible and take your newspaper, and read both. But interpret newspapers from your Bible.'" Dickerson, "The Bible in One Hand and the Newspaper in the Other," n.p.

22. Chong, "Exploring Innovations," 8–9 (emphasis in original). Chong extrapolates McLuhan's observations, drawing on McLuhan, *Understanding Media*, 11.

Words of Warning from the Tower of Babel

However, maybe it is not fair to lay this all at the feet of a smartphone world. Such effects of technology have been coming for a while and have been with us for a while. In 1975, the novelist Walker Percy wrote about the scenario of a man who visits the Grand Canyon.[23] All his life he has seen photos and postcards of the Grand Canyon and finally he is able to visit it. What does he do upon arrival? He takes a photo.

> A man has come to see a postcard and then turns it into a photo. He never sees the Grand Canyon; he is too busy recording it. His present is instantly deferred into the past. . . . [The] tourist is doing something Kierkegaard describes: *remembering the experience while he's still having it*."[24]

Possibly it is simply that smartphone technology has gathered up all the technological advancements over centuries and literally put them in the palm of our hand. So with the invention of writing, spaces between words and the printing press all coaching us to read silently and mentally, have we become deaf? Further, with the advent of the digital age and the invention of the smartphone powerfully applying such technological advancements, we have been coached to read quickly and selectively; have we become blind? We find ourselves in a paradoxical state whereby we are present *and* distracted; close to the action *and* removed from it. I suppose at the heart of all this I am expressing a concern that we run the risk of dehumanizing our experiences of, and engagement with, God. I am expressing a concern that we are running the risk of dehumanizing our experience of, and engagement with, the Scriptures by reducing it to a technological experience and mediating it by virtue of a machine.

Maybe we are living not so much in the Age of the Internet as much as the Age of the Tower of Babel (Gen 11:1–9). Technology has united us with a common means of communication but is it also the means by which our language is being confused? In our attempt to reach the heavens are we in fact being increasingly scattered? Have we arrived and settled at the plain of Babylon (Gen 11:1–2) and the landscape is one where we fail to see how the medium of reading affects our living, fail to recognize the effect of a

---

23. Cited and described by Stokes, "Have We Forgotten?" 41–42.

24. Ibid., 41–42 (emphasis in original). E.g., Adele confronting a fan at one of her concerts who was recording her: "I wanna tell that lady as well could you really stop filming me with that video camera, because I'm really here in real life. You can enjoy it in real life rather than through your camera. Could you take your tripod down? This isn't a DVD. . . . I'm here for real." Ruby, "Adele Calls Out Fan," n. p.

culture of distraction, and where we celebrate the death of distance yet sense a disturbing undercurrent of isolation? To put it bluntly, are we living under the curse of Babel and are increasingly lost for words?

Words of Life from the Good Samaritan

In an article about the effect of communication technology, Pope Francis makes an intriguing and compelling argument about where technology ought to lead:

> The world of communications can help us either to expand our knowledge or to lose our bearings. The desire for digital connectivity can have the effect of isolating us from our neighbors, from those closest to us. We should not overlook the fact that those who for whatever reason lack access to social media run the risk of being left behind.
> While these drawbacks are real, they do not justify rejecting social media; rather, they remind us that communication is ultimately a human rather than technological achievement. What is it, then, that helps us, in the digital environment, to grow in humanity and mutual understanding? We need, for example, to recover a certain sense of deliberateness and calm. This calls for time and the ability to be silent and to listen.
> How can we be "neighborly" in our use of the communications media and in the new environment created by digital technology? I find an answer in the parable of the Good Samaritan, which is also a parable about communication."[25]

The call for silence and a listening disposition resonates. The embedded message of compassion in the parable of the Good Samaritan (Luke 10:25–37) causes us to consider what technology is doing to us. Is our life together being enriched or eroded? Is the way we are reading enhancing our connection with each other or hindering it? In this new Age of the Tower of Babel is the curse of confused communication being advanced or reversed? Earlier I quoted 2 John 12 to illustrate the interplay between technology ("I have much to write to you, but I do not want to use paper and ink") and community ("Instead, I hope to visit you and talk with you face to face."). As preachers, a listening disposition is our end-game. Thomas Merton wrote: "We must remember that the Bible (which we think of as a book to be *read*)

---

25. Pope Francis, "Communication," n. p.

was originally a body of oral traditions meant to be *recited and listened to in a group especially attuned to its message.*"[26]

Over the years when reading drafts of sermons by pastoral staff members or students, I have found myself increasingly saying, "It's time to stop tweaking and working on this sermon. It'll now be in the telling." The sermon was incomplete but only the community, to which it would be preached, in concert with the Spirit, would complete it. The time of study and solitude now needed the complement of community and communication. The time of preparation and use of technology (paper and ink, keyboard and screen) brings the preacher to the moment of delivery (eyes and ears, hearts and minds). If we consider a stark contrast between being in front of a screen engaging with online content and being in front of people engaging with their lives; how might the two be organically and authentically connected? To put it another way, the word needs to become flesh. Again, Pope Francis puts it well with his treatment of the parable of the Good Samaritan:

> It is not enough to be passersby on the digital highways, simply "connected"; connections need to grow into true encounters. We cannot live apart, closed in on ourselves. We need to love and to be loved. We need tenderness. Media strategies do not ensure beauty, goodness, and truth in communication. The world of media also has to be concerned with humanity, it too is called to show tenderness. The digital world can be an environment rich in humanity; a network not of wires but of people. The impartiality of media is merely an appearance; only those who go out of themselves in their communication can become a true point of reference for others. Personal engagement is the basis of the trustworthiness of a communicator. Christian witness, thanks to the internet, can thereby reach the peripheries of human existence.[27]

So, Now What?

So with all this in mind, as we gather in worship and preach the Scriptures in a digital world, *how* do we read? *How* do we live? *How* do we listen? As preachers, how do we retain the integrity of the triad of Spirit-Scripture-Speaker? How do we honor the centuries-old and present-day divine agenda of engaging with humanity so that God's voice might be heard and responded to? The tension is described in Peter's words quoting the prophet

---

26. Merton, *Opening the Bible*, 53–54 (emphasis in original).
27. Pope Francis, "Communication," n. p.

Isaiah:[28] "All people are like grass, and all their glory is like the flowers of the field; the grass withers and the flowers fall, but the word of the Lord endures forever." (1 Pet 1:24–25)

Technological achievements, for all the good they contribute, will be superseded by advances but will never surpass the word of the Lord as *the* means of hearing God and deepening our life in Christ. As preachers we wrestle with faithfully presenting an ancient and timeless text in an apt and timely fashion. The raw material for sermons is unique. Sacred words gifted and graced by the Spirit through lives spanning millennia. Sacred words which cannot be domesticated by paper and ink, keyboard and screen, signal and data. The inescapability of the word of God is that the primary and lasting means of communicating is speech and hearing:

> The interiorizing force of the oral word relates in a special way to the sacral, to the ultimate concerns of existence. In most religions the spoken word functions integrally in ceremonial and devotional life. Eventually in the larger world religions sacred texts develop, too, in which the sense of the sacral is attached also to the written word. Still, a textually supported religious tradition can continue to authenticate the primacy of the oral in many ways. In Christianity, for example, the Bible is read aloud at liturgical services. For God is thought of always as "speaking" to human beings, not as writing to them. The orality of the mindset in the Biblical text, even in its epistolary sections, is overwhelming. The Hebrew *dabar*, which means word, means also event and thus refers directly to the spoken word. The spoken word is always an event, a movement in time, completely lacking in the thing-like repose of the written or printed word. In Trinitarian theology, the Second Person of the Godhead is the Word, and the human analog for the Word here is not the human written word, but the human spoken word. God the Father "speaks" to his Son: he does not inscribe him. Jesus, the Word of God, left nothing in writing, though he could read and write (Luke 4:16). "Faith comes through hearing," we read in the Letter to the Romans (10:17). "The letter kills, the spirit [breath, on which rides the spoken word] gives life" (2 Corinthians 3:6).[29]

How then might we continue to honor and respond to the word of the Lord in ways which are life-giving? There are dispositions and disciplines for preachers which help us to remain switched on, connected, accessible, and interacting; all those digital world verbs.

---

28. Isa 40:6–8.
29. Ong, *Orality and Literacy*, 74.

PART I: TEXT

Ancient SMS Texting and Web 2.0

I am converted to the need to pray the biblical text as part of sermon preparation.[30] The two agencies of this prayerful practice are *lectio divina* and Ignatian Gospel Contemplation. *Lectio divina* has been utilized by the church for about 1,500 years and its most popular form for about 800 years. *Lectio divina* guides the reader in a careful reading and prayerful engagement with the biblical text. Its particular genius is the focus on a word or phrase from the reading which serves as the gateway for deep reflection and response. Ignatian Gospel Contemplation was developed about 500 years ago by the founder of the Society of Jesus (Jesuits), Ignatius Loyola. Ignatian Gospel Contemplation facilitates a careful immersion into the gospel narrative and involves the five senses in praying the passage of Scripture as if you were actually there. The climax of this particular prayer is using the raw material of engaging with the biblical text to then talk with Jesus as one friend with another. With these two prayer disciplines in mind I find an interesting conversation emerges with the challenges and opportunities of preaching in a smartphone world.

One catalyst for this conversation was my twenty-five-year-old son. I was speaking with him about the contours and challenges of a smartphone world and preaching. His response was surely *lectio divina*, with its emphasis on a word or phrase, is no different to my concern about smartphones abbreviating the text. Furthermore, he added, surely the tearing of the curtain in the temple in the gospels is an analogy of the effect of the printing press and smartphone; access to the Scriptures for all.

Quite.

Given I can no longer send my twenty-five-year-old son to his room it seems that I am forced to respond! I need to concede that he makes some telling points.

I suppose that *lectio divina* can be likened to SMS texting insofar as it focuses on a fraction of a larger body of text or passage. And if *lectio divina* is the twelfth-century version of twenty-first century SMS texting, then Ignatian Gospel Contemplation could be the sixteenth-century version of Web 2.0. By virtue of its practice of drawing on the five physical senses and the imagination, it lends itself to an interactive engagement of the passage that is both restricted and released by the text.

So then, what similarities and inspiration do *lectio divina* and Ignatian Gospel Contemplation have for us living with smartphone technology today? I suggest that forming prayerful habits with these two prayer disciplines

---

30. See New, *Imaginative Preaching,* and New, *Live, Listen, Tell.*

might help strengthen our use of smartphone technology today; especially when it comes to our use of Scripture by the agency of smartphones.

Listen!

Lectio divina was developed, in part, as a response to the constant battle with distractions during prayer. *Lectio divina* provided focus for the heart and mind and sought to minimize competing thoughts. This is about concentration. *Lectio divina* draws the prayer into the biblical text by the agency of the Spirit. This is about connection. *Lectio divina* draws the prayer into dialogue with God about the text and about life. This is about communication. *Lectio divina*—ideally—is not so much a way to pray as much as a way to live. The Benedictine monks' pattern of life and prayer concerning *lectio divina* was *ora, labora, lege* (pray, work, read). This is about community.

In a word, what might be *lectio divina*'s lesson for our use of smartphones for engaging and experiencing Scripture?

Listen!

See!

Turning to Ignatian Gospel Contemplation, what might be the points of intersection with the digital age?

Ignatian Gospel Contemplation was developed, in part, as a corrective to excesses of imaginative engagement with the gospel passages. This is about restraint. Ignatian Gospel Contemplation is a journey intended to go from love of God with your heart, soul, mind, and strength to love of your neighbor. This is about relationship. Ignatian Gospel Contemplation involved the prayer drawing on their whole person to ignite the imagination directed by Scripture and the Spirit. This is about revelation. Ignatian Gospel Contemplation created space for people to pray as they could; it did not call them to pray in ways they could not. The vision was for the prayer to talk with Jesus as "one friend to another." This is about reverence.

In a word, what might be Ignatian Gospel Contemplation's lesson in regards to our use of smartphones for engaging and experiencing Scripture?

See!

Conclusion

Both lessons and sentiments from these two prayer disciplines can be captured by John's description of what happened on the island of Patmos (Rev 1:12): "I turned around to see the voice that was speaking to me." I realize it is a literary device ("see the voice") but I like the juxtaposition of seeing and hearing to describe the moment of encounter with the glorified and ascended Christ. I like how listening and seeing are collapsed into one. As mentioned earlier, the power of the digital device is that we now have the means to connect with the Bible and newspaper in the one device; and to access the sacred and profane via the one device. The fight—and it is centuries old—is to engage with the Scriptures and the Spirit even when life seems full of static and fog. Every age presents its own cultural and technological challenges and opportunities and every generation of preachers needs to attend to Spirit and word in ways which authentically engage with their time and place. I am not advocating a repudiation of the digital age. The digital age actually helps facilitate one aspect that the church needs to recover; a sense of wonder:

> One of the surprising aspects of contemporary digital practice is its openness, and even active search, for experiences of enchantment and transcendence. . . . While interest in organized religion may have diminished, digital practice appears to be ignoring those formal boundaries between the secular and the religious, and actively exploring and playing with enchantment and transcendence.[31]

However, there are some things which simply cannot be improved. Scripture is one of those things. The digital age has gifted access to Scripture like never before but the danger embedded within this ready access is the assumption that such convenience easily translates into engagement and experience of the text. Further, there is the danger of allowing the immediacy of this access to set the pace for the reading, reflection, and preaching of the Scriptures. That pace, I suggest, threatens to be too fast for careful and deliberate attention to the word of God. There is no quick and easy way to absorb the message of God. I might be able to microwave a meal in a fraction of the time that it took my ancestors to roast game over an open fire but I still need to chew and digest the food at the same rate. There are no three easy steps we can lean on and no Google search powerful enough. My mind goes to the words in Deuteronomy 8:6 when Israel was on the eve of entering the promised land and Moses recited their experience of God up to that point:

---

31. Horsfield, *From Jesus to the Internet*, 269.

> He [God] humbled you, causing you to hunger and then feeding you with manna, which neither you nor your ancestors had known, to teach you that people do not live on bread alone but on every word that comes from the mouth of the Lord.

Of course Jesus quoted from this text when tempted in the desert (Matt 3:4). In what ways might God be endeavoring to humble us, causing us to hunger? I wonder about this because maybe, just maybe, we are in a digital wilderness of sorts faced with the threat of being lost for words; biblical words. Our digital context can be likened to a wilderness marked by promise and temptation. A place whereby God is humbling us and inviting us to recognize our hunger pangs so that we can learn a crucial spiritual lesson: feed on the word of the Lord. *Feed* on the word of the Lord because our current wandering in this context threatens to starve us of hearing the word from the mouth of the Lord. *Feed* on the word of the Lord because our current wandering in this context threatens to blind us from seeing the works of the Lord. May we pray that we will see and hear. I love the prayer of the great twentieth-century rabbi Abraham Heschel: "I did not ask for success; I asked for wonder. And you gave it to me."[32] When all is seen and heard through our reading, preaching, and living of Scripture, may we know the wonder of life in and through Jesus Christ our Lord and Savior. May we not be lost for words but enlivened by the word.

---

32. Quoted by Samuel H. Dresner in his introduction to Heschel, *I Asked for Wonder*, 7.

Bibliography

Chatfield, Tom. "The Art of Amistics." *New Philosopher* 11 (2016) 78.

Chong, Calvin. "Exploring Innovations, Impacts, and Implications of New Communications and Media Development." *JAET* 18:2 (2014) 93–94.

Dao, Andre. "The End of the World." *New Philosopher* 11 (2016) 55–56.

Dickerson, Tracy. "The Bible in One Hand and the Newspaper in the Other." *Nacreous Kingdom* (blog), 22 October 2010. http://nacreouskingdom.blogspot.co.nz/2010/10/bible-in-one-hand-and-newspaper-in.html.

Dresner, Samuel H. "Introduction." In *I Asked for Wonder: A Spiritual Anthology*, by Abraham Joshua Heschel, edited by Samuel H. Dresner. New York: Crossroad, 2010.

Gamble, Jessa. "Caught in the Net." *New Philosopher* 11 (2016) 64–65.

Hipps, Shane. *Flickering Pixels: How Technology Shapes Your Faith*. Grand Rapids: Zondervan, 2009.

Horsfield, Peter G. *From Jesus to the Internet: a History of Christianity and Media*. Chichester, UK: Wiley-Blackwell, 2015.

Jacobs, Alan. "Christianity and the Future of the Book." *The New Atlantis* 33 (2011) 34.

Keener, Craig S. *Spirit Hermeneutics: Reading Scripture in Light of Pentecost*. Grand Rapids: Eerdmans, 2016.

McLuhan, Marshall. *Understanding Media: The Extensions of Man*. New York: McGraw-Hill, 1965.

Merton, Thomas. *Opening the Bible*. Collegeville, MN: Liturgical, 1970.

Moran, Terence P. *Introduction to the History of Communication: Evolutions and Revolutions*. New York: Peter Lang, 2010.

New, Geoff. *Imaginative Preaching: Praying the Scriptures so God can Speak Through You*. Carlisle: Langham Global Library, 2015.

———. *Live, Listen, Tell: the Art of Preaching*. Carlisle: Langham Preaching Resources, 2017.

Ong, Walter J. *Orality and Literacy: The Technologizing of the Word*. London: Methuen, 1982.

Peterson, Eugene. *Eat this Book: A Conversation in the Art of Spiritual Reading*. Grand Rapids: Eerdmans, 2006.

Phillips, Robin. "Scripture in the Age of Google." *Touchstone* 25:4 (2012) 40–41.

Pope Francis. "Communication at the Service of an Authentic Culture of Encounter." A Message for the 48th World Communications Day, 1 June 2014. https://w2.vatican.va/content/francesco/en/messages/communications/documents/papa-francesco_20140124_messaggio-comunicazioni-sociali.html

Ruby, Jennifer. "Adele Calls Out Fan for Filming Her During Concert: 'I'm Really Here in Real Life.'" *Evening Standard* (31 May 2016) http://www.standard.co.uk/showbiz/celebrity-news/adele-calls-out-fan-for-filming-her-during-concert-i-m-really-here-in-real-lifea3259971.html.

Stafford, Tim. "The Face-to-Face Gospel and the Death of Distance." *Christianity Today* 54:6 (2010) 30–33.

Stokes, Patrick. "Have We Forgotten How to Forget?" *New Philosopher* 11 (2016) 41–42.

Karl Barth's Theology of Preaching

ANDREA MCDOUGALL

KARL BARTH WRITES ABOUT preaching as a pastor, a preacher, and a theologian, and his insights into the task of preaching continue to be relevant and challenging.[1] One of the greatest theologians of the last few centuries, Barth learned firsthand what it is to wrestle, week after week, with the question of what to preach on Sunday morning. Born in Switzerland in 1886, Barth studied theology in Switzerland and in Germany. Then, after two years working for a congregation in Geneva, Barth served as the pastor for the small Swiss industrial town of Safenwil for ten years. Again and again, as he prepared his sermons, he found himself being called back to the Bible: drawn to study the word of God and to seek to hear what God had to say to him and to his congregation. Barth learned that we are to know God by looking to where God chooses to reveal himself: in Jesus Christ as attested to in Scripture. Consequently, Barth insists that preachers are to use Scripture as the

---

1. As a theologian, Barth wrote extensively about preaching, including lectures on homiletics. (See Barth, *Prayer and Preaching*.) Barth's theological understanding of preaching is to be found in various places. See especially Barth, *The Word of God and Theology*a, 101–29; Barth, *The Göttingen Dogmatics*, 30–41, 263–313; and also Barth, *Church Dogmatics*, I/2, 743–58. Some of Barth's sermons have been translated into English: see, for example, Barth, *Deliverance to the Captives*; Barth, *Call for God*; Barth and Thurneysen, *Come Holy Spirit*. Also available is a book containing some of the prayers that Barth wrote to accompany his sermons: Barth, *Selected Prayers*. For an extensive treatment of Barth's thinking on preaching, see Willimon, *Conversations with Barth on Preaching*, and for a detailed examination of Barth's hermeneutics see Burnett, *Karl Barth's Theological Exegesis*. This is not intended to be an exhaustive bibliography of Barth's writing on preaching, but suggestions for interested readers to explore.

foundation for their sermons—the preacher's task is to let the Bible speak. Barth developed a high view of preaching: the preacher and the congregation are to expect that God will speak through the preached word. Through the work of the Holy Spirit, preaching becomes the word of God. Because preaching has to do with both human speech and divine speech, prayer is essential when preparing sermons and when preaching. Before examining Barth's practical insights into the task of preaching, it is instructive to examine the underlying theology.

Barth's theology of preaching can be illustrated by considering the print of the Isenheim altarpiece by Matthias Grünewald that Barth had hanging on the wall in his study for decades.[2] This portrayal of the crucifixion of Jesus Christ parallels Barth's christocentric theology. In the center of the picture, Christ hangs on the cross; there is no attempt made to disguise the agony of this. Nailed to the cross above Christ's head is a sign saying "INRI."[3] Grünewald depicts Christ's importance by painting the figure of Christ far larger than any of the other figures. To the viewer's left is a distraught Mary looking up to Jesus, being supported by the disciple John, and a kneeling Mary Magdalene, also looking up to Jesus. On the other side of Jesus Christ, a lamb holding a cross looks up to Jesus, and John the Baptist stands, looking up to Jesus, holding the open Scriptures in one hand, and pointing to Jesus with his other hand. To draw attention to the way that John the Baptist points away from himself and towards Christ, his pointing finger is slightly elongated. Next to his pointing hand are written the words of John the Baptist from John 3:30: "*Illum oportet crescere, me autem minue*" (He must increase, while I must decrease). In *Church Dogmatics*, Barth writes of the need for Christology to follow the lead of John the Baptist, and point to Jesus Christ while holding the Scriptures: Barth asks, "Could anyone point away from himself more impressively and completely . . . ? And could anyone point more impressively and realistically than here to what is indicated?"[4] As preachers, we too need to follow the lead of John the Baptist. We are to approach preaching by opening Scripture and pointing away from ourselves and towards Jesus Christ; we are to bear faithful witness to Jesus Christ, as attested to in Scripture.

---

2. See p. 26 for a reproduction of this image. Barth himself uses this picture to illustrate his theological stance. See Barth, *Church Dogmatics* I/1, 112; Barth, *Church Dogmatics* I/2, 125.

3. These are the Latin initials for Jesus of Nazareth, King of the Jews (John 19:19).

4. Barth, *Church Dogmatics* I/1, 112.

The Threefold Word of God

Barth believes that preaching is a form of God's self-revelation. He speaks of the threefold word of God: the word of God in Jesus Christ; the word of God in Scripture; and the word of God in preaching. These are not three different words, but three different forms of the one word of God. Jesus Christ is the self-revelation of God; the word of God in Scripture witnesses to the revelation of God in Jesus Christ; and the word of God in preaching witnesses to the revelation of God in Jesus Christ as attested to in Scripture.[5] The term witness is perhaps not strong enough, for Barth believes that Scripture and proclamation do not simply point to the Word of God, but that God actually speaks through the words of Scripture and through preaching.[6] To speak of preaching as the word of God is guaranteed to raise eyebrows, and Barth freely admits that it sounds like arrogance or hyperbole to say that the preaching of the word of God is the word of God.[7]

> But, some might say, how can we theologians come to speak God's word in *our* words? Or, some congregation might say, how can we come to hear God's word in the words of this or that pastor who has nothing to offer us, or in the words of all pastors, none of whom we trust? . . . If we expected to hear God's word more, we would hear it more even in the weak and perverted sermons. The statement that there was nothing in it for me should often read that I was not ready to let anything be said to me.[8]

Barth insists that preaching does not merely point to the word of God: preaching is the word of God, due to "the wholly new reality of the Spirit of

---

5. Ibid., 120–21.

6. This was the conviction of the Reformers: "The preaching of the word of God *is* the word of God" (Second Helvetic Confession, chapter 1).

7. Ibid., 268.

8. Barth goes on to say: "What is needed here is repentance by *both* pastors and congregations. . . . This does not mean that congregations must say Yea and Amen to all the words of their reverend pastors. Pastors are sinners. They are unprofitable servants with all their words even though they do all that they are under obligation to do (Luke 17:10). Nevertheless, they are servants of the Most High (Dan 3:26). They speak in his name. They carry out his commission, which is a reality even today. No matter how well or how badly they do it, this in the presupposition of listening to them. . . . They know fear and trembling whenever they mount the pulpit. They are crushed by the feeling of being poor human beings who are probably more unworthy than all those who sit before them. Nevertheless, precisely then it is still a matter of God's word. The word of God that they have to proclaim is what judges them, but this does not alter the fact—indeed, it *means*—that they have to proclaim it. This is the presupposition of their proclaiming it." Barth, *Göttingen Dogmatics*, 33–35.

God, which we can only await afresh, understand afresh, and need to seek and find and thankfully receive afresh."[9]

Because the preacher is dependent upon the work of the Holy Spirit, prayer is indispensable to the work of sermon preparation. As preachers, we are called to be diligent in our work, but it is prayer, rather than exegesis, that is "the decisive activity" in our understanding of God's Word.[10] We are to pray that God will speak—and that we will hear—as we prepare sermons.

The preacher's reliance on prayer and the work of the Holy Spirit does not, however, negate the need to spend time and effort in sermon preparation: preaching is both a human work and a divine work. What Barth says about the Reformation could also describe his understanding of preaching: "an action of certain [people] and, at the same time, a response on the part of God."[11] Because preaching is a human task, the possibility exists that it may be carried out well or badly; it may be approached profoundly or superficially. Nevertheless, the human task of preaching is blessed by God: the Holy Spirit is at work in the preacher and the hearer wherever the gospel is sincerely preached.[12] The preacher (and the hearers) can be assured that the inadequate human activity of preaching has God's blessing when it is undertaken in obedience to God's command: "Preaching is a human activity and thus stained with sin, but it is also both commanded and blest by God and thus a promise is attached to it."[13]

Scripture is to be the Basis for Preaching

Barth's belief that preaching is the word of God is inseparable from his insistence that preaching is to be based on Scripture; preaching is to convey what God says through Scripture to our current situation. While the question of what Scripture meant to its first hearers is not to be overlooked, Barth emphasizes that the role of the preacher is not to focus on that, but to hear and convey what God says through Scripture to us in our context. Good preaching requires confidence that God does speak to us here and now, and that God "brings to life in this present age the testimony of the prophets and apostles."[14] The preachers' role is to listen to hear what God is saying to us today through Scripture and then to present this word of God to the

9. Ibid., 268.
10. Barth, *Church Dogmatics* I/2, 695.
11. Barth, *Prayer & Preaching*, 9.
12. Ibid., 82.
13. Ibid., 87.
14. Ibid., 105.

congregation.[15] This requires preachers to approach Scripture trustingly, attentively, and expectantly.

Preachers demonstrate their trust in Scripture by using Scripture alone as the foundation for the sermon. Barth insists that giving Scripture this exclusive priority is appropriate, because it is through Scripture that we have the revelation of God in Jesus Christ. Consequently, Scripture is not one of a number of equally valid possibilities for a foundation for preaching. Barth is adamant that "The gospel is not a truth among other truths. Rather, it sets a question-mark against all truths."[16] Every ideology that we are drawn to needs to be examined in the light of God's word, so that our ideas and ideals can be questioned and corrected by the word of God. Barth insists that "the message which Scripture has to give us, even in its apparently most debatable and least assimilable parts, is in all circumstances truer and more important than the best and most necessary things that we ourselves have said or can say."[17] We are not to set any of our ideas or ideologies or our understandings of ourselves and our society alongside, or in place of, Scripture as equally plausible foundations from which a sermon can be built; to do so would permit our philosophies to usurp the place of Scripture. As Barth insists, "Ideas which occupy the mind must be subject to correction by the text of Scripture; one must not adopt the demeanor of one who knows in advance what the truth is."[18] This is not to say that God cannot and will not speak other than through Scripture: God is free to speak through whatever he chooses. As Barth picturesquely states: "God may speak to us through Russian Communism, a flute concerto, a blossoming shrub, or a dead dog," or "through a pagan or an atheist."[19] Yet, while there is no limit on who or what God can speak through, as Christian preachers we are called to proclaim God's word that is heard in Scripture.

While preaching requires God to speak in order to be the word of God, preaching is also a human work that requires preachers to prepare by paying close attention to the text week by week. This requires us as preachers to apply ourselves to rigorous exegesis, including the detailed and arduous work

---

15. "God makes use, according to his good pleasure, of the ministry of the preacher, whose duty is to proclaim to his listeners what God himself has to say to them, by explaining in his own words, a passage from Scripture which concerns them personally." Ibid., 65.

16. Barth, *The Epistle to the Romans*, 35.

17. Barth, *Church Dogmatics* I/2, 719. The preacher "is not required . . . to enlarge on what he thinks about his own life or that of his neighbor, his reflections on society or the world." Barth, *Prayer & Preaching*, 89.

18. Ibid., 91.

19. Barth, *Church Dogmatics* I/1, 55.

of historical and linguistic study. We may protest that this is too demanding in terms of time, or that our ability is limited. Barth, however, has such a high view of preaching that he regards sermon preparation as the minister's prime duty. To show the respect for the text that Barth calls for requires preachers to dedicate a significant amount of time to sermon preparation, to guard against procrastination and sloth, and to spend time learning. The sermon preparation that Barth envisages presupposes a substantial amount of prior knowledge of biblical languages, biblical studies, and theology—Barth would always read the text in the original language, and found it difficult to fathom pastors not doing this. Changing emphases in seminaries and universities in much of the world, however, mean that fewer preachers can engage with Hebrew and Greek.[20] To compensate for this lack, it is necessary to use commentaries to help us with the original languages of the texts, and be diligent in our reading.

Spending so much time in historical study, linguistic study, and exegesis means that as preachers we need to take care not to inadvertently alienate the congregation by overwhelming them with detailed exegetical findings. Preachers need to exercise restraint when deciding what to include in the sermon, for the sermon is not to be used as a platform for us as preachers to showcase our knowledge of biblical criticism or our breadth of reading. The purpose of study and sermon preparation is neither to impress others nor to set ourselves on a pedestal above the congregation: the aim of devoting time to sermon preparation is to pay close attention to God's word, seeking to hear God's word for us in our current situation—as individuals, as a congregation, and as a society. We are called to present the congregation with God's word, not with our own erudite insights (or those of others); for this we need to rely on the same Holy Spirit who inspired the writers of Scripture. This reliance on the Holy Spirit is not to diminish the importance of sermon preparation, nor to diminish the importance of having the sermon written beforehand: we cannot presume that the Holy Spirit will inspire us as we speak. Furthermore, Barth notes that preaching is so significant "that an account will have to be given of every idle word."[21]

The preacher's task is to make the word of God heard, without complicating or distracting from the message.[22] Barth calls us to focus on Jesus Christ, pointing away from ourselves and to Jesus Christ—as John the Bap-

---

20. There are, of course, still places where pastors would be expected to have a good reading knowledge of Greek and Hebrew. In Tubingen in southwest Germany, for example, the German theology students I spoke with were astounded to learn that many pastors in New Zealand could not read Hebrew or Greek.

21. Barth, *Prayer & Preaching*, 100.

22. Ibid., 85.

tist does in Grünewald's *Isenheim Altarpiece*. He urges preachers to "beware of intruding one's own individuality or enlarging on one's personal experience by using illustrations or parables drawn from events in one's own life."[23] Speaking about ourselves leads to the possibility that we, rather than Jesus Christ, will be the focus of the sermon. Barth advises preachers against using personal anecdotes as these can distract the congregation from hearing the word of God. This sounds impersonal, but it is perhaps a useful corrective to the cult of personality and the temptation to use our experience, rather than Scripture, as the foundation for preaching. While I appreciate hearing how others seek to live out the gospel, when preachers deploy illustrations from their own lives the focus can easily move from the person and work of Christ to the person and work of the preacher; the focus can easily move from sharing the good news to being entertaining. Furthermore, such illustrations can alienate the listener by setting the preacher on a pedestal, minimizing the preacher's failings, or telling of their failings in a way that fails to lead the congregation to hear what God is saying to them. Rather than using anecdotes in his sermons, Barth encourages his hearers to identify with him by speaking of their shared situation, and of the offer of forgiveness and grace that God extends to them all, and of the need that they all share for this.

Having emphasized that the role of the preacher is to bear witness to Jesus Christ as attested to in Scripture, Barth is concerned that sermon introductions can interfere with this by leading the hearers to focus elsewhere.[24] An elaborate introduction can divert our thoughts from the word of God, and a lengthy introduction runs the risk of taking too much time, which detracts from the word. Introductions are also intrusive when the preacher attempts to describe the contemporary situation to a congregation who actually know more about this than the preacher does.

Preachers need to avoid overly elaborate introductions, for the preacher is called only to "play the part of a messenger who has a message to deliver; he must not try to build a stair . . . ; he does not have to ascend the heights, for, in truth, what happens is that something comes down from on high to us, but only if, from the start, it is the Bible that speaks."[25] Throughout the sermon, but especially in the introduction, the preacher can be tempted to appeal to some authority other than Scripture, giving another authority priority over Scripture. This focus on Scripture does not mean that the sermon will lack interest: Barth observes that "Scripture is in fact so interesting, it

23. Ibid., 100.
24. Ibid., 110–12.
25. Ibid., 112.

has many new and startling things to tell us, that those who listen cannot possibly be overcome with sleep!"[26]

Because as preachers we are to present God's word which we have heard, we are to approach Scripture expectantly, anticipating that we will hear God speaking. It is not enough to believe that as we study Scripture God is *theoretically* able to speak or that God may *perhaps* speak; we must expect that God *will* speak. Expecting that God will speak means expecting that our own understandings could be called into question; it means approaching Scripture being ready to learn and open to new discoveries.[27]

Choosing a Text

Using Scripture as the basis for preaching raises the question of what text to select each week. Barth recommends either using a lectionary to determine the texts, or else preaching through a book of the Bible. Selecting the text using either of these methods can reduce the temptation for preachers to show a disregard for Scripture by detaching texts from their context. In order to preserve some of the context, the text chosen should not be too brief. Using preselected texts also avoids the temptation to choose the text in order to validate and reinforce what we have already determined to say. This temptation can be particularly insidious when preaching on a theme: Barth warns that preachers of thematic sermons are especially prone to do violence to the text, and also to resist being questioned by the text.[28] Thematic preaching can readily consist of comfortable ideas that conform to ideologies of the day, whereas what the text has to say to us in our current situations is, Barth observes, "generally much less comfortable."[29] A utilitarian use of Scripture—using Scripture as a vehicle to promote an ideology we already hold—is wrong, for the text is to determine the sermon. Scripture does not exist in order to prop up our own ideas or embellish our preconceived sermons. The task of preaching requires us to put our ideas and our comfort to one side, and hear what the Spirit is saying to the church.

Barth notes that "the Christian proclamation is the proclamation of Jesus Christ. He is the Word which became flesh, and therefore he is also the

26. Ibid., 93.

27. This expectation comes from a belief in the inspiration of Scripture that is not simply academic assent. Barth describes it thus: "as regards the 'doctrine of inspiration,' it is not enough to believe in it; one must ask oneself: am I expecting it? Will God speak to me in this Scripture? This expectation must be active; it means giving oneself to the Scriptures, seeking in order that one may be found." Barth, *Prayer & Preaching*, 92.

28. Ibid., 108.

29. Ibid., 108.

word about man."³⁰ Rather than using Scripture to bolster our own ideas, or attempting to extract an idea from the text, preachers are called to see how the text bears witness to Jesus Christ. This focus on the person and work of Christ does not mean that the preacher is to restrict themselves to only preaching from the New Testament. The texts used for preaching must be drawn from across the whole canon of Scripture. The preacher is not to regard the Old Testament simply as a record of historical events, but to recognize that the whole of Scripture witnesses to the revelation of God in Christ Jesus. Barth insists that, although the Old Testament is Jewish, Christian preachers are to read it christologically, for it tells us of "the covenant which God has made with all who are the children of Abraham in faith, and which God has sealed in Jesus Christ once and for all."³¹

As preachers, we are to be wary of relying too heavily on the work of others, and instead *ourselves* bear witness to the gospel of Christ. Now that sermons and commentaries are so readily available on the internet, it is more pertinent than ever to keep in mind Barth's insistence that preachers are to discover *themselves* what *God* has to say to their situation through the text, and not rely too heavily on what others say. Commentaries have their place; they are integral to detailed biblical study, but the preacher is not to abdicate their responsibility to themselves seek to hear what God would say in the context of their own situation, and then present this *in their own words*. The preacher has the dual task of keeping faithful to the text and faithful to life. While others are undoubtedly more erudite and eloquent than we ourselves are, and can express an idea far better than we ourselves can, Barth argues that it is a mistake to think that using the words of others will engage the congregation more, for doing so is likely to distance the congregation.³² Barth warns that "the finest thoughts, once they have been borrowed and transformed on the lips of another, are no longer what they were. Let there be no posturing in borrowed plumes!"³³ When we share what we have discovered as we have studied the Scriptures, when we share what we believe God is saying to us here and now, we speak with far more energy and conviction than when we repeat the words of others. We need to have confidence that God has called us as individuals—not to bring before the congregation the thoughts of others, but to bring what we believe that God is saying to us and our congregation. Rather than misplaced humility

---

30. Barth, *God Here and Now*, 3.
31. Barth, *Word of God*, 25.
32. Barth, *Prayer & Preaching*, 96.
33. Ibid.

(or slothfulness) leading us to lean too heavily on the work of others, we are to rely on the Holy Spirit to speak to us and through us.

How is the Preacher to Relate to the Congregation?

To bear faithful witness to God's reconciling love requires us as preachers to be aware of our own need to be forgiven, and to know God's forgiveness and grace in our own lives. In fact, Barth says that "We become *worthy* of being believed only by acknowledging our own unworthiness."[34] Preachers are not to preach the law—and subsequent condemnation of sin—separately from preaching God's grace. Joseph Newton observes that Barth understands the preacher as "a bringer of the divine word, so far as human words can upbear it, not denouncing men like the prophet, but calling for faith, repentance, obedience, and proclaiming the gospel of reconciliation in which warning is blended with 'the wooing note' of love."[35] As preachers, we are to stand before the congregation as repentant sinners, who know the grace that God offers and who are willing to tell others what this experience of God's grace means for us. In his commentary on the epistle to the Philippians, Barth talks about the propensity each of us can have to set ourselves above or apart from others, and recommends we address this by getting down from our high chair—where we have elevated ourselves in order to look down on others—leaving our own island—where we have chosen to isolate ourselves from others—and going to where others are in order to serve their interests.[36] This, Barth argues, is what it means to have the mind that is appropriate to being in Christ Jesus. This call to humbly serve others is especially pertinent for preachers.

The preacher is to be a person of faith, hope, love, and joy. The preacher is called to have faith in God, the one who loves in freedom, who has spoken, and who will speak again. The preacher is to approach sermon preparation and sermon delivery with hope, hoping expectantly that God will speak again. The preacher is to approach preaching and preparation as an act of loving service, as a task entered into out of love for God and out of love for those to whom the preacher is called to preach. The task of preaching requires the preacher to know and to love those who hear their sermons. Because the preacher brings glad tidings, heralding the good news of Jesus Christ, the preacher is also to be joyful.[37]

34. Barth, *Word of God*, 129.
35. Barth and Thurneysen, *Come Holy Spirit*, xv.
36. See Barth, *Epistle to the Philippians*, 58–59.
37. For the characteristics of a preacher, see Barth, *Prayer & Preaching*, 72, 83, 87,

Preaching God's reconciling love requires preachers to have the courage to present the word of God, even though this challenges them and their congregations and calls for repentance. Preachers are to be aware that we, like the congregation, need to hear the word of God even—and perhaps especially—when it confronts and disturbs. As preachers, we must not allow a fear of discomforting ourselves or alienating our hearers cause us to betray our calling by leading us to refrain from saying what Scripture has to say to us here and now. The word confronts and disturbs, but it does so in order to bring peace. Since as preachers we are called to love our congregations, and not unnecessarily cause offense, this confronting and disturbing word must be brought with gentleness, love, and tact; it is to be accompanied by the word of grace. Preachers are not to hold back from presenting God's "No," God's call to repentance, but this "No" is always to be contained within God's "Yes," God's word of forgiveness and grace. The task of the preacher is not to condemn people or cause them to despair, but to bring the good news of the gospel of Christ: to tell the congregation that God's mercy avails and that it avails for them. This does not mean that the same message will be brought each week: Scripture contains a wealth of riches, and the preacher is to share the variety of these riches with the congregation.[38]

As the sermon is being prepared, the preacher must keep in mind the congregation and the society in which they live, so that Christian truth is set in the context of daily life. The preacher must "know the congregation as individuals; he must be acquainted with the conditions which shape their lives, with their capacities, and their potentialities for good and evil. Only so will he find the means to touch their hearts so that the word may have significance for them."[39] This attention to the congregation and their context helps the preacher to hear what God has to say in today's world. Barth advises preachers "to take your Bible and take your newspaper, and read both. But interpret newspapers from your Bible."[40] Scripture must be allowed to interpret and question our context.

96, 105. Barth's understanding of God as the one who loves in freedom is detailed in Barth, *Church Dogmatics, Volume II/1*, 257–677.

38. Barth, *Prayer & Preaching*, 106.

39. Ibid., 106. Barth also observes that the preacher is not "a hermit dwelling apart from their congregation." Ibid., 97.

40. "Barth in Retirement," n.p.

The Importance of Prayer

According to Barth, prayer has a twofold importance for preaching. We noted earlier the importance of prayer for sermon preparation, for preachers rely upon God to speak as they develop the sermon. In addition, at the time of preaching the preacher and the congregation are to acknowledge their reliance upon God speaking, and petition God to speak to them. Convinced of the importance of prayer to the act of preaching, Barth composed prayers to precede and follow his sermons. Initially, these prayers consisted of a free combination of passages from the Psalms, but later Barth began writing prayers directly related to the topic of the sermon. Barth regarded these prayers for use before and after the sermon as so essential to the sermons that he would only allow his sermons to be published in a book if the accompanying prayers were also included.[41] At approximately two hundred and fifty words each, these prayers are far more substantial than the brief prayers that so often precede or follow sermons. I have found that composing prayers with the Scripture and sermon in mind has sometimes resulted in a reshaped sermon. The following prayer, written to precede a sermon, gives an idea of the nature of the prayers that Barth would formulate.

> Lord, our God, you know who we are: people with good consciences and people with bad consciences—content and discontented, secure and insecure people—Christians out of conviction and traditional Christians—believers, those who half-believe, and unbelievers. And you know where we come from: from a circle of relatives, friends, and acquaintances, or from greater solitude; from peaceful prosperity or from all kinds of difficulty and hardship; from orderly or fraught or ruined families; from a close circle of Christian fellowship or from the margins.
>
> But now we all stand before you; in all our inequality we are equal in this: that we are all in the wrong before you and also between ourselves; that we all some time must die; that we would all be lost without your grace; but we are also equal in that your grace is promised to, and turned toward, all of us through your beloved Son, our Lord Jesus Christ.
>
> We are here together, in order to glorify you, by letting you speak to us. We ask that this may take place in this hour, in the name of your Son, our Lord. Amen.[42]

Composing such prayers is invaluable for preachers as they prepare their sermons, and these prayers are also formative for the congregation,

---

41. Barth, *Selected Prayers*, 6.
42. Barth, *Fünfzig Gebete*, 11. See also Barth, *Selected Prayers*, 11.

as they join in praying that God will speak to them. The prayer that Barth composed to follow this sermon also shows the reliance that we have on God to speak and to help us to hear the good news and live accordingly. This prayer begins:

> Beloved Heavenly Father. We thank you for that eternal, living, saving word, that you have spoken and that you still speak to us in Jesus. But do not let us hear it fleetingly and be too lazy to obey it. Do not let us fall, but remain with your comfort by each of us and with your peace between each of us and our fellow-men. . . .[43]

Barth emphasizes the importance of accompanying sermons with prayer because preaching relies on God speaking and shedding light on our current situation. Consequently, Barth insists that "it is not possible to preach without praying that the words spoken may become the call of God to the congregation; and, moreover, the whole congregation should join in that prayer."[44] Barth's insistence that prayer is indispensable to theology—"The first and basic act of theological work is prayer"—is equally true of preaching: prayer is the first and basic act of preaching.[45] The preacher and the hearers all "necessarily rely on the free grace of God and therefore on prayer."[46] The preacher is to expect that they will hear God speak during sermon preparation; the congregation and the preacher are to expect that they will hear God speak as the sermon is being preached.

Because preachers are called by God and rely on the Holy Spirit, preachers are not to be intimidated by the demands of preaching; nor is preaching to be a source of pride. Barth's insistence that God is the active subject who causes preaching to become the word of God is freeing, for we can be assured that the efficacy of our preaching comes from God speaking, and not from any innate or learned ability that we might have to create eloquent and stirring speech and clever images.[47] We are given the immense task of speaking the word of God, but the enormity of this task is not to crush us: instead, we are to rely on the Holy Spirit to speak the word of God as we immerse ourselves in Scripture. Because the power in preaching

---

43. Barth, *Fünfzig Gebete*, 11–12. See also Barth, *Selected Prayers*, 12.
44. Barth, *Prayer & Preaching*, 98.
45. Barth, *Evangelical Theology*, 160.
46. Barth, *Church Dogmatics* I/2, 755.
47. "Preaching should be an explanation of Scripture; the preacher does not speak 'on' but 'from,' drawing from the Scriptures whatever he says. He does not have to invent but rather repeat something." Barth, *Prayer & Preaching*, 69. "The *promise* of Christian proclamation is this: That we *speak God's Word*." Barth, *Word of God*, 122.

comes from the Holy Spirit, and because the preacher's task is to point away from themselves and to Jesus Christ, preachers must not be puffed up.

Preaching is to be Given Priority

While technology has wrought huge changes in society and in the way in which we access information, Barth's understanding of preaching as a divine and human work still speaks to us today. Barth encourages congregations to take preaching seriously, to expect that, as they listen to the word proclaimed, God will speak to them about their current situation. Barth does not offer any easy answers for the preacher's question of what to preach each Sunday; instead, he calls for time-consuming exegesis and attention to detail, all the while bearing in mind that preaching depends on the work of the Holy Spirit. Barth calls on preachers to take the task of preaching seriously and diligently: to trust Scripture, to pay zealous attention to the text, and to expect that God will speak to us about life here and now. Preachers are not to be overwhelmed by the task: while we are to work hard, we are dependent on the Holy Spirit to speak the word of God and to give us ears to hear, both during sermon preparation, and when the sermon is preached. This reliance on God calls for prayer at the time of preparation and prayer at the time of preaching.

Congregations may seek a pastor who will be a manager or a program developer or a pastoral carer; Barth provides a timely reminder that, of all the many calls on a pastor's time and energy, sermon preparation needs to be allocated a significant amount of time. Barth emphasizes that the preacher's task is not to entertain or give sage advice or provide exegetical teaching: preachers are called to study Scripture, to prayerfully seek what God says to us here and now, and to present that to the congregation. Barth calls preachers away from a reliance on others, on the ideologies, books, and commentaries of others—and away from a reliance on our own ideologies, wisdom, and eloquence—towards a reliance on God. Barth reminds us that as preachers we are called to be faithful to the text, to the community, and, most of all, to Christ.

Bibliography

Barth, Karl. *Call for God.* Translated by A. T. Mackay. London: SCM, 1967.
———. *Church Dogmatics, Volume I, Part 1: The Doctrine of the Word of God.* Edited by G. W. Bromiley and T. F. Torrance. Edinburgh: T. & T. Clark, 1975.
———. *Church Dogmatics, Volume I, Part 2: The Doctrine of the Word of God.* Edited by G. W. Bromiley and T. F. Torrance. Edinburgh: T. & T. Clark, 1956.
———. *Church Dogmatics, Volume II, Part 1: The Doctrine of God.* Edited by G. W. Bromiley and T. F. Torrance. Edinburgh: T. & T. Clark, 1957.
———. *Deliverance to the Captives.* Translated by Marguerite Wieser. London: SCM, 1961.
———. *Epistle to the Philippians: 40th Anniversary Edition.* Translated by James W. Leitch. London: Westminster John Knox, 2002.
———. *The Epistle to the Romans.* Translated from the 6th ed. by Edwyn C. Hoskyns. London: Oxford University Press, 1960.
———. *Evangelical Theology.* Grand Rapids: Eerdmans, 1992.
———. *Fünfzig Gebete.* Zürich: Theologischer Verlag, 2005.
———. *The Göttingen Dogmatics.* Translated by Geoffrey W. Bromiley. Grand Rapids: Eerdmans, 1991.
———. *Prayer and Preaching.* Translated by B. E. Hooke. London: SCM, 1964.
———. *Selected Prayers.* Translated by Keith R. Crim. London: Epworth, 1966.
———. *The Word of God and Theology.* Translated by Amy Marga. London: T. & T. Clark, 2011.
Barth, Karl, and Eduard Thurneysen. *Come Holy Spirit.* Grand Rapids: Eerdmans, 1933.
———. *Come Holy Spirit.* Translated by George W. Richards, Elmer G. Homrighausen, and Karl J. Ernst. Reprint. Eugene, OR: Wipf & Stock, 2009.
"Barth in Retirement." *Time* LXXXI No. 22 (31 May 1963). http://www.time.com/time/magazine/article/0,9171,896838,00.html.
Burnett, Richard E. *Karl Barth's Theological Exegesis: The Hermeneutical Principals of the Römerbrief Period.* Grand Rapids: Eerdmans, 2001.
Willimon, William H. *Conversations with Barth on Preaching.* Nashville: Abingdon, 2006.

PART II

Society

Looking Backward to Look Forward

Insights from the Past for Preaching in the Future

Marc Rader

WHAT IS THE FUTURE of preaching? Is there a future and, if so, how might preaching need to change to meet the needs of a changing culture? As a pastor and a teacher of preachers, I have more than a passing interest in the answer to these questions. I want to be the most effective preacher I can be for my congregation and I want to enable the next generation of preachers to be as effective as they can be.[1] One way to answer these questions about the future of preaching is to look backwards to the history of preaching.

The History of Preaching

The first and most obvious place to begin is with the many examples of effective preaching throughout the history of the Christian church. This great cloud of witnesses presents us with innumerable examples of effective preaching in the past from which we might glean insights to apply to our own preaching in the future. However, when we sit at the feet of those considered to be the most effective preachers of their time—people like John Chrysostom, George Whitefield, and Phillips Brooks, and countless

---

1. I use the qualifier "effective" rather than "great" throughout this essay for a couple of reasons. First, it relates to my understanding of preaching as achieving something in the lives of those who hear it. And second, while the church will benefit from great preachers, effective preachers—whose hearers experience the gospel in what they hear—is perhaps more achievable and realistic.

others—we realise that their sermons, if preached today, would probably not be effective. O. C. Edwards laments "that most Christians today can read few sermons of the past with much edification."[2] The reality is that many, if not all, effective sermons appear to be non-transferable. The reasons are obvious. For one thing, the most effective sermons are often linked to a particular congregational context. For example, the power of John Chrysostom's Statue Sermons—considered to be some of the most powerful sermons the bishop of Antioch preached—is linked, in no small part, to the context of fear that gripped the city after widespread rioting. Different concerns occupy our churches today.

Less obvious, but no less important, is the change in methods of biblical interpretation. The allegorical method of interpretation, which dominated much Christian preaching for over a thousand years, has largely been displaced by historical-critical methodologies. Add to these critical elements of a sermon the use of time-specific illustrative references, and differences in culture generally, and it is no surprise that there are few sermons that we could profitably use as examples of effective preaching in our contemporary age.

If the sermons of the great preachers of the past are not transferable, then help for the future of preaching might be gained not from reflecting on the sermons of an individual preacher but from reflecting on the preaching of effective preachers across the ages. And when we look at the woods instead of the trees we see, first of all, a general consensus regarding the features common to effective preaching that are, shall we say, transcendent. These include speaking clearly with a unity of thought, using engaging illustrative material, keeping one's congregation's needs in mind, personal integrity, and the like. Against such things there appears to be no law. These same things (with some minor differences) fill homiletics textbooks, course outlines, and evaluative instruments; and so they should. Effective preaching through the ages has been, and will continue to be, characterized by these things even though the emphasis on particular aspects will vary "in the details of volume, of grasp, of relative importance, and of presentation."[3]

As helpful as this is, however, it does not provide us with much more direction for the future of preaching than do the individual examples of effective preaching. To keep doing what we have been doing, with only minor changes, does not seem to reflect the level of challenge we are facing in our present time. Effective preaching has never been, nor will it ever be, simply a matter of adhering to the rules of sermon preparation and delivery. If it were as simple as this there would be many more effective preachers (although

---

2. Edwards, *A History of Preaching*, 832.
3. Dargan, *A History of Preaching*, 39.

there would also be many more effective preachers if more preachers did adhere to those rules!). While these sermonic elements may be the same yesterday, today, and forever, what constitutes effective preaching itself is not so static. In other words, it was not merely John Chrysostom's expertise in rhetorical eloquence or stirring use of illustrations that made him such an effective (and great) preacher.

In view of this, does the past offer us any help for negotiating the future of preaching? I believe it does, but its value does not lie in either the specific examples of individual preachers or in the general principles of effective preaching. Rather, direction for the future of preaching lies at the intermediate level of historical reflection. It is with this not-too-general yet not-too-specific perspective that some of the influences that continually shape preaching become clear. It is my contention that the intermediate history of preaching demonstrates that the pulpit is reactive to, and reflective of, its context. In particular, the pulpit reflects three contexts: 1) what is happening in the wider culture; 2) what is happening in the academy, especially in relation to biblical hermeneutics and theology; and 3) the challenges facing the congregations of that culture.

The genesis of this contention occurred when I overlaid a history of Christian preaching on top of a more general history of the Christian church. What struck me as I read—and I readily acknowledge that I am more of a keen hobbyist than a bona fide historian—was that there appeared to be a strong correlation between the preaching of a particular period and the context in which that preaching occurred. In fact, the characteristics of the preaching of a particular period were almost impossible to describe without reference to the wider context. It also seemed to me that as historians of Christian preaching described the preaching of particular periods they tended to use several common categories: the use and interpretation of Scripture; the role of the preacher; the place and function of the sermon in worship; sermon forms and delivery; theological themes that are addressed; and common topics and sermon content.[4] These categories provide a useful framework for comparing and contrasting various periods of preaching. Using these categories, let me provide some examples of this relationship between preaching and its context. In each example that follows I will seek to draw attention to the broad characteristics of the period (of which the great preachers of the age appear to be exemplars) and the context that goes some way to explaining those features.

---

4. This is an expanded list based in part on a similar list in ibid., 30.

Preaching and its Context in the Patristic Period

To begin with, let us briefly consider the patristic period. Even though we have limited evidence of the preaching of this period of Christian history we can identify several broad characteristics of preaching. Regarding the use and interpretation of Scripture, preachers utilized the apostolic tradition, the Hebrew Bible, and, increasingly, the New Testament. One can readily identify contextual factors that might have influenced this, such as the simple fact that the New Testament canon was not yet fully formed. Preaching was rarely expositional. The Scriptures were used mainly in quotation and application.[5] This would change significantly in connection with developments within the academy. The grammarian-trained Origen, who confined himself to explaining a text, adopted a more expositional model of preaching.[6] The expository sermon, along with the Alexandrian typological interpretation of Scripture, became increasingly common.[7]

Preaching was also increasingly seen as the exclusive task of an official class of men, men of the apostolic succession who could protect the church against false teaching and heresy. They preached in the context of worship, primarily to believers. The form of the sermons in the early part of this period was generally the homily—a conversation or talk. Dargan writes that "[These homilies] were without much logical order, and give little if any indication of a previously prepared outline."[8] It is when we turn to the theological themes of the time that we most clearly see the correlation between preaching and its context. The theological themes found in the patristic preaching include the primacy of the church, its unity and universality, and doctrinal guidance aimed at counteracting heresy. Alongside these topics, the sermons show an interest in the glory of martyrdom—in a context of persecution, should we be surprised?—and ethical guidance against sexual sins (with an emphasis on the virtue of chastity), sins of excess (e.g., drunkenness and excessive luxury), and sins of speech (e.g., lying and blasphemy), especially in contrast to the wider, hostile, pagan culture.[9]

---

5. Ibid., 41.

6. Edwards, *A History of Preaching*, 31–46, for an excellent discussion of the connection between Origen's background and his homiletics.

7. Dargan, *A History of Preaching*, 41.

8. Ibid., 41.

9. Dunn-Wilson, *A Mirror for the Church*, 31.

Preaching and its Context in the Fourth Century

We can observe similar correlations between the preaching of the fourth century and its context. In terms of the use and interpretation of Scripture, the canon of the New Testament was largely settled, and increasingly formed the basis of sermons. Dargan states:

> Preaching [was] largely exposition of Scripture, often on a short text, sometimes continuous on whole books or parts of books, or on subjects. Doctrine also becomes now increasingly important as homiletical material; but with it, according to the personality of the preacher, is often mingled some speculation and philosophising.[10]

The preaching was, by this time, restricted to the bishops and presbyters and there was what Dargan calls a "culture of ministry," which refers to the impact in the pulpit of an increasing number of cultured and educated elites. Sunday worship was the regular time for preaching, but as the church calendar became more established, preaching on festival days became more common.

Perhaps the biggest difference is in the miscellaneous nature of the congregations and the form of the sermon. With imperial patronage, people flooded into newly built basilicas and chapels, bringing their cultural expectations into the nave with them. Rhetorical flourish and ostentatious displays in formal religious ceremony were expected. Worship became more elaborate and the preaching in this period reflected this shift. The sermons were what Dargan calls a "discourse": "Retaining the Scriptural motive and tone, and in large degree the familiarity of the homily . . . the *logos*, or oration, of this age is more assimilated to the classic models of oratory."[11]

The content of the sermons also reflected the church's growing wealth and power. Gone were the simple homilies exhorting perseverance in the face of persecution. In their place were rhetorically ornate ethical appeals to an increasingly nominal parish. These sermons assumed the authority of the church and were largely focused on pastoral concerns that were apt for the day: economic and social disparity in the church, the dangers of sin, especially sexual sin (with a growing emphasis on the virtues of chastity—remember the wider monastic movement that had become influential in this period), and the "duties of religion."[12]

---

10. Dargan, *A History of Preaching*, 70.

11. Ibid., 70.

12. These common traits are found in Dunn-Wilson's description of Ambrose, Augustine, and Chrysostom in Dunn-Wilson, *A Mirror for the Church*, 88–117.

The most effective preachers of any period typically exemplify the characteristics of their era. In the fourth century, we should not be surprised, therefore, that someone like John of Antioch, later called Chrysostom, should be a successful preacher. Born into a wealthy, aristocratic family, trained by the famed rhetorician Libanius, influenced by Antiochene, exegesis, and the burgeoning ascetic movement, John was a product of his age and the perfect pulpit match for the time.

Preaching and its Context in the Early Middle Ages

The same correlation between preaching and society was evident in the early middle ages. A general decline in intellectual activity and a tendency to imitation was mirrored in the pulpit. Allegorical interpretations of Scripture dominated medieval sermons, along with the homiliary (collections of sermons for use by the clergy). As the Roman Catholic Church filled the void left by the removal of imperial authority, prelates often neglected preaching in order to attend to their significantly increased administrative duties.

The development of a sacramental theology and liturgy reduced the importance of the sermon in the context of worship and reframed the role of the clergy from that of preacher to priest.[13] Sermons were taken up with festivals, saints' days, and other matters of church discipline (e.g., penance, fasting, alms, and other meritorious works).[14] "This led to the preaching of church discipline rather than Christian morals, of penance rather than repentance."[15] Monastic and churchly virtues received more emphasis relative to other topics.[16]

Once again, we find these characteristics exemplified by the great preachers of the age, such as the Venerable Bede (ca. 673–735), an English monk who, according to Edwards, was one of the last polymaths in history—"one of the last people to know almost everything that was known at his time."[17] Bede was a preacher. His writings contain fifty homilies on the Gospels. They focus primarily on the nativity and resurrection, with some

---

13. Dargan observes that, theologically, the growth of liturgy and other forms of worship in the Middle Ages preserved a place for preaching but also made the "spoken word of far less relative value." Dargan, *A History of Preaching*, 109.

14. This list of topics, taken from Leo the Great's preaching, was typical of the age. Dargan, *A History of Preaching*, 124.

15. Ibid., 110.

16. Ibid., 137.

17. Edwards, *A History of Preaching*, 144.

homilies for saints' days and other holy days.[18] Edwards describes Bede's preaching as follows:

> There is a short introduction, stating why his congregation [of monks] should ponder the words of the Gospel passage that has just been read to them. Then the passage is examined, but Bede does not feel compelled to comment on every word or even every verse, because it is the pericope as a whole that he wishes to be understood. He explicitly teaches a fourfold interpretation, but seldom deals with more than the literal and perhaps one spiritual meaning. He uses allegorical interpretation regularly but with restraint."[19]

Preaching and its Context in the Scholastic Period

In his allegorical method, scholastic divisions and headings,[20] and use of *exempla* from everyday life, the Franciscan preacher and "friend of the poor,"[21] Anthony of Padua (c. 1195–1231), exemplifies much of the preaching of the late middle ages. The sermons of the Scholastic period reveal what we might expect in a time of economic growth, social change, a rising merchant class, increased urbanization, developing intellectual and spiritual appetites, the birth of modern universities, the waxing of papal influence and Roman liturgy, and the irreverence, ignorance, and superstition characteristic of the Middle Ages. Lecoy de la Marche's summary of the sermons of this period point to the correlative character of the preaching in the thirteenth century:

> [The preachers] pointed out to us the weaknesses of the prelates and monks, the abuses of power by the princes, the robberies of the lords and their retainers, the ambitions of the burghers, the ruses of the merchants and usurers, the coarseness of the sailors, of the labourers, of the servants, the artifices and coquetry of the women, the peccadilloes of the students. They have given us in a rapid view the state of knowledge, the received ideas in the matter of government, of commerce, of education, the development given to each branch of the human sciences.[22]

---

18. Ibid., 146.
19. Ibid., 147.
20. Dargan, *A History of Preaching*, 256.
21. Larsen, *The Company of Preachers*, 122.
22. Dargan, *A History of Preaching*, 228.

Preaching and its Context in the Reformation

In the Reformation period the correlation between context and preaching is perhaps most easily observed. With the seismic shifts in biblical interpretation, there was little allegory in the Reformers' preaching. With the rejection of much of the sacramentalism of Roman Catholicism, the sermon became the centerpiece of Protestant worship. The pastor's central work was preaching, and preaching was largely an exposition of the word. Theologically, the great theme of the Reformation dominated: justification by grace through faith in Christ. Preachers warned against the errors of belief from which the Reformers sought to extricate the church, such as penance, purgatory, and prayers to the saints.

Sermon forms were similar to those which had preceded the Reformation, but not identical. Dargan's description is helpful:

> There is less of logical analysis and of oratorical movement in the sermons of the Reformers than in those of many of their predecessors and followers. But still there is no complete recurrence to the old loose homily, no entire renunciation of the more compact homiletical structure which was largely the gift of scholasticism to the pulpit.[23]

Luther and Calvin (among many others) are exemplars of this kind of preaching and in their sermons we see the correlation between preaching and the wider context.

Preaching and its Context in Nineteenth-Century America

The Protestant Reformation might have spawned a plethora of denominations and national churches, but the correlation between context and pulpit can still be discerned. For example, consider Phillips Brooks (1853–1893), one of the most influential American preachers in the nineteenth century. His famous definition of preaching as "truth through personality" is more than a catchy phrase; it reflects the romanticism and "liberalism" of nineteenth-century New England. As Hughes Oliphant Old incisively observes, this definition places authority not in the text of Scripture (which had been eroded by biblical criticism), but in the heroic personality of the preacher.[24] The romantic ideal of the artistic soul also influenced Brooks's view

---

23. Dargan, *A History of Preaching*, 380.
24. Old, *The Reading and Preaching of the Scriptures*, 495.

of inspiration,[25] as well as his understanding of the purpose of preaching to move souls.[26] Emphasizing the incarnation rather than the atonement, he believed that in Christ, men and women were able to cultivate their essential "richness and potential" toward ideal humanity.[27] Preaching topical sermons rather than textual ones, Brooks's ministry was "gracious and beneficent,"[28] representative of an intellectually respectable Christianity.[29]

Preaching and its Context in Early Twentieth-Century England

In *Varieties of English Preaching* 1900–1960 Horton Davies identifies several cultural, theological, and academic trends in the early twentieth century and shows how they were manifested in English pulpits during that period.[30]

According to Davies, preaching became more subdued. This was due, he argues, to an increased suspicion towards rhetorical oratory in the wake of political dictators, and relentless attacks on Christian faith and morality represented by Darwin and Freud, along with rapid political and social changes in Europe and Africa and the impact of entering the nuclear age: "Interim judgments and shortened horizons are the order of the day. Inevitably, the trumpet speaks with an uncertain sound . . . expressed in the appropriate mode of a confidential tone, not with oratorical certitude."[31] The decline of religiosity in England and the passing of the heyday of the popular preacher also had a significant impact on church life and preaching according to Davies. Gone were the days of pulpit personalities, those flamboyant and authoritarian preachers who drew large crowds but didn't build congregations. In their place were smaller congregations with a preacher who was conceived as "a first violinist in the orchestra of faith, rather than as a soloist."[32] The influence of radio and television, along with these shifts in the function of the preacher, also impacted the length of sermons which were nearly half as long as their Victorian predecessors.

Davies also traces the impact of prominent theological trends on the English pulpit. The "New Theology" (the English equivalent of the American Social Gospel) resulted in preaching that was filled with social compassion,

25. Ibid., 498.
26. Edwards, *A History of Preaching*, 640.
27. Old, *The Reading and Preaching of the Scriptures*, 490.
28. Turnbull, *A History of Preaching*, 110.
29. Old, *The Reading and Preaching of the Scriptures*, 488.
30. Davies, *Varieties of English Preaching*.
31. Ibid., 22.
32. Ibid., 20.

spoke of Christ not as Savior but as philanthropist and social reformer, and minimized the universality of sin.[33] Writing after the waning of the New Theology, Davies notes its ongoing legacy in the pulpit, especially in the condemnation of racism and other prejudices that "thwart the love of the neighbor."[34] The Neo-Orthodox movement, which emphasized those elements jettisoned by the New Theology, renewed concern for biblical dimensions of grace, sin, and eschatology, and the kingdom of God as the "rule of God actualized in every age . . . inaugurated and sustained by God in crisis and perfected in eternity . . . neither planned by men nor gradually achieved by them."[35] These theological and hermeneutical trends also produced a renewed emphasis on exegetical preaching, and help to explain the decline of pulpit personalities. While "Victorian preaching 'stars' ascended their pulpits or platforms, as Moses had descended from Sinai, to thunder forth the Divine will to expectant crowds," their twentieth-century successors were far less likely to be so colorful or eccentric.[36]

The Reactive and Reflective Nature of the Relationship Between Preaching and its Context

Clearly, then, there is a correlation between preaching and its context. Preaching both reacts to, and is reflective of, its context. Dargan states this principle in his description of the preaching of the patristic period: "We shall have frequent occasion to observe that preaching, like all other special institutions, is responsive to general influences; and so it shared, more or less directly, in the whole character and movement of the age."[37] When he turns to the early medieval period he states:

> The general law of reaction is noticeable in the history of preaching, as it is in other histories. . . . The reaction was to be expected, and it came swiftly and sadly enough. This natural ebb-tide was concurrent with a rough sea of storm and turmoil in the world. The times were evil indeed. Barbarism threatened without and corruption sickened within the church as well as the state. The general corruption on morals affected balefully the lives of the clergy as well as the laity. Ambition, place-hunting, selfishness,

33. Ibid., 25.
34. Ibid., 26.
35. Ibid., 28.
36. Ibid., 17–18, 28.
37. Dargan, *A History of Preaching*, 33.

greed, and even worse things were not unknown among those whose business it was to live as well as preach the gospel."[38]

Again, in relation to the seventh and eighth centuries, Dargan writes that, "Preaching, as usual, shared and to some extent reflected the character of the age. There were materials and qualities of it common to both sections of the church and world."[39]

Dargan is not alone in describing the correlation between preaching and context as reflective. In his concluding thoughts O. C. Edwards observes that,

> In addition to the qualities of preachers, there must be considered as well the characteristics of the times in which they preached. There have been many different kinds of preaching in history, and they all were probably related to what was going on in the society in which they arose.[40]

What is noteworthy is that the direction of influence appears to be from the context to the pulpit. This is important to note since it defines the relationship between them as reflective rather than as primarily participatory[41] or reciprocal.[42] This is most easily demonstrated, as we have seen in the examples above, in the correlation between the cultural context and its preaching. The influence of imperial patronage on the preaching in the fourth century or the stagnation of intellectual endeavor on the pulpit of that period are easily discerned.

The same reflective correlation is evident in the hermeneutical and theological emphases of the day. Edwards points out that, "The way [Scripture] is explicated reflects the principles of biblical interpretation in vogue at the time."[43] Paul Scott Wilson makes the same sort of observations in his brief history of preaching when he identifies biblical studies, theology,

---

38. Ibid., 109.
39. Ibid., 132.
40. Edwards, *A History of Preaching*, 831.
41. Craddock argues "preaching *participates* in those contexts. Preaching is not only set in tradition but is itself an act of traditioning, not only done in a pastoral context but is itself a pastoral act." Craddock, *Preaching*, 47. Italics added.
42. This is Edwin Dargan's term. He argues that "preaching has shaped events, and events have affected preaching." Dargan, *A History of Preaching*, 8. This is ultimately unconvincing, apparently, even to Dargan, who repeatedly admits that preaching "has, sometimes for the better and sometimes for the worse, received moulding from contemporary customs and standards of ethics" and that in some areas, such as arts and science, "[preaching] has received more than it has given" (*A History of Preaching*, 9).
43. Edwards, *A History of Preaching*, 832.

language, and art as fields that have been of particular help to preachers.[44] These influences are, however, a little more difficult to identify than the cultural influences for three primary reasons.

First, theological and hermeneutical trends tend to be slower to develop and change.[45] For instance, Antiochene exegesis, with its emphasis on the literal rather than the allegorical meaning of Scripture, was one of the dominant methods of interpretation for over a century.[46] John Chrysostom was clearly influenced by, and represented, this exegetical approach. However, compared to the sudden seismic cultural shift that Constantine ushered in, biblical hermeneutics did not change significantly in this period. Likewise, the allegorical interpretation of Scripture which dominated biblical scholarship for over a thousand years profoundly shaped the preaching of tens of thousands of preachers including Anthony of Padua, but its ubiquity made its influence less immediate. When, however, there are significant shifts in theology or hermeneutics, these influences can be discerned in the pulpit. For example, we have already noted the seismic shifts that influenced the Reformation hermeneutic and the influence of postmodern hermeneutics on the New Homiletic and the development of inductive models of preaching.[47]

A second reason that theological or hermeneutical trends are more difficult to trace is they are mediated by preachers. While culture has what might be called a first-degree influence on preachers, theology and hermeneutics have a second-degree influence. In other words, cultural values tend to be learned informally and intuitively, while theology and hermeneutics are learned more formally. From the restriction of preaching to the bishops in the second century to the denominational seminaries and colleges of today, theology and hermeneutics have formed part of the instruction of preachers. The degree to which these trends are evident in the pulpit is dependent upon the degree of engagement, understanding, and integration of those trends by the preacher. The aptitude of a preacher to apply theological

---

44. Wilson, *A Concise History of Preaching*, 178.

45. However, this appears to be changing in contemporary hermeneutics with new methodologies appearing at an ever-increasing rate. See, for instance, Thiselton, *New Horizons in Hermeneutics: The Theory and Practice of Transforming Biblical Reading* or, for a more accessible text, Bray, *Biblical Interpretation: Past and Present* .

46. Gerald Bray discusses both Antiochene and Alexandrian exegesis in the period of 326–451: *Biblical Interpretation*, 104–107.

47. Edwards describes this as "a loss of confidence in the ability of language to describe reality or to convey univocal meaning" (*A History of Preaching*, 799). DeBona cites McClure's observation that the New Homiletic "found support and insight in literary, rhetorical, and reader-response criticisms that were more concerned with the 'how' of the text . . . than with its 'what.'" See DeBona, *Fulfilled in Our Hearing*, 175.

and hermeneutical insights varies from preacher to preacher. The influence, therefore, tends to be indirect.[48]

Third, theological and hermeneutical emphases are often localized. Dunn-Wilson's comment about the early church is apt: "We may refer to 'the early church' [or any era] as though it were monochrome, but we know that its congregations have always been a maelstrom of conflicting theologies, liturgies, and customs."[49] Similarly, the congregational needs that preachers address in their sermons, while sharing some of the monochromatic nature of the wider culture, are also localized. We can, however, trace the pastoral concerns of preachers in various periods as they relate to the wider cultural context. For example, sermons that emphasize the glories of martyrdom and encourage the congregations to live distinctly Christian lives are reflective of the cultural opposition to Christianity in the patristic period.

Looking Forward

Having looked backwards, we can now turn our attention to our contemporary situation and the question which opened this essay, "What is the future of preaching?" If it is true that preaching reacts to, and reflects, the context in which it is performed, this has important implications for how we preach in the face of changes in culture, hermeneutics, and theological emphases.

There is a Future for Preaching

The first implication of this intermediate perspective on the history of preaching is that, whatever the future holds, there will be a place for preaching. Put simply, preaching certainly has a future! As Edwards points out, we have examples of preaching from every period of Christian history and, if history is anything to go by, it will continue to be the case into the future. Christian preaching has proven to be remarkably resilient and responsive to whatever is happening in church and society. At the risk of oversimplifying, as long as things are happening, there will be preaching!

---

48. This might explain Wilson's query about why there is not a more direct link between biblical criticism and preaching in the history of preaching. Dunn-Wilson, *A Mirror for the Church*, 179.

49. Ibid., 122.

Preaching Will Change

A second implication is that preaching will change in order to remain effective. This is not a matter of "must," but a matter of course. Preaching has always reacted to, and reflected, its context, and that will continue to be the case.

The more pressing question is how it will change. If preaching is reactive to, and reflective of, its context, then we only have to look to our current and emerging contexts to begin to identify how preaching will change. And the good news is that the significant changes in our culture, hermeneutics, and theology are being analyzed already. It is common in recent homiletic texts to discuss the shifting context in which we preach. Reflections on the impact of postmodernity and the advent of television, not to mention other forms of digital media, are readily available. Likewise, there are many excellent resources reflecting on the influence of changing hermeneutical disciplines on the pulpit.[50]

These summaries of the changes that are unfolding usually conclude with a question about the significance for preaching. Alec Gilmore, in *Tomorrow's Pulpit*, summarizes the answers that are generally given:

> At the risk of slight exaggeration the picture [of change] just presented tends to produce one of two reactions. Either it leads one to say that the day of preaching therefore is done or it leads one to say that whatever happens in the world around us, preaching is always vital and we must go on doing it [as we have always done it]. Neither reaction is very helpful, for the one is too sweeping and the other too stubborn.[51]

Cahill describes the responses to the New Homiletic and inductive sermon forms in a similar way: "The question of sermon form cannot ultimately be a matter of either *status quo* or *going with the flow*."[52]

Historical reflections suggest that preaching will continue to react to, and reflect, its context and that these correlations will be found in how preachers use and interpret the Bible, in the role of the preacher, in the place and function of the sermon, in the sermonic forms and other matters of delivery, and in the theological themes and topics that are found in sermons.

---

50. On the impact of postmodernity see Johnson, *Preaching to a Postmodern World*, Lose, *Confessing Jesus Christ: Preaching in a Postmodern World*, Webb, *Comedy and Preaching*, and Webb and Kysar, *Preaching to Postmoderns*. For reflections on media and imagery see Blackwood, *The Power of Multi-Sensory Preaching and Teaching*, and Jonker, *Preaching in Pictures*. For hermeneutics see Gibson, *Preaching to a Shifting Culture* or Wright, *Telling God's Story*.

51. Gilmore, *Tomorrow's Pulpit*, 15.

52. Cahill, *The Shape of Preaching*, 23. Italics original.

And even though our historical perspective on effective preaching today is prone to near-sightedness, we can observe the changes to preaching in some of the categories (albeit some are clearer than others). For example, the insights of the New Homiletic drew attention to the shifts in culture that necessitated a change in how preaching was conceived and delivered. Edwards describes the New Homiletic as descriptive rather than prescriptive and uses Don M. Wardlaw's analysis of contrasts presented by the New Homiletic. These contrasts include: from deductive to inductive models, from analytical development of timeless truths to a development that has movement, from left brain to right brain, from the explicit to the suggestive, from authoritarian to relational, from the work of the isolated scholar to more collaborative models.[53] In these contrasts we are confronted with one view of how the role of the preacher has changed and how sermonic forms and delivery need to change. I will return shortly to some other areas where I suspect preaching will need to change.

The Kind of Preachers the Future of Preaching Requires

The reflective relationship between culture, theology, hermeneutics and preaching points to the general shape of things to come and has several implications for preachers who desire to become or remain effective preachers—and for those who train them.

For one thing, preachers and homileticians will need to be light on their feet and swift to engage with and describe the latest trends in culture, theology, and hermeneutics, and outline their implications for effective preaching. Preaching will, therefore, benefit from a multi-disciplinary approach that seeks to integrate wider cultural, theological, and hermeneutical currents.

Preachers will also need to cultivate an ability to exegete their culture as well as the Scriptures. Leonora Tubbs-Tisdale makes this point in *Preaching as Local Theology and Folk Art*:

> Good preaching not only requires its practitioners to become skilled biblical exegetes. It also requires them to become adept in "exegeting" local congregations and their contexts, so that they can proclaim the gospel in relevant and transformative ways for particular communities of faith.[54]

---

53. Edwards, *A History of Preaching*, 799–801.
54. Tubbs-Tisdale, *Preaching as Local Theology and Folk Art*, xi.

Tubbs-Tisdale here raises a fault line of concern for many evangelical preachers, namely the potential sacrifice of biblical truth at the altar of relevance. There is, of course, a distinction that must be maintained between relevance for the sake of relevance and relevance for the sake of the gospel, but this is precisely what the great preachers of the past have done.

Speculations on the Future of Preaching

Can more be said about the future of preaching? At least in the corner of the world where I preach, there are several aspects of culture, theology, and hermeneutics that would appear to be important for the pulpit. At the risk of being too programatic, I conclude with a few suggestions about where the pulpit may need to be more reflective. I readily acknowledge that these insights are not self-contained or discrete; they are interconnected. They are also not unique or original to me, but represent the trends in homiletics that have struck me as most significant in my reading, teaching, and personal reflection on preaching.

First, speech-act theory, socio-rhetorical considerations, canonical considerations, and a growing emphasis on the hearer (among others) have all influenced the way the Bible is read and, therefore, how it is preached. The impact of these hermeneutical trends will continue to be felt in the development of inductive models of communication, in more informal forms of preaching, and in the emphasis on narrative.[55]

Second, while theological emphases vary from place to place and from denomination to denomination, preachers cannot ignore them. In the West, it is generally understood that we are now living in a post-Christendom world in which the church is increasingly marginalized. Into this new reality there is a renewed interest in ecclesiology and missiology and these must be integrated into the preaching of the church.[56]

Third, the pulpit will have to wrestle with the influence of social media on our lives. Not only does social media invite and expect participation, it has also had significant influence in shaping our post-truth society. The implications for preaching are significant. How can we invite more

---

55. Kysar and Webb, in *Preaching to Postmoderns*, state the principle of reflective practice of preaching as they conclude their introduction to various interpretive methodologies and their impact on preaching: "We are convinced that the issues involved in the multiplication of interpretive methods and the resulting methods themselves are important for preachers. If you believe that Scripture remains essential to the life of faith and to preaching, then you are—we believe—obliged to understand what is happening in biblical interpretation today." (xxx).

56. See Johnson, *The Mission of Preaching*.

participation and engagement in our preaching? How can we equip our congregations to critique what they hear in their social media networks? How can we preach the eternal word of God in a world of "likes" and here-today, gone-tomorrow viral ideas?

In these and many other areas the pulpit will inevitably reflect the cultural, theological, and hermeneutic influences of the day. I am convinced that the history books of the future will include descriptions of preachers from the mid-twenty-first century whose preaching was effective because it was typical of the times and places they ministered. Will we join them? Will we read and think and pray and experiment and evaluate and, by all means possible, preach?

Bibliography

Blackwood, Rick. *The Power of Multi-Sensory Preaching and Teaching*. Grand Rapids: Zondervan, 2008.

Bray, Gerald. *Biblical Interpretation: Past and Present*. Downers Grove, IL: IVP Academic, 1996.

Cahill, Dennis M. *The Shape of Preaching: Theory and Practice in Sermon Design*. Grand Rapids: Baker, 2007.

Craddock, Fred. *Preaching*. Nashville: Abingdon, 1985.

Dargan, Edwin C. *A History of Preaching, Volume 1: From the Apostolic Fathers to the Great Reformers, AD 70–1572*. Grand Rapids: Baker Book House, 1974.

Davies, Horton. *Varieties of English Preaching, 1900–1960*. London: SCM, 1963.

DeBona, Guerric. *Fulfilled in Our Hearing: History and Method of Christian Preaching*. New York: Paulist, 2005.

Dunn-Wilson, David. *A Mirror for the Church: Preaching in the First Five Centuries*. Grand Rapids: Eerdmans, 2005.

Edwards, O. C. *A History of Preaching*. Nashville: Abingdon, 2004.

Gibson, Scott M., ed. *Preaching to a Shifting Culture*. Grand Rapids: Baker, 2004.

Gilmore, Alec. *Tomorrow's Pulpit*. Guildford, UK: Lutterworth, 1975.

Johnson, Graham. *Preaching to a Postmodern World*. Grand Rapids: Baker, 2001.

Johnson, Patrick W. T. *The Mission of Preaching: Equipping the Community for Faithful Witness*. Downers Grove, IL: IVP Academic, 2015.

Jonker, Peter. *Preaching in Pictures*. Nashville: Abingdon, 2015.

Kysar, Robert and Joseph M. Webb. *Preaching to Postmoderns: New Perspectives for Proclaiming the Message*. Hendrickson, MA: Peabody, 2006.

Larsen, David L. *The Company of Preachers: A History of Biblical Preaching from the Old Testament to the Modern Era*. Grand Rapids: Kregel, 1988.

Lose, David J. *Confessing Jesus Christ: Preaching in a Postmodern World*. Grand Rapids: Eerdmans, 2003.

Old, Hughes Oliphant. *The Reading and Preaching of the Scriptures in the Worship of the Christian Church, Volume 7: The Modern Age*. Grand Rapids: Eerdmans, 2007.

Thiselton, Anthony C. *New Horizons in Hermeneutics: The Theory and Practice of Transforming Biblical Reading*. Grand Rapids: Zondervan, 1992.

Tubbs-Tisdale, Leonora. *Preaching as Local Theology and Folk Art*. Minneapolis: Fortress, 1997.

Turnbull, Ralph G. *A History of Preaching, Volume 3*. Grand Rapids: Baker, 1974.

Webb, Joseph M. *Comedy and Preaching*. St. Louis: Chalice, 1998.

Webb, Joseph M. and Robert Kysar. *Preaching to Postmoderns*. Hendrickson, MA: Peabody, 2006.

Wilson, Paul Scott. *A Concise History of Preaching*. Nashville: Abingdon, 1992.

Wright, John W. *Telling God's Story*. Downers Grove, IL: IVP Academic, 2007.

Word Made Flesh

The Fundamentals of Cross-Cultural Preaching

ROBERT SMITH JR

"JESUS LOVES ME" is a song that is popular in Sunday schools, camps, mission outreaches, and many other venues which teach children of any culture the truth of its title. The song reflects God's plan to include all nations, tribes, peoples, and tongues in his family.[1] The song embodies a principle that is of enormous relevance to preaching in our world today: it is personal, salient, and reaches across cultures.

The Bible is replete with stories of cross-cultural ministry. From Genesis 12:3, where God promised Abram all families of the earth would be blessed through him, to Revelation 7:9, God shows his plan of inclusion and preachers can infer their need to be cross-cultural and relevant in their preaching. In a well-known narrative God tells Jonah, the Hebrew prophet, to preach cross-culturally to the Ninevites, the enemies of Jonah's people. Jonah's reaction to the mission reveals the attitude of his heart: he was willing to be among people of a different culture as long as he did not have to deliver a message of salvation to people he did not like, understand, or know. (The sailors on the voyage from Joppa were not Hebrews. The people of Tarshish where he chose to go were not Hebrews either. Moreover, both groups were polytheistic.) After strong, unpleasant compulsion, Jonah ultimately delivered the salvific message to the people of a culture he disdained.

God commissions preachers in every generation to preach the gospel across cultures. Compelled by the love of Christ we are to make disciples of all nations. Today this does not necessarily mean traveling to a far-off

---

1. See Rev 7:9.

land. We are living in a time of unprecedented population movement. According to the United Nations Population Fund, in 2015 some 244 million people were living outside their country of origin.[2] As preachers, to start and remain intentionally within one's own culture is to violate the Great Commission. Sermons which address only one culture are often preached by preachers who only keep one eye open. Any driver who drives a car with one operative eye is considered suspect. How should society consider a preacher who preaches with only one operational eye?

Charles Colson of Prison Fellowship, in his work, *Loving God*, laments the habit the church has of evangelizing and entertaining itself instead of connecting with its unchurched neighbors.[3] The implication of his message is "we must needs go through Samaria" (John 4:4). We must needs go beyond the boundaries of our cultural comfort zones. Howard Thurman did. He pastored the Church for the Fellowship of All Peoples in San Francisco, California (the only church of that kind at the time). Every Sunday he stood up before people of African-American, Euro-American, Asian, and Hispanic descent. Do we? Or are we hemmed in by our own culture?

James Earl Massey, the former dean of the School of Theology of Anderson University and the former dean of the Chapel at Tuskegee University, believed preachers can maintain their heritage and take the best of other cultures to produce sermons that will receive an effective hearing cross-culturally. He did not believe in living at the extreme of any culture. The question for him is not, "What is the best preaching tradition, black or white?" The question is: "Can you take and use the best of any preaching tradition to effect a receptive hearing cross-culturally?" His answer is a resounding, "Yes!"

John Jasper (1812–1901), an African-American preacher, could not read and had no formal education. He was a building laborer and a tobacco factory worker. A man who could himself barely read taught Jasper how to read the Bible. John Jasper memorized and contextualized the Bible, and the rest is history. The learned black and white of Richmond, Virginia went to hear John preach, for he was a man who transcended racial and ethnic lines.

The church is still heavily laden with cultural attitudes that hinder our preaching. We can adopt the attitude of the one who wants to quarantine other cultures. It is the attitude of *isolation*. It is the attitude of the priest and the Levite who see someone from another culture needing ministry but who pass on the other side (Luke 10:31–32). This attitude must die. The attitude of *accommodation* and compromise must die as well. This is the attitude of

---

2. United Nations Population Fund, "Migration," n. p.
3. Colson, *Loving God*, 192.

Simon Peter who ministers to the believing Gentiles in Antioch but ignores the Gentiles when the Jews arrive (Gal 2:11–14).

Then there is the attitude of prophetic reform. It is the attitude of *transformation*. It is the attitude of the Lord Jesus, who says to Simon Peter when he has the vision on the housetop, "Whatever I have cleansed, do not call common" (Acts 10:15). This means everyone is a candidate for our ministry and our church. There will be people of every tribe, kindred, nation, and tongue in the eschaton (Rev 5:9; 7:9). If they will be with us in heaven then they need to be in the church on earth with us now.

This is a pressing issue for the church and its preaching. The church in the West is facing rapid social change. Take New Zealand, for example. Like many prosperous Western countries, it is experiencing a migration growth. According to Gareth Meech, the General Manager of Census 2013, "People born overseas now make up more than a quarter of New Zealand's population."[4] The Asian population including Filipino, Indian, Chinese, and Korean has grown exponentially. Additionally, the Maori population still strives for equality and acceptance. These realities must not be ignored. Failure of the German church and government to teach acceptance of the Jews in Germany led to the Holocaust. Helmut Thielicke, the German theologian-ethicist, spoke out when he was in Germany and warned preachers while preaching in America. He said, "Preaching in this land needs the same directions, the same urgency, the same clarity with respect to America's guilt for her treatment of Negroes and other non-white members of her country."[5] In Germany and America many preachers chose to yield to the government's dictates driven by prejudice and classism instead of adopting Peter's dictum of Acts 5:29, "We must obey God rather than man." How will preachers of influential congregations in any country preach when increasing numbers of other cultures show up in their churches? Will they modify their approach to cross-cultural hearers while remaining true to the content of the gospel? Will they address those hearers, or exclude them?

Speaking Bilingually

In Isaiah 36:11–17 we read this fascinating exchange:

> Eliakim, Shebna, and Joah said to the field commander, "Please speak to your servants in Aramaic, since we understand it. Do not speak to us in Hebrew in the hearing of the people on the wall."

---

4. The Office of Ethnic Communities, "Culture and Identity in New Zealand," n. p.
5. Duke, "The Preaching of Helmut Thielicke," 292.

But the commander replied, "Was it only to your master and you that my master sent me to say these things and not to the men sitting on the wall who, like you, will have to eat their own filth and drink their own urine?"

Then the commander stood and called out in Hebrew, "Hear the words of the king, the great king of Assyria. This is what the king says: Do not let Hezekiah deceive you. He cannot deliver you. Do not let Hezekiah persuade you to trust in the Lord when he says, 'The Lord will surely deliver us. This city will not be given unto the hand of the king of Assyria.'"

"Do not listen to Hezekiah. This is what the king of Assyria says, Make peace with me and come out to me. Then every one of you will eat from his own vine and fig tree and drink water from his own cistern, until I come and take you to a land like your own, a land of grain and new wine, a land of bread and vineyards."

It is odd this text is chronicled not only in II Kings 18, but in Isaiah 36 and 2 Chronicles 32 as well. Since it is mentioned three times, it must be significant. The pagan king offers some interesting dynamics for cross-cultural communication. Here is the background: in 722 BC the northern kingdom was dismantled, and Shalmanazzar, the king of Assyria, took the northern kingdom into captivity. Then there is a change in the throne room. The new king is Sennacherib, king of Assyria, and he is marching on the southern kingdom. In fact, he is dismantling the forty-five cities. Hezekiah the king of Judah tries to pay him off, but his resources are dwindling to nothing—the treasures of the temple are emptying and even the gold is stripped off the doors. Rabshakeh is sent by his king Sennacherib to come to the wall of Jerusalem and demand an unconditional surrender. Hezekiah sends his embassy, his negotiating committee, headed by the palace administrator, Eliakim, to negotiate with Rabshakeh.

Rabshakeh the spokesman for the Assyrian king says, "Hear this: don't you Jews rely upon yourself. If I gave you 2,000 horsemen, you wouldn't have enough riders to put on them. Don't trust in your power. Don't trust in Egyptian power, because the Egyptians are unreliable. They're like a splintered reed that punctures your hand. Don't trust your God, because your God cannot deliver you." When Eliakim heard him speak he said, "Don't speak in Hebrew. If you speak in Hebrew, the people who are on the wall, who are monolingual, will understand, and the people behind the wall who are monolingual also will understand. Pandemonium, riot, and insurrection will take place, and we will not be able to have meaningful negotiations. Since we, the representatives of Hezekiah, are *bilingual*, speaking Aramaic and Hebrew, and you are bilingual, speaking Aramaic and Hebrew, do not communicate to the masses in Hebrew. Don't speak cross-culturally—speak in Aramaic so that only you and we understand, and the folk on and behind the wall do not get the message."

Rabshakeh was a cross-cultural communicator in 2 Kings 19. He spoke loudly in Hebrew saying, "Don't trust in your God. Where are the other gods—the king of Separvaim, the king of Arpad, the gods of Hena, the king of Harmath, the gods of Ivvah? Where are they? They are lying in the dust and so will your God be in the dust. So do not choose death, choose life. If you want to surrender, then you will be able to eat from your own vine, sit under your own fig tree and drink from your own cistern." This man was a good cross-cultural communicator because he was willing to speak the language of the people instead of the official language only. He knew how to get people to move in Assyria and he knew how to get people to move in Jerusalem although he sought to move the Israelites from trusting their God. He used cross-cultural communication.

Preachers must preach in such a way that we use both the language of Zion on Sunday morning and the language of the ghetto on Monday. We have to preach in such a way that we can take the message of Bethlehem and relate it to Auckland. We have to preach in such a way that we can take the message in Cairo and relate it to Canberra. We have to preach in such a way that we can take the message of the New Jerusalem and preach it in Newcastle. We have to take God's message from the sanctuary to the street and from the pulpit to the pavement.

Joseph, the son of Jacob, is bilingual. Joseph knows how to speak his public language, Egyptian. But when he sees his brothers are repentant (especially Judah) and bemoans the fact they sold him into slavery, he puts the Egyptians out, quits using his public language, and starts talking to his brothers in his private language (Hebrew). Daniel is a bilingual communicator. He knows how to speak Chaldean, or Babylonian, and he knows how to speak Hebrew. In fact, the book of Daniel is bilingual. Chapter 1 and chapters 8–12 are written in Hebrew because they address issues concerning Hebrew people. But chapter 2, verse 4, opens up with this statement: "In Aramaic the astrologers said to the king, 'O King Nebuchadnezzar live forever, tell us the dream and we will interpret it.'" So chapter 2, verse 4 to the end of chapter 7 is written in Aramaic because it addresses Aramaic speakers—the Chaldeans, the Babylonians—and it is talking about things affecting them. Rabshakeh is efficiently bilingual. He knows the idioms or the linguistic nuances and was able to speak confidently to King Nebuchadnezzar in a language he understood, and speak convincingly to Aspenaz, the king's eunuch. The king trusted Daniel over the entire province of Babylon. This undoubtedly required proficient and masterful linguistic nuances designed to lead, persuade, engage, and encourage people in various levels of society.

Understanding Idioms

When we preach cross-culturally we must not only see faces, we must know what connects with the minds of the people whose faces we see. Dr. Brian Hicks, who taught missions at The Southern Baptist Theological Seminary, talks about going to a service where a friend of his, a white preacher, was preaching in a black church. The emotional temperature of the worship service started rising, and the hearers engaged vigorously in call-and-response. Finally, an old lady stood up and said, "You better shut your mouth!" Dr. Hicks said that his friend sat down because he did not understand the black idiom. She was really saying to him, "Go on and preach!" We must take time to learn and understand *idiomatic expressions* popular in different cultures. How are we going to talk about hell as a dreaded hot place when we are talking to Eskimos who live in cold temperatures and want warmth? In North America "hot as hell" is an idiomatic expression readily understood as undesirable. To Eskimos, however, we should make hell look not like a furnace, but like the most wet, cold, and miserable dwelling. How will we preach about Jesus being the Bread of Life in Indonesia and in India, when in Indonesia and India bread is white man's food? We can emphasize the dynamic equivalent, not the literal equivalent. In those cultures Jesus the Bread of Life can be understood as Jesus the Rice of Life. We would have to change our metaphor in Indonesia and in India in order to communicate the meaning of the metaphor.

Dr. Hicks also relays a story of missionaries who were preaching to natives in a certain indigenous area. While translating the first chapter of John, they came to verse 29: "Behold the Lamb of God who comes to take away the sin of the world." In that culture, a lamb was the most impure, filthy animal on the face of the earth. But the sacrosanct, the sacred, the holy animal was the pig. The missionaries took "lamb" from their translation and wrote, "Behold the Pig of God that takes away the sin of the world." The burden of emphasis in the translation was not about pig or lamb; it was about purity.

We have to appreciate the idiomatic expressions, cell-phone language, and the nuances of the communities in which we preach. Paul was effective because he understood Greco-Roman philosophy. In Acts 17:28, after going to Mars Hill and talking to the philosophers, Paul did not directly quote the Bible. He talked about the truth, its source, and about the matter of epistemological evidence—what is truth? He says in Acts 17:28, "We are his offspring, as your poets say." People will hear us better when they know we have read their literature, understood their culture, and are using illustrations from their *sitz im leben* (situation in life).

Adapting to our Audience

Rabshakeh was not only *bilingual* and *idiomatically expressive*, but he was an *audience adapter*. He could stand in Assyria and be with the movers and the shakers and be successful. He could come to Jerusalem and issue a stern ultimatum that would bring the king to his knees. He was an audience adapter. Martin Luther King, Jr., was an audience adapter. He could stand in the Washington Cathedral and talk about the ubiquitous nature of human sin. He could go down to the Ebenezer Baptist Church in Atlanta, Georgia and say, "Jesus is a rock in a weary land, a shelter in a time of a storm." King was able to upshift and downshift according to his hearers.

These are some of the same reasons Paul was effective as a crosscultural communicator. He spoke to the people in terms they understood. In Acts 17, Paul starts where the people are. He enters the city of Athens and sees monuments dedicated to all kinds of gods—gods like Hades the god of the underworld, Hermes the god of speed and commerce, Aphrodite the goddess of beauty, Apollo the god of the sun, Artemis the god of the moon, Nike the goddess of victory, Eros the god of love, Poseidon the god of the sea, and Zeus the chief of the gods. Paul sees a monument dedicated to the unknown God and says, "I want to acquaint you with the one you don't know. I know him, and I want you to know him." Paul began to talk about God. He did not talk about *messias* or *christos*. *Messias* is not a word that connects in the Greco-Roman milieu. The Greeks' allegiance was to a *kyrios* (lord), but not the kind of *kyrios* familiar to a Jewish perspective. The Greeks had no king but Caesar. So Paul preached to them in terms they could understand and finally closed with the resurrection. Some of the listeners became upset and mocked Paul. However, Dionysius, Damaris, and a number of others heard Paul and believed. Paul enters a Jewish synagogue in Antioch of Pisidia in Acts 13 and begins his message in the Jewish Scriptures. Starting with the patriarch, Abraham, he goes through the Jewish Scriptures and concludes with the resurrection. Some of his hearers are upset. Others ask him to come back the next Sabbath to preach the gospel to them (Acts 13:42). Paul adjusted his message style according to the culture of his audience and in each situation won an effective hearing.

Jesus stands above everyone as a cross-cultural communicator. In John 4 Jesus meets a woman in the daytime. He addresses her racial struggles—Jews and Samaritans had no dealings with each other. He deals with her liturgical struggle—Samaritans believed Mount Gerizim was the proper, designated place of worship while Jews believed the proper place of worship was Jerusalem. Jesus also addresses her moral dilemma—Where's your husband? She had been married five times and was living with a man who was not her husband. Jesus addresses her spiritual need—He asked her for a drink of water using the question as a platform to reveal the living water he could give her which would, like a spring, erupt into everlasting life. She returns to her community and says to the men—"Come see a man who told me everything that I ever did—is this not the Christ?" (John 4:29).

Jesus saw the Samaritan woman during the *day*. However in John 4:3 Jesus sees a Jewish man, Nicodemus, at *night*. Nicodemus wants to know how a man can be born again, but does not want to approach Jesus in front of a crowd of witnesses (John 4:3). Jesus did not try to help Nicodemus understand the new birth experience abstractly and conceptually. Instead Jesus appealed to Nicodemus' tactile sense. "Put your hand out here, Nicodemus. What do you feel?" "I feel the wind." Jesus asked, "Where is it going?" Nicodemus admitted, "I don't know." Jesus replied, "And where has it been?" Nicodemus acknowledged, "I don't know." Jesus concluded, "That's how the Spirit is. He blows where he wills, and you do not know where he comes from, or where he is going." As a teacher of the Law, Nicodemus is accustomed to thinking through analogies. Jesus answered in a manner familiar to his culture.

Jesus knew Thomas had doubts about Jesus' physical and bodily resurrection and would need to touch the wounds in order to believe. So Jesus invited Thomas to touch him. In that same chapter there is a woman named Mary Magdalene. She presses upon Jesus and wants to cling to him. Jesus responds, "Don't touch me. Don't hold on to me for I have not yet returned to my Father" (John 20:17). Mary felt she needed to touch Jesus, but did not need the touch to secure her faith. Thomas did need the touch and Jesus allowed it. Jesus addressed each according to their personal need for their spiritual growth. There is a blind man who gets touched one time by Jesus and receives blurred vision. He sees men who resemble walking trees. Jesus touches him a second time and he sees clearly. There is another man who has been born blind and has never seen the rose in its crimson splendor or the lily in its purple purity. Jesus stops by the roadside, sets up a pharmaceutical practice, spits in the ground and mixes his spit with dust. Jesus puts this salve on the man's eyes and sends him to wash in Siloam. The man obeys Jesus and after one touch and washing in the pool of Siloam, he is able to see. Finally, there is blind Bartimaeus. He says to Jesus, "Lord, I want to see." Without any touch, Jesus pronounces Bartimaeus will have his sight—and he does. Jesus chose his approach according to his audience and his goal. As Jesus' disciples, we must learn to communicate cross-culturally in order to obey the Great Commission.

Building Rapport

A primary step in cross-cultural communication is building rapport with people. One of the white students at The Southern Baptist Theological Seminary went to Africa as a missionary and tried to forge a rapport with the African people she was serving. When it was time to eat she thought they would give her an individual plate. However, there was a large bowl called the community bowl and everyone put their hands in the same bowl filled with something she did not recognize. She realized to be effective in preaching to the African people, she would have to eat with them from the same bowl. She did and they accepted her because she was identifying with them. Ezekiel identified with the exiles in Babylon. In Ezekiel 3:15, for seven days he sat where they sat and did not open his mouth. He listened, observed, and paid attention to the Jewish exiles as they sat at the river Chebar. After seven days, God called Ezekiel to the plains to give him a message for the people. After spending time with the people and with the Lord, Ezekiel was able to preach the word of the Lord to the people.

When we are invited to preach in a context different from our own we need to invest time in learning our listeners' history. Several years ago I made a contextual mistake while preaching at the Greater New Hope Missionary Baptist Church in Cincinnati, Ohio. I received positive and encouraging comments from people who came up to speak to me after the benediction. However, one African-American young woman said, "Sir, thank you for the word. You explained the Scripture well." Then she started to ask me a series of questions. "Aren't there any African-American attractive women? Aren't there any African-American scholars? Aren't there any African-Americans who have been successful in life?" She interrogated me on these lines because I used illustrations and quotes from the white experience, not from the cultural experience of the congregants. Years later I had the privilege of being the pastor for a week at the Indian Assembly at the Falls Creek Camp outside of Oklahoma City, OK. I prepared to preach by researching their history in America. I used illustrations from their history. I called them "Indians" instead of Native Americans because I learned they preferred the term Indian over Native American. The congregants appreciated my efforts and I received an extremely warm reception from the Indian audience. I connected with them throughout the week because I used their idiomatic expressions and applied the biblical text in their cultural context.

Dr. Timothy George, dean of Beeson Divinity School at Samford University in Birmingham, Alabama, preached at the Greater New Hope Missionary Baptist Church where previously I had failed to culturally adapt the sermon. He preached about the bones of Joseph using the bones metaphorically to represent vestiges of worship we should retain in the church: the altar, the Bible, the Lord's Supper, baptism, fellowship, etc. During his conclusion, he started reciting from the richness of the African-American religious tradition. He said, "African-Americans know how to be faithful to God, and how to praise God. I hear you say that you thank God that your bed was not your cooling board and your covers were not your winding sheets. In your prayers you say, 'Lord, I come to thee knee-bent and body-bowed. This evening, our heavenly Father, once more and again a few of your handmade servants bow down before thee. We come to you like empty pitchers before a full fountain desiring to be filled.'" The African-American worshippers stood and supported him vocally because he was telling the story of their experience using their language and their idioms. Dr. George had spent time in the African-American community and their churches. He spent time inquiring about the African-American culture. His efforts enabled him to honor the African-American heritage and connect with the African-American congregants when he spoke to them without losing his cultural identity or being condescending.

I often preach in white contexts and have found congregants want me to be culturally authentic—that is comfortable in my own skin—without being culturally exclusive. About twenty years ago an article in *Ebony* magazine featured Barry White, the musical artist. In the article, "Barry White: Comeback of the Nineties," Barry White made a statement adaptable to cross-cultural preaching. He said, "I learned how to change my style without losing my soul."[6] Preachers have to change our style to preach cross-culturally without losing our soul.

On his *Preparation for Preaching* outline Ray Stedman relays his well-known belief that the Bible is not twenty centuries old. He posits the Bible is one century old repeated twenty times. What worked in the first century of biblical exposition will work today. We do not need to adjust the Bible, we just need to trust the Bible and adjust our approach to delivering it to our contemporary audience so we can be effective in any cultural context.[7] When my professor and mentor, the late James W. Cox, was about

---

6. Chappell, "Barry White," 52–58.
7. Steadman, "Preparation for Preaching," n. p.

70 years old I invited him to preach at the New Mission Baptist Church in Cincinnati, Ohio, where I pastored for twenty years. He said, "Now, Robert, I only preach about twenty minutes." I said, "Now, Dr. Cox, you have as much time as you need. They'll sit and wait on you because I normally preach about an hour." Dr. Cox preached, and Dr. Cox preached for nearly 50 minutes. He couldn't stop because of the momentum which the call and response built. He was energized and he mounted up with wings like an eagle after he mounted the pulpit.

God communicates to us cross-culturally. Hebrews 1:1 states, "God, in sundry times and diverse places spoke unto us by the prophets. In these last days, he has spoken unto us by his dear son." John 1:14 states, "The word was made flesh and dwelt among us, and we beheld his glory, the glory of the only-begotten of the Father, full of grace and truth." Preachers are called to preach the word to all people in season and out of season. We must preach cross-culturally with the burning lips of Isaiah: "Woe is me, for I'm undone. I'm a man of unclean lips, and I dwell in the midst of people with unclean lips" (Isa 6:5). We must preach cross-culturally with the fiery mouth of Jeremiah: "[The word is] like fire shut up in my bones. I was weary of holding it in; indeed I could not" (Jer 20:9). We need to preach cross-culturally with the kind of "The Lord took me up" calling of Amos who said, "I was not a prophet, nor the son of a prophet. I was a sycamore fruit-picker and a herd-gatherer. But while I was doing my job, the Lord took me up" (Amos 7:14–15). We need to preach cross-culturally with the "I can't help it" conviction of Peter and John who could not help but speak the things they had seen and heard (Acts 4:20). We need to preach cross-culturally with the "Woe is me" urgency of Paul who acknowledged, "Woe is me if I preach not the gospel of Jesus Christ" (1 Cor 9:16). We must preach Jesus cross-culturally for by his grace alone he saves all cultures.

Bibliography

Chappell, Kevin. "Barry White: Comeback of the Nineties." *Ebony* (May 1995) 52–58.
Colson, Charles. *Loving God*. Rev. ed. Grand Rapids: Zondervan, 1996.
Duke, Robert W. "The Preaching of Helmut Thielicke." *Theology and Life* 7 (1965) 292.
The Office of Ethnic Communities. "Culture and Identity in New Zealand." 17 April 2014. http://ethniccommunities.govt.nz/story/culture-and-identity-new-zealand
Steadman, Ray. "Preparation for Preaching." http://www.discipleshiplibrary.com/pdfs/K410.pdf
United Nations Population Fund. "Migration." http://www.unfpa.org/migration.

Preaching with Vulnerability

Self-disclosure in the Pulpit

SIMON MOETARA

PHILLIPS BROOKS MEMORABLY DESCRIBED preaching as "the bringing of truth through personality."[1] While William Willimon believes that Brooks's definition strikes experienced preachers as "essentially right,"[2] he also expresses concern at some contemporary homiletical practice: "We have got the personality thing down fairly well. It's the truth thing that may be in peril."[3] For some today, the concern is that the focus is weighted too much towards personality at the expense of faithfulness to biblical truth, or that the quality of delivery takes precedence over the content of the message.[4] We must declare, therefore, right from the start, that the proclaiming of scriptural truth is indispensable to biblical preaching. However, it is not a case of *either* truth *or* personality, but of *both* truth *and* personality. The person of the preacher is a vital component of the preaching event. Almighty God speaks the life-giving word, but he speaks it through frail and finite human beings: through George Herbert's "brittle crazie glasse," Pascal's "feeble earthworm," Schaefer's "glorious ruin"—through the likes of you and me.[5]

---

1. Brooks, *Lectures on Preaching*, 5.
2. Willimon, *Pastor*, 157–58.
3. Willimon, "Naked Preachers Are Distracting," 62.
4. See, for example, White, "Not in Lofty Speech or Media," 133.
5. Herbert, "The Windows," 59; Pascal, *Pensées*, 64; Winter, *When Life Goes Dark*, 198.

Brooks elaborates: "The truth must come really through the person, not merely over his lips . . . through his character, his affections, his whole intellectual and moral being. It must come genuinely through him."[6] Brooks is calling attention to the human and incarnational aspect of preaching.[7] Like it or not, the sermon is filtered through the preacher's personality type, through his or her personal experiences and theology, sense of humor, gender, ethnicity, and culture. For this reason, Johnson highlights the importance of honoring "the ecology of our personhood" in our preaching, realizing that who we are will come through in our preaching no matter how much we might wish it to be otherwise.[8] Christian truth takes the form of a message which, through the distinct traits of the individual preacher, is "transmuted into a witness."[9] As a witness, the preacher "shares personal experiences, values, and feelings that reveal Jesus Christ in [his or her life]."[10]

Self-disclosure in the Pulpit

This brings us to the issue of the preacher's self-disclosure. Lee Ramsay helpfully describes self-disclosure as referring to "those elements within the sermon in style and substance that disclose the personhood of the preacher and that selectively incorporate the preacher's life experiences . . . for the purpose of elucidating the gospel."[11]

The preacher's sharing of her life experiences as part of the preaching event is a key component of Brooks's personality aspect through which truth is conveyed. Jeffrey Arthurs and Andrew Gurevich believe a major reason why preaching which uses self-disclosure works is that it is incarnational; it helps preachers to "stand between two worlds by embodying the message."[12] The gospel is intended to be embodied, instilled, and experienced. As Day has it, sharing one's personal story in preaching expresses something of who you are and "must surely put flesh on abstract declarations."[13]

Paul Windsor, Director of Langham Preaching, speaks of the importance of the preacher's personal work in their preparation:

---

6. Brooks, *Preaching*, 8.
7. McClure, *Preaching Words*, 103; Heisler, *Spirit-Led Preaching*, 97–98.
8. Johnson, *The Glory of Preaching*, 174.
9. Lischer, *The Company of Preachers*, 15.
10. Arthurs and Gurevich, "Self-Disclosure," 217.
11. Ramsay, "Getting Personal," n. p.
12. Arthurs and Gurevich, "Self-Disclosure," 216–17.
13. Day, *Embodying the Word*, 22.

> Particularly in today's world, unlike two generations ago, the preacher needs ... to be able to find the right level of drawing in their own story, their own illustrations from their own personal life, their own observations. Transparency, authenticity, passion; these kinds of things are very important.[14]

This raises an important question: If who we are is an essential element of our preaching, and sharing personally is part of our witness for Christ, how much disclosure is appropriate from the pulpit?

Homileticians have been divided on this topic. For example, on one side of the debate, David Buttrick believes that personal illustrations will always "split consciousness," causing the listener to focus on the speaker and not the message, and asserts, "To be blunt, there are virtually no good reasons to talk about ourselves from the pulpit."[15] On the other side, John Claypool, inspired by Henri Nouwen, calls for preachers to dare to make available to others what they have learned through "an honest grappling with their own woundedness." "I can help most," says Claypool, "when I am honest enough to lay bare my own wounds and acknowledge what is saving and helping me."[16] Thomas Long declares that most preachers occupy a middle ground.[17]

It is a fine line we tread as preachers between preaching Christ and him crucified (1 Cor 2:2) and parading ourselves. Despite the ongoing debate, when we turn to the pages of Scripture we find a number of examples of personal vulnerability in public preaching. Isaiah speaks about his own sinfulness (Isa 6:5); Jeremiah about his shock, fear, and agony (Jer 1:6; 20:14–18); Amos about his humble roots (Amos 7:14); and Habbakuk about his struggle and questions (Hab 1:2). In the New Testament, the Apostle Paul is very transparent about his humanity and weakness. He refers to his own distress and anguish (2 Cor 2:4), his weakness and fear (1 Cor 2:3; 2 Cor 7:5; 12:9), acknowledges himself to be a sinner (1 Tim 1:12–17), and speaks of his previous persecution of Christian believers (1 Cor 15:9; Phil 3:6). Paul presents the mortal "earthen vessel" in order to better display the contrasting "surpassing greatness of power" that belongs to God (2 Cor 4:7 NASB), and so models how the preacher's story can exalt Christ, "when it

---

14. Windsor, "Preliminary Session," *One Step Ahead Preaching: Discovering New Skills in Preaching* DVD.

15. Buttrick, *Homiletic*, 142.

16. Claypool, *The Preaching Event*, 87.

17. Long, *The Witness of Preaching*, 221. One example would be Fred Craddock, who states that, "self-disclosure in moderation is appropriate in preaching." Craddock, *Preaching*, 209.

contrasts for the hearers the weakness of the preacher and the strength of the Lord."[18]

Self-disclosure in preaching is about not only whether personal stories are permissible, but also whether such stories, "reveal or mask the preacher's true self."[19] This does not call for airing one's dirty laundry, but, as Christian psychologist David Benner puts it, seeking to turn up as who I am *in reality* and who I am becoming as I seek after God.[20] C. S. Lewis called for such authenticity from our true self when he advised that the prayer preceding all prayers is, "May it be the real I who speaks. May it be the real Thou that I speak to."[21] Benner states that our true-self-in-Christ is vital for genuine authenticity. In contrast, our false self is pretending, knowingly or unconsciously, to be someone we are not. It is a self we create, package, and retail in the belief that it will earn us love based on what we do, what we have, and what others think of us.

This is particularly an issue in a world saturated with virtual reality and social media, where the temptation to construct and inhabit a false self is very strong. There are any number of social platforms from which we can explore questions of identity and social connection. We might use Twitter, Instagram, Snapchat, upload video to YouTube, or swipe right on the online dating site Tinder, all accessible on our cell phones or tablets. Facebook users choose how to best present themselves with user profiles that are clear constructs, containing both truth and artifice, digital selves that "become fractured, confused reflections of a person, never wholly unreal, but never wholly real either—a seeming half-truth."[22] As one pastor asks in using Facebook for social interaction, "Am I interacting with their vulnerable and far more beautiful real self or their ideal self?"[23] In an increasingly online world, the preacher is called to witness to the Word made flesh "in a world where flesh and words are becoming segregated."[24] Hooke believes being our true selves is a necessary component of good preaching because "it is as [the preacher] displays how the Christian faith makes sense of her life that others come to believe it for themselves."[25] As preachers we must resist the allure of the "false self" to perform, discard the facades we adopt as strate-

---

18. Eswine, *Preaching to a Post-Everything World*, 88.
19. Hooke, *Transforming Preaching*, 11.
20. Benner, *The Gift of Being Yourself*.
21. Lewis, *Prayer*, 83.
22. Boon and Sinclair, "A World I Don't Inhabit," 104.
23. Evenson, "Pastor on Facebook?" 331.
24. Thoren, "The Pastor on Facebook," 279.
25. Hooke, *Transforming Preaching*, 11.

gies to avoid vulnerability, and the fronts we create to cover our pride, pain, or fear.[26] We must strive to live authentically before God, and bring our true self, appropriately and yet genuinely, into the pulpit.

Eswine calls for the Christian preacher to pursue a "redemptive vulnerability." As preachers, we are "clay jars," accepting the limitations of human existence, but we also hold out the "treasure" of the gospel and demonstrate that true power and redemption rests not with us, but with Christ.[27] I believe this redemptive vulnerability and willingness to disclose the preacher's true self has much to offer in our contemporary world. To demonstrate this I will discuss the benefits of self-disclosure and preaching in two contexts: first, in New Zealand (my context), the preacher's self-disclosure models an alternative to a dominant cultural model of masculinity (one that is afraid of showing weakness, views emotional expression as unmanly, and chooses to suffer in silence); secondly, appropriate self-disclosure offers a necessary corrective and challenge to Pentecostal-Charismatic theology and praxis in the areas of leadership and suffering.

Vulnerability, Preaching, and "Kiwi" Masculinity

Conceptions of masculinity in Aotearoa-New Zealand have been heavily influenced by a number of influential images, such as the pioneer, the rural man of the land, the patriotic soldier, and the rugby hard man.[28] Theologian and psychotherapist Philip Culbertson argues that New Zealand's settler history provided the foundation for a new definition of Kiwi masculinity: The Man Alone.[29] The idealized Kiwi bloke has been described as, "a stoic, Man Alone figure, who provided for his family but was emotionally removed from them."[30] Historian Jock Phillips writes of the psychological injuries that have resulted from these stereotypical notions of masculinity:

> Men afraid to admit weakness, fear, or defeat suffered in silence or channeled their feelings into bitterness or self-contempt. Men thinking it a weakness to express emotion, found it difficult to communicate and were locked into a lonely isolation. . . . Men's

26. Benner, "Touched by an Author," 49; Benner, *The Gift of Being Yourself*, 61–89.
27. Eswine, *Preaching to a Post-Everything World*, 89; Eswine, "Redemptive Vulnerability," n.p.
28. Culbertson, "Men's Quest for Wholeness," 1–19; Phillips, *A Man's Country*.
29. Culbertson, "Men's Quest for Wholeness," 4. The kiwi is a flightless bird native to New Zealand and a national symbol. The term "Kiwi" is used widely as the colloquial term for New Zealanders.
30. Hume, "Man (Still) Alone," n. p.

frustration at their inability to communicate effectively poisoned their sexual relations or else found an outlet in violence.[31]

The quest to embody the strong, silent "kiwi bloke" has had significant consequences for men "in terms of poor levels of health, and high rates of imprisonment, domestic violence, suicide, and divorce."[32] Mike King, founder of The Key to Life Charitable Trust, believes our "harden up, stay staunch attitude" needs to change and calls for an attitudinal change at a societal level.[33] This is also an issue at earlier stages of life. The "stoic male" ideal produces boys who "cannot express their feelings, suffer from depression and anxiety, and lack the resiliency to bounce back after hardship."[34] Counselor Stephen Gaddis cites research saying, "We live in an anti-relational, vulnerability-despising culture, one that not only fails to nurture the skills of connection, but actively fears them."[35]

We can find inspiration for preaching with redemptive vulnerability and contesting unbiblical ideas of masculinity in the example of the Apostle Paul. In his message of the cross Paul purposefully distances himself from the Greco-Roman ideals regarding honor/shame, strength/weakness, and masculinity.[36] He is eager to show how the cross and resurrection not only set the basic pattern of Christian discipleship, but also the content and manner of his preaching.[37] Paul's coming to the Corinthians "in weakness and in fear and in much trembling" (1 Cor 2:3) is an intentional choice that places him in direct contrast with the popular orators of his culture.[38] For example, when Paul's personal presence is criticized as "unimpressive" and his speech "contemptible" (2 Cor 10:10), Larson contends that the attacks must be understood in terms of "a cultural context that held authority, rhetorical skill, and masculinity to be almost synonymous."[39] Paul comes as an "anti-rhetor"

31. Phillips, *A Man's Country*, 289.
32. Paris et al., Introduction to *The Life of Brian*, 14.
33. King, "New Zealand needs," n. p.
34. Casteix, "Boys Don't Cry? Sure They Do, and We Need to Embrace it," n. p.
35. Gaddis, "Cool/Manly?" 49; citing Real, *How Can I Get Through to You?*
36. Shi, *Body Language*, 72.
37. Knowles, *We Preach Not Ourselves*, 255.
38. Thiselton, *The First Epistle to the Corinthians*, 213. Garland identifies a range of opinions on Paul's weakness that caused himself or others to question his efficacy for the role: "an unimpressive presence, a repellent physical malady, his toiling with his hands, his relative impoverishment, his vulnerability to persecution, his refusal to play to the crowds with silver-tongued oratory." Garland, *1 Corinthians*, 84–85.
39. Larson, "Paul's Masculinity," 91. Larson contends that Paul may have encountered resistance from some potential male converts because the weakness embraced by Paul was "strongly associated with femininity."

seeking to reflect "a humiliated, crucified messiah."[40] For Paul the Christian minister's weakness is "the point where the deepest integration of his life and his message is possible."[41] Foster describes this as the "cross life," a life that reflects the cross in terms of submission and service.[42] Paul refuses to acquiesce to accepted cultural norms regarding masculinity, and chooses to seek God's glory rather than man's, his commitment being "to true godliness and not manliness."[43]

Paul helps us to see that in God's kingdom, being powerless, tender, and vulnerable is not a sign of weakness, but is, on the contrary, a precondition of strength. Also, real masculinity examined in the light of the cross "can be emotional, vulnerable, weak, and full of grace as much as it is strong, confident, and disciplined."[44] The myth that sharing the more vulnerable aspects of our selves undermines masculine strength must be confronted and challenged. Christian counselor Jane McWilliams believes it is imperative that preachers, in order to facilitate social change, confront the cultural discourses around topics such as hierarchies of masculinity, patriarchy and homo-social theory: "We need men to be speaking into it, men to be vulnerable and sensitive and authentic and to speak into and stand up to behaviors and stereotypes and norms . . . The more men who will be willing to be vulnerable around these things, the better." McWilliams carries on to say that preaching "is a must" to address these issues.[45]

One important way in which preachers can help is by modeling aspects of the journey of growth in the life of faith.[46] The modeling hypothesis in communication studies posits that one person's self-disclosure serves as a model for the self-disclosure of others.[47] Arthurs and Gurevich refer to the "spiral effect" as "one self-disclosure begets another, usually deeper, one."[48] Through self-disclosure, we show respect for our listeners by trusting them with our story, and, by the Spirit's prompting, invite others to look more truthfully at their own need for courage and grace.

Everything within us may rail against dropping the mask of sophisticated respectability, but the urge to conceal must be resisted. In Brené

40. White, "Not in Lofty Speech," 132–33.
41. Bauckham, "Weakness," 4.
42. Foster, *Celebration of Discipline*, 145.
43. Shi, *Body Language*, 72.
44. Pyle, *Man Enough*, 109.
45. McWilliams, personal communication, 5 May 2016.
46. Mulligan and Allen, *Make the World Come Alive*, 30.
47. Tardy and Dindia, "Self-Disclosure," 236.
48. Arthurs and Gurevich, "Self-Disclosure," 220.

Brown's words, "we must dare to show up and be seen."[49] Ralph Lewis and Gregg Lewis speak of the importance of "risking ourselves" for meaningful ministry: "That personal risk is the price of involvement; the preacher becomes vulnerable. Love and ministry always extract that price."[50] The preacher is asked "to show up, to claim and own his words and his beliefs, to inhabit them fully, and to offer them to the hearer."[51]

Preaching with appropriate levels of personal vulnerability is, for me, part of living Foster's "cross life." It is tempting as a preacher to hide, to "lie about myself and by doing so to perpetuate the lies we all carry round with us."[52] As a preacher I could perpetuate idealized notions of masculinity through subtle comments that ridicule weakness, or by always presenting myself as strong, denying fear, never needing help. A form of courage often disregarded in our ideas of masculinity is, "the courage to be vulnerably honest about who [we] are and what [we] can and cannot do."[53] Chris Neufeld-Erdman maintains that personal vulnerability in preaching is "about being as real about God and gospel and kingdom as I can be," which means "I can't help but show up in the room in all of my humanness."[54]

And so I risk myself; I become vulnerable, and share as an act of love. I share about the fear I felt at becoming a father for the first time, but how God has helped me to enjoy the role. I share of my grappling with the darkness of depression, and how God and a number of his people comforted me and journeyed with me toward healing. I share about how ignorant I was in my early years as a husband, but how God in his grace convicted me, and showed me how to better honor the wife of my youth.

And after I share, people open up. A parent reveals the impact my vulnerability had for a teenage son. A brother sends me a letter telling how he has been inspired to be more open and honest in his marriage and more gentle with his children. An older man meets with me and confesses a sinful secret. As Brown affirms, "Vulnerability begets vulnerability; courage is contagious."[55] Such sharing may at times leave one feeling what Brown labels "a vulnerability hangover,"[56] but while at times risky, such vulnerable preaching is still valuable. By modeling a redemptive vulnerability, such

---

49. Brown, *Daring Greatly*, 2.
50. Lewis and Lewis, *Inductive Preaching*, 23.
51. Hooke, *Transforming Preaching*, 12.
52. Neufeld-Erdman, *Ordinary Preacher*, 43.
53. Pyle, *Man Enough*, 123.
54. Neufeld-Erdman, *Ordinary Preacher*, 45.
55. Brown, *Daring Greatly*, 16.
56. Ibid., 13.

unhealthy cultural norms as our "harden up, stay strong" attitude are challenged and there is opportunity for different conceptions of masculinity to be explored.

Vulnerability, Preaching, and Pentecostal-Charismatic Approaches to Leadership and Suffering

Pentecostal-Charismatic Approaches to Leadership

Vulnerability in preaching is also of benefit in the area of Pentecostal-Charismatic leadership and consequent issues relating to power and authority.[57] Pentecostal historian Brett Knowles notes a trend in pentecostal leadership in the late twentieth century which he calls "pastoral theocracy."[58] This is the idea that, "the pastor is God's agent" and that "God rules the church through the pastor and his appointed leaders."[59] Alan Jamieson observes that this trend brought a new emphasis on charismatic leadership based on extraordinary qualities or individual gifts, and produced an authoritarian leadership style. The result was that Pentecostal pastors appeared to hold much greater power than ministers in traditional churches; they "expected leaders to lead" and congregations were given little say in decision-making.[60]

While many leaders in their confessional theology advocate servant leadership as practiced by Jesus Christ, Roger Heuser and Byron Klaus observe that not many openly recognize "the dissonance or ambiguity of an operational theology that in practice embraces an autocratic, 'controlling' leadership in a religious hierarchy."[61] This is at odds with Paul's "strategic subversion of the secular, egotistical leadership norms of his day," a leadership approach which Julien Ogereau believes provides a compelling challenge to "the self-sufficient, self-confident, self-assertive, and self-made leader oftentimes enthroned as paradigmatic for Western church leaders."[62] Don Barry, senior leader of Gateway Church in Hamilton, New Zealand, re-

---

57. What I discuss in this section may well be pertinent to other areas of the body of Christ, but I speak particularly in regards to Pentecostal-Charismatic leadership as it is the approach with which I have the most experience and involvement.

58. Knowles, *Transforming Pentecostalism*, 173, 175.

59. Knowles, personal communication, 27 May 2016.

60. Jamieson, *A Churchless Faith*, 25.

61. Heuser and Klaus, "Charismatic Leadership Theory," 161. As Okesson notes, servant leadership has become "especially convenient within Christian circles for 'business-as-usual' under the glossy veneer of doing it for Christ." Okesson, "'Are Pastors Human?'" 133.

62. Ogereau, "Paul's Leadership Ethos," 33.

fers to this leadership model as the "man of God" syndrome, which tends to place leaders on pedestals.[63] Although it can be constructive, at its worst this approach can potentially result in a domineering and autocratic leadership style, cults of personality, a sense of entitlement, a perception of questions as troublesome, a lack of accountability, the abuse and misuse of power, and distance between the preacher and the people.[64]

Expectations on leadership can also be unreasonable and onerous. We live in a culture enamored with entertainers and heavily influenced by media, with voracious demands for greater quality and excellence. For many contemporary churchgoers, preachers become performers with a celebrity status similar to that of the orators of Paul's time.[65] Eddie Kaufholz, concerned with the moral failure of a number of prominent church leaders and the current church models that produce celebrity ministers, laments the situation in which many church leaders find themselves: "It must be a lonely life not really being vulnerable or known." He goes on to say:

> We must do whatever we can do make the role of a pastor one that truly allows for a person to be a human . . . [and] to not allow these men and women to be consumed by our expectations and worship of them. Because when we do this, we kill our pulpit and make humans out to be the gods they were never meant to be.[66]

With all of these factors taken together, it is easy to see why the "man of God" syndrome—whether enforced from above by the leaders themselves or generated from below by the consumptive desires of those who would follow—can be detrimental to the ongoing well-being of both the minister and church community.[67]

Adopting a stance of redemptive vulnerability in ministry is one way to address such issues. A leader's unexamined interior life can result in disaster for leader and organization.[68] Henri Nouwen's call for ministers to be "articulators of inner events" is an important one. When we as ministers "become familiar with the complexities of our own inner lives," and "discover the dark corners as well as the light spots," we are able to "ar-

---

63. Barry, personal communication, 5 June 2016.

64. Olson, "Pentecostalism's Dark Side," 29; Knowles, *Transforming Pentecostalism*, 242; Crawley, "Questioning 'the Man of God,'" n.p.; Trammel and Moll, "Grading the Movement," 38–41; Lewis, "Why Have Scholars?," 74–76.

65. White, "Not in Lofty Speech," 133.

66. Kaufholz, "The Mega-Problem," n. p.

67. See Fraser and Brown, "Navigating the Treacherous Waters," 94–109.

68. Heuser and Klaus, "Charismatic Leadership Theory," 166.

ticulate" these discoveries to others.[69] Such articulation must be sensitive to the human condition, as it encourages people to recognize their own inner struggles. Reflecting the modeling hypothesis, the pastor is able to disclose their own journey, thoughts, and experiences, as they gain self-awareness and understanding, and this self-disclosure "invites others to be honest with their lives."[70]

Julie Ma and Wonsuk Ma recognize that Pentecostalism has revealed the shadow side of power orientation, and that the "powerfulness" of Pentecostal Christianity frequently leaves its leaders susceptible to temptation. For this reason, they maintain it is critical to expand the concept of power to include weakness and humility.[71] The fifth point of Windsor's LUCIS model of preaching for Kiwi audiences is helpful here: self-deprecation.[72] Self-deprecation helps us, in Murray Robertson's words, to not take ourselves too seriously.[73] While most often understood in the area of humor, self-deprecation can also refer to an attitude of "modest self-presentation."[74] Zhu Hua links self-deprecation with the Māori value of *whakaiti*, i.e., being humble and modest.[75] Humility is a trait valued by New Zealanders in leadership. Jeffrey Kennedy points out that high levels of performance must be balanced by "a somewhat modest, self-deprecating attitude."[76] As Jo Brosnahan, founder of Leadership New Zealand, succinctly states, "Kiwis like humility."[77] Humility helps us to "step outside the box of self-importance," and "brings us down to earth: it is living leadership *with* others, not above them."[78] Through self-deprecation, preacher and listener are on the same level. This removes any sense of the preacher being "above" the audience, and closes the distance between them.

Dan Allender believes that a Christian leader's admission of weakness removes "the dividing wall of hierarchy" and "false assumptions about people in power," and proves false the myth that the leader is "imbued with

---

69. Nouwen, *The Wounded Healer*, 42.
70. Chartier, *Preaching as Communication*, 34.
71. Ma and Ma, *Mission in the Spirit*, 39.
72. The five points are: Laidback, Understated, Casual, Informal, and Self-deprecating. Murray Robertson presentation; Paul Windsor interview with Stephen Worsley, See "Session 5: Communication," in Worley, *One Step Ahead Preaching* DVD.
73. Ibid.
74. DeLamater et al., *Social Psychology*, 154.
75. Hua, "Identifying Research Paradigms," 16.
76. Kennedy, "Leadership and Culture in New Zealand," 422.
77. Bland, "Leaders of the Pack," n. p.
78. Spiller et al., *Wayfaring Leadership*, 63.

superhuman 'stuff.'"[79] This holds true for self-disclosure in the preaching event. I must resist unrealistic views and expectations of authority, accept my humanity, and adopt the role of a servant. In following Christ's example of coming not to be served but to serve (Mark 10:45), I reject worldly games of ambition and seek to be free from concerns of authority and status. As Richard Foster puts it, in the discipline of service, "We become available and vulnerable."[80] Don Barry acknowledges the difficulties such vulnerability might cause, but calls for preachers to be honest about their pain and brokenness. "In a beautiful irony," he says, "I have found, rather than undermining leadership authority, vulnerability and honesty actually increases [sic] credibility and therefore authority."[81] Appropriate self-disclosure in preaching also offers an important corrective to Pentecostal-Charismatic attitudes toward suffering.

Pentecostal-Charismatic Views of Suffering

Pentecostal-Charismatic Christianity affirms a belief in triumphant Christian living and "an emphasis on power to overcome problems in one's life."[82] We can see this in Johnathan Alvarado's endorsement of Pentecostal preaching, with "its themes of victory through the cross of Christ or power in the blood of the Lamb or the anointing of the Holy Spirit," and its ability to transform hearers "into an empowered community of overcomers ready to take on the world!"[83] This is indeed true, and provides great courage, hope, and comfort for believers.

However, other Pentecostals see this homiletical emphasis on victory as problematic. For example, Keith Warrington notes that Pentecostals have tended to concentrate on the glory of the cross rather than the suffering which, despite some exceptions, has largely been neglected.[84] Pentecostal preachers often do not tackle the problem of unanswered prayers or disillusioned faith. Much of Pentecostal-Charismatic preaching and testimony

---

79. Allender, *Leading with a Limp*, 172–73.
80. Foster, *Celebration of Discipline*, 165.
81. Barry, *Water Under the Bridge*, 185.
82. Kärkkäinen, *Toward a Pneumatological Theology*, 167.
83. Alvarado, "Worship in the Spirit," 150.
84. Warrington, *Pentecostal Theology*, 303; cf. Ma, "Asian (Classical) Pentecostal Theology in Context," 75. In recent years a number of Pentecostal missiologists and scholars, aware of this lack, have begun exploring the theme of suffering in the Christian life, e.g., Menzies, "Reflections on Suffering," 141–49; Mittelstadt, *The Spirit and Suffering in Luke-Acts*; Warrington, *Healing and Suffering*.

is intended to "increase and strengthen faith," and so tends to focus on "success" stories.[85] However, theodical concerns are deeply rooted within narratives of healing and the miraculous. Daniel Castelo provides a strong challenge, averring that the Pentecostal worldview, as typically formulated and promulgated, "cannot account—either conceptually or practically—for those cases in which healings and miracles do not occur," and, as such, Pentecostals and Charismatics are "often impoverished, given their tradition's resources, to account for how life is."[86] Veli-Matti Kärkkäinen acknowledges the importance of talk of faith, power, healing, and miracles for Pentecostal-Charismatic Christians, but sees as more problematic the inevitable "questions of life" and how to face "the dark side of life."[87] An inclination towards emphasizing victory and the miraculous can lead to contrary circumstances being perceived as a potential threat. This in turn can lead to much damage for people already hurting; as Castelo puts it, "We would rather feel guilty (or deem others as guilty) than to admit we do not know God's ways."[88]

To address this gap, Kärkkäinen helpfully draws on Luther's theologies of the cross and of glory.[89] As Luther puts it, the theologian of glory, "does not know God hidden in suffering. Therefore, he prefers works to suffering, glory to the cross, strength to weakness, wisdom to folly, and, in general, good to evil."[90] A theology of glory preaches the cross as "just another technique for getting what we want;"[91] by contrast, a theology of the cross "accepts the difficult thing" and "looks directly into pain, and "calls a thing what it is."[92] This challenges Pentecostals to provide space for both the miraculous and for suffering within their understanding and approach to Christian living. For Warrington, the victory and glory connected with the

85. Castelo, "What if Miracles Don't Happen?" 167.
86. Ibid., 237.
87. Kärkkäinen, *Pneumatological Theology*, 167; Bruce Stevens, an Australian clinical psychologist and theologian, notes a shift in Australian Pentecostal preaching from a pre-WWII affirmation that believers will suffer in this life to a denial of negative feelings in the 1960s and the emergence of a form of preaching "that was impatient with suffering and anything less than being victorious in Christ." Stevens contends that our culture tends to support the pervasive use of the psychological mechanism known as the "manic defense" (i.e., a psychological way of avoiding the recognition or feeling of a negative emotion). In this culture Pentecostalism jettisoned its earlier healthy recognition of suffering, and is now associated with an overemphasis on a theology of victory and little interest in a theology of suffering. Stevens, "'Up, Up and Away,'" 285–86, 294.
88. Castelo, "What if Miracles Don't Happen?" 242.
89. See Kärkkäinen, "Theology of the Cross," 150–63.
90. Madsen, *The Theology of the Cross*, 74.
91. Willimon, *Proclamation and Theology*, 69.
92. Tchividjian, *Glorious Ruin*, 9.

cross have been comprehended in triumphalistic terms, while vital biblical themes such as victory through suffering, strength through weakness, and light through darkness have been generally disregarded. Warrington issues the following challenge:

> The recognition of the place of suffering in Pentecostal theology needs to be redeemed as an integral aspect of an authentic spirituality that acknowledges the value of suffering in the life of the believer and does not simply attempt to exclude it or assume that its presence is intrinsically illegitimate.[93]

Many believers today, influenced by a culture infused with individualism and self-help philosophy, assume a right to happiness and divine provision of pleasant experiences. The idea that God could use suffering in our lives as a means to instruction and growth is a scandalous and repugnant idea to many believers.[94]

To this end, Castelo sees the idea of the believer as "empowered for witness" as including the power to engage in longsuffering as a witness to the Spirit's presence and power in our lives, and to be aided by the Spirit "to endure suffering and pain with the prospect that these do not have the final say in our lives' meaning and significance."[95]

Through appropriate self-disclosure, the preacher can model living in the eschatological tension between the "already" and the "not yet," between the suffering present and the glorious future.[96] She can acknowledge the reality of pain and suffering, and, rather than minimizing or avoiding it, call it what it is in light of God's grace in Jesus Christ, thereby providing a message of hope. Empowered to witness, she can speak of the Spirit's strength and presence in the midst of suffering, testifying to God's goodness.

To this end, Barry advocates a "willingness to disclose the darker parts; the broken regions; the parts that we are tempted to skillfully manage and re-represent like a spin doctor might, rather than telling the raw, unflattering truth."[97] In this way, we acknowledge that the notion of suffering is redeemed as a valuable and integral element in the development of the life and mission of a believer.[98]

---

93. Warrington, *Pentecostal Theology*, 303.
94. Warrington, "Suffering and the Spirit in Luke-Acts," 31–32.
95. Castelo, "What if Miracles Don't Happen?" 237.
96. Hoekema, *The Bible and the Future*, 68–75.
97. Barry, *Water Under the Bridge*, 175.
98. Warrington, "Suffering and the Spirit," 31.

For Kärkkäinen, the church is not a showplace for the successful, but a healing "hospital" for the suffering and needy.[99] The awareness that the preacher is vulnerable in the same ways as the congregation can help listeners to identify with the preacher and feel their own vulnerability validated, while also sensing that "such vulnerability is 'safe' in the grace of God."[100] As the preacher shares of her journey through pain and suffering, others are validated and encouraged to reflect honestly on their experience.

And so I share: in one sermon, I share about the silent grief of miscarriage and attendant shattered dreams and turbulent emotions, while in another I share of my overwhelming sorrow at the death of my beloved father. I share my struggles with health concerns, all the while declaring God's faithfulness and lordship through it all. The preacher can engage in self-disclosure as part of a pastoral response to suffering that, with the empowerment of the Holy Spirit, can give voice to human lament, support listeners in facing reality, help to make suffering bearable, strengthen faith, and enable a sense of joy.[101]

Guidelines for Appropriate Vulnerability in Preaching: How Much is Too Much?

There is no "one-size-fits-all" formula for healthy vulnerability in preaching, but there are some good guidelines to consider. Self-disclosure is not meant to be a technique, but a style of life.[102] As Willimon points out, "To intentionally pepper my sermon with doses of predetermined authenticity is to be, well, inauthentic."[103] According to Chartier, preachers should be consistent, practicing self-disclosure in all areas of life and ministry.[104] If the pulpit is the only place where people are permitted to see into the preacher's life, self-disclosure will be perceived as insincere or manipulative.

Self-disclosure must be regulated by the principle of appropriateness in order to have a positive effect.[105] There needs to be discernment, sensitivity, and wisdom in the use of personal disclosure. Robinson shares the example of a pastor preaching on lust who admitted, "I know the power of sexual temptation. There are times when I still lust after women. In fact, standing

---

99. Kärkkäinen, *Pneumatological Theology*, 178.
100. Mulligan and Allen, *Word Come Alive*, 29, 30.
101. Aden and Hughes, *Preaching God's Compassion*, 51.
102. Palmberg and Scandrette, "Self-Disclosure," 218.
103. Willimon, "Naked Preachers," 62.
104. Chartier, *Preaching as Communication*, 39.
105. Chen, "Intercultural Effectiveness," 395.

here this morning, looking out at this congregation, I've lusted after some of you."[106] Too much information! Such inappropriate sharing shatters the effectiveness of the sermon and becomes a barrier to the message (and likely leaves people wondering, "Has he been looking at me?").

Chartier argues that preachers should present a balanced self-picture with regards to two areas: first, with respect to the past and the present; and second, with respect to personal strengths and weaknesses.[107] As a general rule, sharing about an event from the past is easier for people to handle. Robinson's general rule on unresolved issues is also helpful: "If you haven't worked a situation through to a biblical solution, it's not ready to use as an illustration."[108] However, although speaking about the past is less risky, Chartier argues that while revealing past experiences might aid people in identifying with the preacher's struggles, disclosing what is happening in the present "has the power of immediacy, and people recognize the trust the preacher has in them when such vulnerable self-data is presented."[109] Again, wisdom and discernment are required. A balanced self-picture is also required in terms of personal strengths and weaknesses. If we disclose only stories of weakness, we can present a totally negative view of human experience. On the other hand, if we share only positive and victorious stories, we run the risk of presenting an idealization of the preacher's experience as one like us in every way, but without sin, which will ultimately ring hollow. Rather, the Christian life "consists of the interplay of both victories and defeats," and so the preacher is encouraged to share both, so that the congregation "will be encouraged toward both genuine repentance and joyous celebration."[110]

Self-disclosure should also be related to the needs of others, rather than self-centered.[111] In other words, sharing information about oneself should be genuinely designed to encourage the congregation's self-exploration, instead of a means of achieving the preacher's personal catharsis. Ramsay cautions that preaching might be used subtly or not so subtly as a means to gain ego satisfaction for the preacher, and, rather than being an event proclaiming the gospel, the sermon becomes "a moment of pastoral confession, attention-seeking or, worse yet, psychological exhibitionism."[112]

106. Robinson, "Bringing Yourself into the Pulpit," 131.
107. Chartier, *Preaching as Communication*, 42.
108. Robinson, "Bringing Yourself into the Pulpit," 130.
109. Chartier, *Preaching as Communication*, 40.
110. Arthurs and Gurevich, "Self-Disclosure," 226.
111. Chartier, *Preaching as Communication*, 40.
112. Ramsay, "Self-Disclosure," n. p.

The preacher must also be aware of her audience. Day makes an important point: "A congregation that knows you (and likes you) will make allowances. A strange congregation can jump to conclusions which are unwarranted."[113] How well you know (and are known) by the people to whom you are preaching will impact on the level of self-disclosure you employ. This is an important part of "exegeting the audience."[114]

Self-disclosure should always be in service to the message of the sermon, and true to God's work in our lives.[115] Illustration should be message-focused. Shauna Hannam says, "If that personal story makes the preacher the protagonist over and above Jesus Christ, that's a problem. . . . All of our preaching should point to what God has done in Jesus Christ and continues to do for us and with us through God's Holy Spirit."[116] Keith Willhite proposes a very helpful "Illustration Hierarchy."[117] He posits that the most effective type of illustration is one from the experience of both the speaker and the listener, which not only creates high audience connection, but also serves the message by fulfilling the purpose of application and validation of your intended point.

Final Thoughts

Willimon asserts that personal references in preaching and the preacher's exposure of self are "some of the most dangerous, theologically questionable of homiletical practices—and among the most essential."[118] It can indeed be risky, but also very valuable. My desire and intention has been to live authentically before people in a fitting manner, whether with students, my children, rugby teammates, or within the church community. This also impacts my preaching. It has been my experience that as I have sought to sensitively share my highs and lows, my triumphs and my trials, people have been more open to God's transforming word, and encouraged to examine their own hearts with greater ease. And I endeavor to share not from the lofty platform of an expert dispensing pearls of hidden wisdom, but rather from the perspective of a fellow traveler on the journey with *whānau* (family) toward greater intimacy with Christ. I have sought to do this—to use Mackay's famous analogy—not from the safe and shaded distance of the

113. Day, *Embodying the Word*, 21.
114. Carter, et al., *Preaching God's Word*, 84–98.
115. Smith, *The Vulnerable Pastor*, 174.
116. "Preaching Moment 75: Shauna Hannan."
117. Willhite, *Preaching with Relevance without Dumbing Down*, 112.
118. Willimon, "Foreword," 12.

balcony, but from the outlook of the dusty road where "life is tensely lived," and "concern is never far from the wayfarer's heart."[119] As I share, I am aware of some of the circumstances in the lives of many of those listening: a brother battling a debilitating disease; another grieving the loss of a loved one; a family recently immigrated trying to make a home in a strange land; a couple trying to conceive; a sister battling with doubts about her faith; a teenager struggling with bullying. And before this diverse group of precious people, I stand to share not only God's word, but myself as well.

As Stowell puts it, "True transparency in preaching enables people to see right through us to Jesus."[120] I draw on the words of Richard of Chichester's prayer in desiring that, with each passing day, our people may see him more clearly, love him more dearly, and follow him more nearly.[121] Because in the end, our preaching is about him, *his* greatness and mercy, *his* worthiness to be worshiped and obeyed. I think as preachers we can learn to be more vulnerable, more at home with our weakness and humanity. I have found this approach to be beneficial for myself and for those listening, and with this in mind I believe our people will benefit from preachers willing to share not only the gospel but their lives as well (1 Thess 2:8), so that, ultimately, God is glorified.

---

119. Mackay, *A Preface to Christian Theology*, 29–30.
120. Stowell, "Keep it on Christ in You," 61.
121. English, *Theology Remixed*, 129.

Bibliography

Aden, LeRoy, and Robert G. Hughes. *Preaching God's Compassion: Comforting Those Who Suffer.* Minneapolis: Augsburg, 2002.

Allender, Dan B. *Leading with a Limp.* Colorado Springs, CO: WaterBrook, 2006.

Alvarado, Johnathan E. "Worship in the Spirit: Pentecostal Perspectives on Liturgical Theology and Praxis." *Journal of Pentecostal Theology* 21 (2012) 135–51.

Arthurs, Jeffrey, and Andrew Gurevich. "Theological and Rhetorical Perspectives on Self-Disclosure in Preaching." *BSac* 157:626 (2000) 217.

Barry, Don. *Water Under the Bridge: Loads of Other Stuff too: A Journey into Values-Shaped Leadership.* Auckland: Castle, 2015.

Bauckham, Richard. "Weakness—Paul's and Ours." *Themelios* 7:3 (1982) 4.

Benner, David G. *The Gift of Being Yourself: The Sacred Call to Self-Discovery.* Downers Grove, IL: IVP Academic, 2004.

———. "Touched by an Author: An Interactive Review of *True Self/False Self: Unmasking the Spirit Within* [by] M. Basil Pennington." *Conversations* 1 (2003) 49.

Bland, Vikki. "Leaders of the Pack." *New Zealand Herald* (18 July 2006). http://www.nzherald.co.nz/vikki-bland/news/article.cfm?a_id=224&objectid=10391878.

Boon, Stuart, and Christine Sinclair. "A World I Don't Inhabit: Disquiet and Identity in Second Life and Facebook." *EMI* 46:2 (2009) 104.

Brooks, Phillips. *Lectures on Preaching.* New York: E. P. Dutton & Company, 1878.

Brown, Brené. *Daring Greatly: How the Courage to be Vulnerable Transforms the Way We Live, Love, Parent, and Lead.* New York: Penguin, 2012.

Buttrick, David G. *Homiletic: Moves and Structures.* Philadelphia: Fortress, 1987.

Carter, Terry G., et al. *Preaching God's Word: A Hands-on Approach to Preparing, Developing, and Delivering the Sermon.* Grand Rapids: Zondervan, 2005.

Casteix, Joelle. "Boys Don't Cry? Sure They Do, and We Need to Embrace It." http://www.stuff.co.nz/life-style/parenting./big-kids/five-to-ten/82987791/boys-dont-cry-sure-they-do-and-we-need-to-embrace-it.

Castelo, Daniel. "What if Miracles Don't Happen? Empowerment for Longsuffering." *Journal of Pentecostal Theology* 23 (2014) 237.

Chartier, Myron R. *Preaching as Communication: An Interpersonal Perspective.* Nashville: Abingdon, 1981.

Chen, Guo-Ming. "Intercultural Effectiveness." In *Intercultural Communication: A Reader,* edited by Larry A. Samovar, Richard E. Porter, and Edwin R. McDaniel, 393–401. Boston: Wadsworth, 2009.

Claypool, John R. *The Preaching Event.* San Francisco: Harper & Row, 1989.

Craddock, Fred B. *Preaching.* Nashville: Abingdon, 1985.

Crawley, David Raymond. "Questioning 'the Man of God': Selina's Story." *Australasian Pentecostal Studies* 18 (2016) http://aps-journal.com/aps/index.php/APS/article/view/9487/9498.

Culbertson, Philip. "Men's Quest for Wholeness: The Changing Counselling Needs of Pakeha Males." *Universitas* 2 (2006) 1–19.

Day, David. *Embodying the Word: A Preacher's Guide.* London: SPCK, 2005.

DeLamater, John, et al. *Social Psychology 8th Edition.* Boulder, CO: Westview, 2015.

English, Adam C. *Theology Remixed: Christianity as Story, Game, Language, Culture.* Downers Grove, IL: IVP Academic, 2010.

Eswine, Zack. *Preaching to a Post-Everything World: Crafting Biblical Sermons that Connect with our Culture*. Grand Rapids: Baker, 2008.

———. "Redemptive Vulnerability." *Leadership Journal* (30 October 2013). http://www.ctlibrary.com/le/2013/november/redemptive-vulnerability.html.

Evenson, Kae. "Pastor on Facebook? Not for Me." *Word and World* (1 January 2010) 331.

Foster, Richard. *Celebration of Discipline*. Rev. ed. London: Hodder & Stoughton, 1989.

Fraser, Benson P., and William J. Brown. "Navigating the Treacherous Waters of Celebrity Culture: A New Challenge for Evangelicals." In *Evangelical Christians and Popular Culture, Volume 3*, edited by R. H. Woods, Jr., 94–109. Santa Barbara, CA: Praeger, 2013.

Gaddis, Stephen. "Cool/Manly? Boys Growing into Good and Gorgeous Men." *NZ Journal of Counselling* 26:4 (2006) 49.

Garland, David E. *1 Corinthians*. Baker Exegetical Commentary on the New Testament. Grand Rapids: Baker, 2003.

Heisler, Greg. *Spirit-Led Preaching: The Holy Spirit's Role in Sermon Preparation and Delivery*. Nashville: B&H, 2007.

Herbert, George. "The Windows." In *The Works of George Herbert*. Hertfordshire, UK: Wordsworth Editions, 1994.

Heuser, Roger, and Byron D. Klaus. "Charismatic Leadership Theory: A Shadow Side Confessed." *Pneuma* 20:2 (1998) 161.

Hoekema, Anthony A. *The Bible and the Future*. Grand Rapids: Eerdmans, 1994.

Hooke, Ruthanna B. *Transforming Preaching*. New York: Church, 2010.

Hua, Zhu. "Identifying Research Paradigms." In *Research Methods in Intercultural Communication: A Practical Guide*, edited by Zhu Hua, 16. Chichester, UK: John Wiley & Sons, 2016.

Hume, Tim. "Man (Still) Alone." *Sunday Star Times* (1 January 2009). http://www.stuff.co.nz/sunday-star-times/features/feature-archive/the-state-of-men/134892/MEN-S-SERIES-Man-still-alone

Jamieson, Alan. *A Churchless Faith: Faith Journeys Beyond the Churches*. London: SPCK, 2002.

Johnson, Darrell W. *The Glory of Preaching: Participating in God's Transformation of the World*. Downers Grove, IL: IVP Academic, 2009.

Kärkkäinen, Veli-Matti. "Theology of the Cross: A Stumbling Block to Pentecostal/Charismatic Spirituality?" In *The Spirit and Spirituality: Essays in Honor of Russell P. Spittler*, edited by Wonsuk Ma and Robert P. Menzies, 150–63. London: T. & T. Clark, 2004.

———. *Toward a Pneumatological Theology: Pentecostal and Ecumenical Perspectives on Ecclesiology, Soteriology, and Theology of Mission*, edited by Amos Yong. Lanham, MD: University Press of America, 2002.

Kaufholz, Eddie. "The Mega-Problem Behind the 'Falls' of Megachurch Pastors." *Relevant* (12 July 2016). http://www.relevantmagazine.com/current/mega-problem-behind-falls-megachurch-pastors#Kwb6fIzlTWVj29g4.99

Kennedy, Jeffrey C. "Leadership and Culture in New Zealand." In *Culture and Leadership Across the World: The GLOBE Book of In-Depth Studies of 25 Societies*, edited by Jagdeep S. Chhokar and Felix C. Brodbeck, 422. Mahwah, NJ: Lawrence Erlbaum Associates, 2007.

King, Mike. "New Zealand Needs to Focus on Suicide Prevention NOW." http://www.entrehub.org/#!New-Zealand-needs-to-focus-on-suicide-prevention-NOW/c1fdu/57b54b540cf21c87f5075bb0

Knowles, Brett. *Transforming Pentecostalism: The Changing Face of New Zealand Pentecostalism, 1920–2010*. Lexington, KY: Emeth, 2014.

Knowles, Michael P. *We Preach Not Ourselves: Paul on Proclamation*. Grand Rapids: Brazos, 2008.

Larson, Jennifer. "Paul's Masculinity." *JBL* 123:1 (2004) 91.

Lewis, C. S. *Prayer: Letters to Malcolm*. London: Fount, 1977.

Lewis, Paul W. "Why have Scholars Left Classical Pentecostal Denominations?" *Asian Journal of Pentecostal Studies* 11:1–2 (2008) 74–76.

Lewis, Ralph L., and Gregg Lewis. *Inductive Preaching: Helping People Listen*. Wheaton, IL: Crossway, 1983.

Lischer, Richard, ed. *The Company of Preachers: Wisdom on Preaching, Augustine to the Present*. Grand Rapids: Eerdmans, 2002.

Long, Thomas G. *The Witness of Preaching*. 2nd ed. Louisville: Westminster John Knox, 2005).

Ma, Julie C., and Wonsuk Ma. *Mission in the Spirit: Towards a Pentecostal/Charismatic Theology*. Oxford: Regnum, 2010.

Ma, Wonsuk. "Asian (Classical) Pentecostal Theology in Context." In *Asian and Pentecostal: The Charismatic Face of Christianity in Asia*, edited by Allan Anderson and Edmond Tang, 75. Baguio City, Philippines: Regnum/APTS, 2005.

Mackay, John A. *A Preface to Christian Theology*. New York: MacMillan, 1941.

Madsen, Anna M. *The Theology of the Cross in Historical Perspective*. Eugene, OR: Wipf & Stock, 2007.

McClure, John S. *Preaching Words: 144 Key Terms in Homiletics*. Louisville/London: Westminster John Knox, 2007.

Menzies, William W. "Reflections on Suffering: A Pentecostal Perspective." In *The Spirit and Spirituality: Essays in Honor of Russell P. Spittler*, edited by Wonsuk Ma and Robert P. Menzies, 141–49. London: T. & T. Clark, 2004.

Mittelstadt, Martin William. *The Spirit and Suffering in Luke-Acts: Implications for a Pentecostal Pneumatology*. New York: T. & T. Clark International, 2004.

Mulligan, Mary Alice, and Ronald J. Allen. *Make the World Come Alive: Lessons from Laity*. Danvers, MA: Chalice, 2005.

Neufeld-Erdman, Chris. *Ordinary Preacher, Extraordinary Gospel*. Eugene, OR: Cascade, 2014.

Nouwen, Henri. *The Wounded Healer: Ministry in Contemporary Society*. New York: Doubleday, 2010.

Ogereau, Julien M. "Paul's Leadership Ethos in 2 Cor 10–13: A Critique of 21st-Century Pentecostal Leadership." *Australasian Pentecostal Studies* 13 (2010) 33.

Okesson, Gregg A. "'Are Pastors Human?' Sociological and Theological Reflections on Ministerial Identity in Contemporary Africa." *AJET* 27:2 (2008) 133.

Olson, Roger. "Pentecostalism's Dark Side." *Christian Century* (7 March 2007) 29.

Paris, Anna et al., eds. *The Life of Brian: Masculinities, Sexualities, and Health in New Zealand*. Dunedin, New Zealand: University of Otago Press, 2002.

Pascal, Blaise. *Pensées* 131. Harmondsworth, UK: Penguin, 1966.

Phillips, Jock. *A Man's Country? The Image of the Pakeha Male—A History*. Rev. ed. Auckland: Penguin, 1996.

"Preaching Moment 75: Shauna Hannan." https://www.youtube.com/watch?v=Pie77qBcIbc.

Pyle, Nate. *Man Enough: How Jesus Redefines Manhood*. Grand Rapids: Zondervan, 2015.

Ramsay, Lee. "Getting Personal: Self-Disclosure and Preaching." http://www.ministrymatters.com/all/entry/2928/getting-personal-self-disclosure-and-preaching.htm.

Real, Terrence. *How can I get Through to You?* New York: Fireside, 2002.

Robinson, Haddon. "Bringing Yourself into the Pulpit." In *Mastering Contemporary Preaching*, edited by Bill Hybels, et al. Leicester, UK: InterVarsity, 1989), 131.

Shi, Wen Hua. *Paul's Message of the Cross as Body Language*. Tubingen, Germany: Mohr Siebeck, 2008.

Smith, Mandy. *The Vulnerable Pastor: How Human Limitations Empower Our Ministry*. Downers Grove, IL: IVP Academic, 2015.

Spiller, Chellie, et al. *Wayfaring Leadership: Groundbreaking Wisdom for Developing Leaders*. Wellington, NZ: Huia, 2015.

Stevens, Bruce. "'Up, Up and Away': Pentecostal Preaching and the Manic Defence." *AJPS* 9:2 (2006) 285–86, 294.

Stowell, Joe. "Keep it on Christ in You." *Leadership* 22:2 (2001) 61.

Tardy, Charles H., and Kathryn Dindia. "Self-Disclosure: Strategic Revelation of Information in Personal and Professional Relationships." In *The Handbook of Communication Skills*, edited by Owen Hargie, 236. New York: Routledge, 2006.

Tchividjian, Tullian. *Glorious Ruin: How Suffering Sets You Free*. Colorado Springs, CO: David C. Cook, 2012.

Thiselton, Anthony C. *The First Epistle to the Corinthians*. The New International Greek Testament Commentary. Grand Rapids: Eerdmans, 2000.

Thoren, Amy C. "The Pastor on Facebook: Boldly Going Where Everyone Else Goes." *Word and World* 30:3 (2010) 279.

Trammel, Madison, and Rob Moll. "Grading the Movement." *Christianity Today* 50:4 (April 2006) 38–41.

Warrington, Keith. *Healing and Suffering: Biblical and Pastoral Reflections*. Carlisle, UK: Paternoster, 2005.

———. *Pentecostal Theology: A Theology of Encounter*. London: T. & T. Clark, 2008.

———. "Suffering and the Spirit in Luke-Acts." *JBPR* 1 (2009) 31–32.

White, Adam. "'Not in Lofty Speech or Media:' A Reflection on Pentecostal Preaching in Light of 1 Cor 2:1–5." *JPS* 24 (2015) 133.

Willhite, Keith. *Preaching with Relevance without Dumbing Down*. Grand Rapids: Kregel, 2001.

Willimon, William. "Foreword." In *Preaching Autobiography: Connecting the World of the Preacher and the World of the Text*, edited by David Fleer and Dave Bland, 12. Abilene, TX: ACU, 2001.

———. "Naked Preachers Are Distracting." *Christianity Today* 42:4 (June 1998) 62.

———. *Pastor: The Theology and Practice of Ordained Ministry*. Nashville: Abingdon, 2002.

———. *Proclamation and Theology*. Nashville: Abingdon, 2005.

Winter, Richard. *When Life Goes Dark: Finding Hope in the Midst of Depression*. Downers Grove, IL: IVP, 2012.

Worsley, Stephen. "Session 5: Communication." *One Step Ahead Preaching: Discovering New Skills in Preaching* DVD. Wellington, NZ: Stephen Worsley, 2009.

PART III

Listener

Engaging the Listener

Passionate, Pointed, and Prophetic Preaching

LAURIE GUY

"It only takes a spark to get a fire going."[1]

"While I mused, the fire burned; then I spoke with my tongue."

(Ps 39:3)

WHERE IS THE SPARK in preaching today? Where are the Richard Baxters who preach as never to preach again, and as a dying man (or woman) to dying men and women? Where is the "bristling, crackling, and thundering" of a George Whitefield, as Edwin Gaustad described him?[2] Martyn Lloyd-Jones spoke of forgiving preachers for the feeblest of sermons if only they would give him a sense of the presence of God.[3] Where is that sense today?

All this is to raise the question of the purpose of preaching. What does it do? For many the purpose of preaching is to declare the word of God. And so the phrase, "biblical preaching," is much in vogue. Much as I endorse biblically based preaching, I hesitate to say that this is a completely satisfactory response.

---

1. Opening words of the song "Pass it on" written by Kurt Kaiser in 1969.
2. Gaustad, *The Great Awakening in New England*, 25.
3. Lloyd-Jones, *Preachers and Preaching*, 97.

The Word of God

My hesitation relates, firstly, to the phrase "word of God." Most of us may be Protestant, deeply grasped by the *ad fontes* (back to the source) principle of the Reformation with a commitment to the word of God. What, however, is that "word"? Lazy and reductionist thinking equates "word of God" with the "Bible." Yes, the Bible is the word of God. But so also is the triune God himself. The Word was (and is) God; and that Word became flesh (John 1:1, 14). So Jesus, the Son, is that Word.

I sat for two years under the ministry of a preacher who was not really an expositor. But he deeply loved Jesus. And he preached Jesus. This rational academic (me) heard the word of God for two years. It was inspiring. Transformative.

Not only is the word of God the text of Scripture and the person of Jesus. It is also, thirdly, a spoken, a living word. The word of God that came to Jeremiah was not the Bible; it was a quickened word, a living word, a word from God for those people at that time.

Is the word of God the Bible, or is it Jesus, or is it the living word that is sharper than any two-edged sword (Heb 4:12)? Or is it all three? The Hebrews text speaks of the living word but it goes on to speak of appearing before God or Christ. This may suggest a dance, an interweaving of Bible, Jesus, and an applied living word. So the goal of preaching will not be simply to explain the Bible. The goal will also be to bring Christ, to bring the living word, to the congregation.

Remember the first early witness of Papias in AD 130 to the existence of four Gospels? Alongside the four Gospels, however, Papias noted the spoken word, the oral message, something he called "the living and abiding voice," which in his view was even better.[4]

The task of the preacher is not simply to explain the Bible but, on the basis of that Bible, to bring that living word of God to today's world. The preacher needs to have a transformative goal. To inform, yes; to inspire, yes; but also to bring change. And she or he needs to have the sense, "To the best of my conscience I have brought the particular word of God, the word that God would declare, to these people in their situation today." Biblical preaching, preaching the word of God, is not simply explaining the Bible.

---

4. Eusebius, *Church History*, III.39.4.

Expository Preaching

My second hesitation concerning so-called biblical preaching relates to the common practice of equating it with expository preaching. Expository preaching may simply mean Bible-based preaching. I am fully supportive of Bible-based and Bible-aligned preaching. However, in many circles expository preaching is understood more narrowly as the unfolding of the meaning of a substantial portion of Scripture. And commonly this systematic unfolding of a passage of Scripture is the recommended and normal, and perhaps even the only, mode of preaching.

Once such advocate of this view is leading American pastor and journalist Ed Stetzer. In his view "verse-by-verse exposition is the best form of preaching."[5] He also comments:

> I find my approach to preaching aligns with Tim Keller's approach, and he probably explains it better than I do. At *Christianity Today* he said that the majority of preaching in the church should be verse-by-verse, and should be expositional. In my view, it should be specifically verse-by-verse exposition working through books of the Bible, as that's the best way to teach and shape a congregation.[6]

Tim Keller himself defines expository preaching as "the systematic explanation of Scripture." He states further:

> I would say that expository preaching should provide the main diet of preaching for a Christian community. Why? Here is the main reason (though of course there are many others): Expository preaching is the best method for displaying and conveying your conviction that the whole Bible is true. This approach testifies that you believe every part of the Bible to be God's word, not just particular themes and not just the parts you feel comfortable agreeing with.[7]

Keller's explanation seems rooted in the struggles of American fundamentalism and its successors against modernism and its successors. It may be a subsidiary justification; but as a "main reason"?

Finally, I turn to leading Canadian pastor Darrell Johnson. He argues that the word of God "makes things happen": "it not only informs, it

---

5. Stetzer, "Thinking about Expository Preaching," n. p.
6. Ibid., n.p.
7. Keller, *Preaching*, 32

performs, it transforms."[8] He then asks how the speaking of human words becomes the word of God. His response follows: "[T]he answer I want to commend to all who preach is in *expository preaching*. It is the only place I know where I can stand and have any confidence that what I say is what the living God is saying. It is the only place I know where we mere humans can dare to say or think, 'Thus says the Lord.'"[9] Johnson then goes on to damn topical preaching with faint praise: "Yes, there is a role for sermons other than expository ones. So-called topical preaching, for example, does sometimes participate in God's transformation of people's lives."[10]

Johnson prefaces all this with scriptural support from Luke 24:27 (the Emmaus Road encounter). Ironically, Luke 24:27 exemplifies what Johnson damns with faint praise—topical preaching. The topic of Luke 24:27 is the nature of the messiahship of Jesus, and Jesus establishes this from texts from many parts of the Old Testament, "beginning with Moses and all the prophets."

It is not my purpose to criticize expository preaching as such. After all, it is one of the options I myself employ. However, I do want to question the near idolatry that some accord to this approach. And I want to propose other key elements and approaches that ought to feature in our preaching.

What then are my reservations in relation to expository preaching (understood as the systematic unfolding of a passage of Scripture)? The first is that while it is commonly claimed to be "biblical preaching," it is seldom, if ever, the method exemplified in the Bible itself. One can commonly find textual preaching in Scripture, as well as topical preaching, and also preaching based not simply on specific texts but on the profound, undergirding theology out of which the texts arise. Examples of that undergirding (or overarching) theology include Jesus' teaching on the two great commandments, his teaching on marriage and divorce, and Paul's breathtaking declaration that the whole of the law is summed up in one word: "You shall love your neighbor as yourself" (Rom 13:10).

A second concern relates to the audience. Skilled expositors sparkle, penetrate, and uplift. But many expositors are not so skilled. So what emerges? Too often verse-by-verse expository preaching is the same old thing, boring, and irrelevant. This is not the fault of expository preaching *per se*, but a common weakness of expositors is saying in workmanlike fashion what is already patent in the text and already known to the audience. And this may commonly lead to boredom.

---

8. Johnson, *The Glory of Preaching*, 25.
9. Ibid., 53–54.
10. Ibid., 54.

I cannot get past the haunting words of Harry Emerson Fosdick to the effect that people won't come panting to the doors of the church to find out what happened to the Jebusites last week.[11] The problem is that a lot of expository preaching insufficiently considers the situation and concerns of the audience. The primary focus of Johnson, for example, in *The Glory of Preaching*, is the text. A consequence is that he rejects explicit application of that text to the audience, stating: "I repeat: the pressure to apply is a modernist pressure, not a biblical pressure."[12]

I recognize that Johnson is using the word "apply" quite narrowly to argue that preachers should not feel an obligation to always tell their listeners what they must "do" as a result of the sermon. And I note that he does urge preachers to draw out the *implications* of the text for their listeners. However, I suspect that many of his readers fail to appreciate the distinction, and pull back from connecting the word of Scripture with the lives of their listeners.

I contrast this lack of audience focus with a comment from Ian Grant, former national director of Youth for Christ New Zealand, and subsequent founding leader of the Parenting Place: "My big question when I am doing my thing in preaching is, 'What are they doing?'"[13] That is an audience-centered approach. We need sparkling, penetrating, and pertinent preaching where the common people hear us gladly (Mark 12:37). General, rational Bible teaching is unlikely to do this. The audience is an essential part of the mix.

A third concern about expository preaching relates to the wiring and gifting of the preacher. Preaching may be instructional or persuasive; it may focus towards the head or the heart; it may be educational or exhortatory. Audiences may leave with the sense of having learned something, or they may leave with a sense of warmth and encouragement. Both are valid outcomes. Preachers come with varying giftings and varying wirings: teacher, prophet, exhorter, encourager, evangelist. One size does not fit all. And expositional preaching does not fit all. It best fits the teaching personality, much less so the encourager personality. Overemphasis on the expositional model leaves some preachers struggling with Saul's armor, a method (or weaponry) not appropriate to their personal wiring. Preaching is "truth *through personality*."[14] For some, expository preaching does not fit personality.

11. Fosdick's actual statement was this: "Only the preacher proceeds still upon the idea that folk come to church desperately anxious to discover what happened to the Jebusites." See Miller, *Harry Emerson Fosdick*, 342.

12. Johnson, *The Glory of Preaching*, 159.

13. Spoken to Carey Baptist College homiletics courses taught by the author in the mid-1990s.

14. A famous definition articulated by nineteenth-century preacher Phillips Brooks.

Some devotees assert that expositional preaching is *the* way to go. I rather see expositional preaching as one option amongst many; one arrow—maybe a commonly used arrow—but one arrow only, in the multitude of arrows in the preacher's quiver. Select it by all means. But don't be blind to other arrows, and don't insist that everyone else must use your preferred arrow.

The issue should not be whether expository preaching, in the sense of preaching systematically on a sizeable unit of Scripture, is the way to go. More to the point is the conviction that Scripture ought fundamentally and ultimately to be the source and control for the sermon, however that is done. But what should such preaching be achieving? I have suggested that the goal of the preacher is to bring the living word of God to the audience, to bring about transformation. And I would suggest that three key qualities are needed for such transformation.

Passionate Preaching

The first of these is preaching that is passionate. This may sound odd coming from a retired academic who has lived so much of his life out of his head. However, there are two reasons for being passionate. First, it is the *gospel* that we are preaching—good news. We preach to issues of life and death (1 Cor 1:18). We preach to people often carrying enormous and hidden burdens: suffering, doubt, fear, desolation. We preach to people for whom this may be their last or only sermon. Hence the words of Richard Baxter: "I preached as never sure to preach again, and as a dying man to dying men."[15] Can we simply deliver workman-like sermons, given both the gospel and the human condition? Can we simply be orderly and rational? The greatest danger for me and the church is not the fire, but the refrigerator. Preaching must be passionate.

And preaching must be passionate because passion is crucial to the goal of transformation. Augustine spoke of people sinking to lower levels or rising to higher levels. What makes the difference? Love. Desire. In his words, "love lifts us up"; by love, he said, we are carried whithersoever we are carried.[16] It is love, it is desire, that transforms. So the issue is one of changing love or desire, of stirring love or desire. Evoking that love is more likely to come from a warm heart than a cool head. Listen again to Augustine:

See Brooks, *Lectures on Preaching*, 5.

15. Baxter, "Love Breathing Thanks and Praise," 40.
16. *Confessions*, XIII.9; also *City of God*, XI.28.

> If . . . the hearers require to be roused rather than instructed, in order that they may be diligent to do what they already know, and to bring their feelings into harmony with the truths they admit, greater vigor of speech is needed. Here, entreaties and reproaches, exhortations and upbraidings and all the other means of arousing the emotions, are necessary.[17]

Following Cicero, Augustine urged preachers to do three things: to teach, to delight and to move.[18] Charles Simeon was of similar persuasion: "The understanding must be informed, but in a manner . . . which *affects the heart*; either to comfort the hearers, or to excite them to acts of piety, repentance, or holiness."[19]

Walter Hollenweger is an elderly Pentecostal-turned-Presbyterian church historian. He has an intriguing dedication in his book, *The Pentecostals*: "To my friends and teachers in the Pentecostal Movement who taught me to love the Bible and to my teachers and friends in the Presbyterian Church who taught me to understand it."[20] Is it the Presbyterians or the Pentecostals who are more likely to stir up transforming desire in their preaching?

Princeton Seminary president emeritus John A. Mackay is reported as saying, "If it is a choice between the uncouth life of the Pentecostals and the aesthetic death of the older churches, I for one choose uncouth life."[21] Mackay is right in the way he has framed the issue. Do we, however, have to make such an either-or choice?

The ideal is both head and heart, wonderfully exemplified in a preacher like John Wesley. Often, however, particularly with educated clergy, the focus is too much on the head. Richard Baxter stressed the importance of speaking to the heart: "In the study of our sermons we are too negligent, gathering only a few naked truths, and not considering of the most forcible expressions by which we may set them home to man's consciences and hearts."[22] And this is not simply better techniques and content. It must come deeply from within. Heart will speak to heart. Let the word dwell in our hearts. And let us speak it out with passion as well as reason—"logic on fire . . . theology coming through a man [or woman] who is on fire!"[23] Preaching must be passionate.

17. *De Doctrina Christiana*, IV.4.
18. Ibid., IV.12–13.
19. Packer, "Expository Preaching," n. p.
20. Hollenweger, *The Pentecostals*, xvii.
21. Sherrill, *They Speak with Other Tongues*, 161–62.
22. Baxter, *The Reformed Pastor*, 147.
23. Lloyd-Jones, *Preachers and Preaching*, 97.

Pointed Preaching

The second quality that I want to stress is that preaching should be pointed. I recall hearing of a preacher who began his preaching one Sunday by saying that he had had many complaints during the week. The criticism was that he'd had far too many points in his previous sermon; so this week his sermon would be pointless. And some are.

When I say that a sermon should be pointed, I mean that preaching should fundamentally have a single aim, not go in a number of directions. Points taken from a biblical passage may easily develop in different directions. The outcome is shotgun divergence rather than a .303 rifle, single-shot approach. We should heed the words of three past leading preachers and teachers. First, Charles Simeon: "I think that every sermon should have, like a telescope, but one object in the field."[24] Secondly, J. H. Jowett: "I have a conviction that no sermon is ready for preaching ... until we can express its theme in a short pregnant sentence as clear as crystal."[25] Thirdly, Professor Ian Pitt-Watson: "Every sermon should be ruthlessly unitary in its theme. This is the first and great commandment."[26]

How can one reduce a passage to a single aim? F. B. Meyer spoke of reading and rereading a passage until one finds a crack, a hinge in the passage. That is where one should focus. Meyer exemplified his point by taking the passage about Aaron and Hur holding up the arms of Moses to pray on the mountainside. "Then came the Amalekites." For Meyer that was the hinge. People pray. And then they are plunged into the hard realities of life. What then?

When I was a pastor I had a former student of Laidlaw College in the congregation. He told me of a sermon he preached in a Laidlaw sermon class on the parable of the prodigal son. He now recognized that the sermon was a dog's breakfast. The lecturer in charge of the class asked him what really impressed him about the parable. The answer was the love of the father. "Preach on that then," was the advice of the lecturer. That sort of advice leads to single-focus preaching, pointed preaching.

Prophetic Preaching

The third key quality of a sermon is that it be prophetic. That sounds risky, especially if one understands the prophet to be an automaton receiving from

---

24. Stott, *Between Two Worlds*, 225.
25. Jowett, *The Preacher*, 134–35.
26. Stott, *Between Two Worlds*, 226.

above, and understands the message as future prediction. Neither of those features is fundamental or even usual to prophecy. Jeremiah, for example, received a word while watching pot-making (Jer 18:1–11). His message spring-boarded off that pot-making experience. It focused on the present, while warning of future destruction unless present attitudes changed.

What is fundamental to prophecy is an immediate word, a quickened word of God, bringing together biblical truth and the immediate situation of the hearers. I commend this definition: "Take the word of God, and take the world of God, and bring them together; and then you will have prophecy."[27] This suggests a person soaked in Scripture and prayer. It suggests also a person soaked in the world. The latter soaking is not gained simply from newspapers, books, and movies. These will inform, but at a distance. Much better is personal engagement, living in the world—not in the study or in the cloister, but living in the raw world—profoundly experiencing that world, and having ongoing relationship with those who are not yet Christ-followers—exactly the life exemplified by Jesus himself.

When I was a new missionary in Papua New Guinea, a senior missionary told me that the indigenous people would be watching me for several months before coming to an assessment of me, an assessment that would subsequently be hard to shake. In some cases, said that missionary, they would note that the missionary largely stayed in his office, and would scornfully describe him as *"man bilong opis"* (man stuck in his office). And that may describe some of today's preachers.

In the first year of my law studies at university, I studied Cicero's *Pro Milone*, his lawyerly defence of Milo. I was struck by a particular technique of Cicero. He commonly stated, "But someone will say," and then gave his powerful rebuttal. He knew the other side of the argument and spring-boarded off it to put forth his own case. We need to know firsthand the other side of the argument, and that can be a spring-board to our preaching.

My own practice as a preacher has always been to belong to a non-Christian organization that will bring me into close relationship or encounter with wider society. This has included tennis clubs and the social times that follow tennis matches. Most recently it has included volunteering half a day a week at a Citizens Advice Bureau in one of the poorest areas of Auckland. I experience so much, from the trivial and banal ("please go on the internet and tell me who has been selected for the national netball team") to the complex, profound, and moving. One interview etched in my memory is a story of ghastly living (drugs included), arising out of shocking

---

27. Spoken to me by Mike Riddell, a faculty colleague at Carey Baptist College, in the 1990s.

experiences in childhood. A week later the person called in again and thanked me profusely for listening, saying if I had not done that she would have gone under a train. It is experiences such as this that etch into our gut an awareness of the world out there and the marvelous good news, the life and hope, that the gospel brings.

So it is that connection with humanity, as well as Scripture and prayer, that will fuel the living, prophetic word. Is there any word from the Lord for our world, our society, our city, in 2017? Is there a living word, sourced and immersed both in the text of Scripture and in the lives of our listeners?

This chapter may have seemed to downplay expository preaching. I have done this largely out of a concern that too much expository preaching today insufficiently considers the audience that is in front of the preacher in church, and insufficiently considers the potential audience that is out there in the wider world. I do, however, warmly welcome expository preaching where it has a deep sense of its audience, where it is both faithful to the Scriptures and sensitive to the listeners. Biblical preaching that is passionate, pointed, and prophetic. It is through such fiery preaching—"bristling, crackling, and thundering" preaching—that God renews this world.

Bibliography

Augustine. *The City of God.* Translated by Henry Bettenson. Harmondsworth, UK: Penguin, 1972.

———. *Confessions.* Translated by Vernon J. Bourke. Washington, DC: Catholic University of America Press, 1966.

———. *De Doctrina Christiana. Oxford early Christian texts.* Edited and translated by R. P. H. Green. Oxford: Clarendon, 1995.

Baxter, Richard. *The Reformed Pastor.* Edited by William Baxter. Reprint. Edinburgh: Banner of Truth Trust, 1974.

Brooks, Phillips. *Lectures on Preaching.* New York: E. P. Dutton & Co., 1907.

Maier, Paul L., ed. *Eusebius: The Church History; A New Translation with Commentary.* Grand Rapids: Kregel, 1999.

Gaustad, Edwin. *The Great Awakening in New England.* New York: Harper, 1957.

Hollenweger, Walter. *The Pentecostals.* London: SCM, 1972.

Johnson, Darrell W. *The Glory of Preaching: Participating in God's Transformation of the World.* Downers Grove, IL: IVP Academic, 2009.

Jowett, J. H. *The Preacher: His Life and Work.* London: Hodder & Stoughton, 1912.

Keller, Timothy. *Preaching: Communicating Faith in an Age of Skepticism.* New York: Viking, 2015.

Lloyd-Jones, D. Martyn. *Preachers and Preaching.* Grand Rapids: Zondervan, 1971.

Miller, Robert Moats. *Harry Emerson Fosdick: Preacher, Pastor, Prophet.* Oxford: Oxford University Press, 1985.

Packer, J. I. "Expository Preaching: Charles Simeon and Ourselves." https://www.monergism.com/expository-preaching-charles-simeon-and-ourselves-j-i-packer.

Sherrill, John. *They Speak with Other Tongues.* London: Hodder & Stoughton, 1965.

Stetzer, Ed. "Thinking about Expository Preaching: Part 2." http://www.christianitytoday.com/edstetzer/2016/february/thinking-about-expository-preaching-part-2.html.

Stott, John R. W. *Between Two Worlds: The Challenge of Preaching Today.* Grand Rapids: Eerdmans, 1982.

Free-for-all

How a Culture of Giving Voice Shapes Preaching

JODY KILPATRICK

WHEN I ARRIVED AT Ponsonby Baptist Church in 2004, I pegged Mary as the quintessential school ma'am of a bygone era. I quickly learned that despite firm ideas and a somewhat prickly interface, Mary was sparkly, intelligent, and humane. She had many interests, with her finger on more pulses than most of us could count. She read widely—literature, biography, history, philosophy, the *New Zealand Herald*. She was very interested in the arts, driving herself off to concerts in the Town Hall well into her eighties. She loved nature and gardens, and she loved being in the thick of things. In her rich and busy life, God was the giver, the initiator; grace and faith could only and always be the gift of God.

When Mary stood up to speak during free-for-all, we never knew if it would be to review the new Johnny Cash movie, expound on a Bible verse or the theology of Martin Luther, or simply commend "all you clever people who knew about the clocks" (the day she was caught out by Daylight Saving). She spoke most weeks, sometimes more than once if she remembered a forgotten point or wanted to respond to someone who spoke after her. She listened closely to the concerns and opinions of others, asking after specific situations when I saw her during the week, sending her love or flowers from her garden to those who were struggling.

For me, Mary personified the spirit of free-for-all: expansive, eclectic, conviction with room for difference, relationship at the heart. In this chapter I will explore the long-standing tradition of free-for-all at Ponsonby Baptist

Church, and the way it can work with preaching to develop a congregation's ability to listen to the transforming voice of God in our midst.

Ponsonby Baptist is a small-city fringe church, with sixty to seventy people in attendance each Sunday. I have been the sole charge minister and main preacher for the last twelve or so years. The church tends to attract people with a strong sense of social justice, expressed collectively through CORT—a housing trust providing homes for people on low incomes in Auckland—and individually through vocations and causes. It is a church that appeals to people deconstructing and reconstructing their faith. Diversity, participation, and inclusiveness are highly valued.

Located in a central suburb of Auckland, the church reflects the tone of the neighborhood, while drawing attendees from all over the city. Originally a working-class area, it is now predominantly (though by no means exclusively), upper-middle class, with Ponsonby Road known for its dining and shopping establishments, art galleries and nightclubs, and the annual Pride Parade. "Post-gentrification Ponsonby and Freemans Bay remain distinctly tolerant and liberal urban neighborhoods, where residents are not inclined to accept unwanted developments or injustices lying down."[1]

Free-for-all began during Ivan Howie's time as part-time minister of the church (1982–1983). Ivan confessed he could not recall whether it had been his idea or not: "I like to think of these ideas rising among us," he says, but it "seemed like a significant thing to do."[2]

His instinct served the church well. Free-for-all is a firmly established element in our services, like a call to worship or a benediction. We always have this slot, even if we know the day won't be particularly conducive to it (such as when the service contains extra content or the congregation will have lots of guests). I suppose we cannot imagine public worship without the possibility of hearing from any and every voice.

Our services have a reasonably typical Baptist mix of Scripture, prayer, music, and preaching. We also have a regular slot called "contemporary reading," a short reading (or song, or video clip) chosen and given by a rostered volunteer. This reading might be overtly Christian, or the reader might offer the links to faith. Like free-for-all, it is significant input unmediated by the preacher or service leader.

Free-for-all occurs towards the end of our church services, either immediately or soon after the sermon. In planning the service I aim to allow 20 minutes for it, though of course the time taken varies week to week.

---

1. Carlyon and Morrow, *Urban Village*, 272.
2. Howie, personal communication, September 2016.

During free-for-all anyone who wishes can air their concerns and opinions. This could be a prayer request for a friend: "My friend is in hospital, waiting for test results. I asked if she wanted our church to pray, she said yes." It could be a challenge to the sermon, "It's true the Gospels emphasise how fickle the disciples were when Jesus was in trouble, but notice how faithful the women were, standing at the foot of the cross." Or it could be a comment on current events that invites action, "Here's what I did when I discovered my bank invested in weapon manufacturing..."

One person left his hat at a concert in the church building on Saturday evening. When he came to retrieve it the next morning, he decided to stay for the service:

> After the sermon there was an announcement of "Free-for-All." This was a new concept for me. One young man stood and said that he just wanted to praise God because it was five months since he had had his last drink. His statement was one of the reasons I stayed at Ponsonby Baptist.

Anyone can speak in free-for-all. This includes visitors who are looking for money and small children. It is not a platform for the "wise" and "upstanding." It really is free for all. As one person told me, "However skillful the leader, there's the potential for this part of the service to be out of control; elements of novelty and danger. It's not always an easy time."

People stay where they are and a microphone is passed to them. They might stand or sit to speak. They are asked to give their name. The facilitator is typically (though not always) up front at the lectern, also with a microphone. The facilitator is the host, responsible for giving a brief overview of what free-for-all is, inviting, encouraging, and sometimes sensitively limiting contributions, and praying to conclude.

The style of closing prayer varies. Some facilitators work through a list, covering each comment with a sentence of prayer. Others might have us say together "Lord hear our prayer" after every comment has been made. Others might use a prepared prayer published in a book, or written that morning using snatches taken from the whole service. Others still might invite us to say the Lord's Prayer together. Following free-for-all we either have a hymn and then the benediction, or just the benediction:

> The Lord bless you and keep you; the Lord make his face to shine upon you, and be gracious to you; the Lord lift up his countenance upon you, and give you peace. (Num 6:24–26).

As one person pointed out to me:

After the "disorder" of an impromptu, unscripted session, the ancient traditional words are sung in unison, standing together, with a deep sense of how we need the Lord to bless and keep all of us. That moment can be poignant or strengthening, depending on what has gone before.

Some weeks the free-for-all consists of a collection of comments on how nice the flowers look and prayer requests for people most of us don't know. Which is to say, it is not always a time of rigorous engagement. But other weeks there will be sustained discussion about the Bible passage and sermon, a global situation, a personal situation, or an issue our church is facing.

What are the Dangers or Limitations of Free-for-all?

According to the dictionary, a free-for-all is "a disorganized brawl or argument,"[3] chaotic, and unruly. While the congregation has enjoyed some heated disagreements and controversial topics over the years, our free-for-all is typically a supportive time of processing out loud, respectful discussion, some jokes, and some tears. But there are dangers.

Sometimes there is aggression, ranting, swearing, accusation. Sometimes there are interminable stories that don't seem to have a point. Sometimes there is unsettling unbelief. One person told me:

> It's an opportunity to be heard because I feel unheard in my life, usually. All week I have to be careful about what I say. If I'm feeling a bit crazy and want to go "blah" I imagine the house is bugged so I don't. But with a church you've got to be honest.

There is a risk that proclamation and worship are lost in a jumble of disjointed comments towards the end with free-for-all. This means we need to craft the service to limit the possibility of clutter—a tension we usually manage. Often the person facilitating free-for-all will jot down lines from other parts of the service and use them in their concluding prayer. This is a way of keeping our focus on intentional expressions of worship alongside a myriad of other comments. We also have a wonderful music group, and their music is an important element that offers balance to our talk. And we sing the same benediction to close each service.

There is also the risk that, during some phases of church life, a few voices can dominate. Sometimes people don't have any or many public spaces for expression. Sometimes people need an outlet at a certain time of their life. Sometimes people just like to have their say. It is a tension to make

---

3. Collins English Dictionary.

sure there is time and space enough for everyone who might wish to talk. Some facilitators might ask "Is there anyone we don't often hear from with something to say?" or pointedly ask an individual "Tell us how the PhD is coming along." Very occasionally the facilitator will thank someone who has been talking for a long time and try to shift attention to someone who is waiting to speak.

People also tend to share responsibility for bringing balanced perspectives and responding to each other. It does not fall to the facilitator or pastor. This is something the community has learned together over time, and something to which we bring skills from other areas of life. Once someone commented that children didn't have enough discipline, and advocated smacking on occasion. The person sitting next to them said into the microphone as it was being passed back to the isle, politely and briefly, "I think there are ways of setting limits that don't rely on smacking."

Of course, people engage on different levels. Not everyone experiences free-for-all as a profound exchange of their innermost thoughts and feelings. The forum (talking to sixty or so people) does not suit everyone's style. Those who do not feel able to speak to the group—maybe they feel too fragile or too nervous—might choose to ask someone else to speak on their behalf. Since our morning tea is partway through the service (or, once a month, at the start), there is time for people to chat before the free-for-all forum. Sometimes this sharpens a resolve to ask for prayer, sometimes it gives opportunity to find someone to speak on their behalf, sometimes a simple conversation over morning tea alleviates the need to address the entire congregation.

The practice probably only works, as it stands, in a small church of less than 100 people. Our experience has been that when there are over eighty people, fewer people are willing to speak, and engagement lessens—it becomes a series of disconnected sound bites. If we regularly had larger numbers in attendance we would probably try a mix of spontaneous comments and prayer requests with five or so reflectors, people who were lined up that morning to make a response to the sermon, service, and current events. We would need to make an effort to include every person who was willing in semi-regular rotation.

Yes, hearing from people can be risky, dangerous even. All the more reason to do it.

What is Expressed in the Practice of Free-for-all?

Free-for-all is really just an "open mic" time. Plenty of churches do something similar, but at Ponsonby Baptist it has been used consistently week in and week out for nearly thirty-five years. In the process, it has shaped the theology of the gathered community. Certainly, my own theology and practice as a pastor and preacher have been profoundly shaped by participating in it for over a decade. Quite apart from the content of each free-for-all, the very practice of free-for-all sends an important message.

Giving Voice and Decentralizing Power

When I first preached at Ponsonby Baptist I thought, "Oh dear, people can answer back," but over time that became "Oh wow, everyone has a voice." I've learned that giving voice is an extremely valuable thing to do. Whether it's biblical or not depends on how you read the Bible, but I believe the multiple voices of Scripture, and the different ways they are expressed, are useful clues to hearing the voice of God.

One Sunday an attendee, usually a very affirming and obliging presence, sat at the back of the congregation belting out her own words during the singing. Someone politely tried to shush her—she was most indignant: "I need to have my voice!" I've pondered that often—that day her voice was unsettling, uncomfortable, and made me nervous; but why shouldn't the gathered body of Christ hear her? Why should her voice only be acceptable when it was modulated and conformed?

It's tempting for those of us with power to define the terms of what is required to have a valid voice in church. Speaking in church (in many contexts I'm familiar with) is for the educated, thoughtful, articulate, those who are mobile enough to climb the stage, or tall enough to reach the microphone.

My understanding has been challenged and extended by theology from the margins, and by voices from the margins. Published and spoken theology tends to go through a vetting process before it can get to people. Voices don't.

For example, Ponsonby Baptist has strong, long-standing links with people who identify as part of the mental health community—who as part of our faith community often bring the incredibly generous gift of honesty and a lack of pretense. This is not to say that those who self-identify in this way lack education, thoughtfulness, or articulation. Far from it. But if we limited ourselves to hearing only from those who are "qualified" (to sign up for rosters, be contacted about upcoming opportunities, prepare a sermon, lead worship) we'd be missing out on some very important perspectives.

I was struck recently by Meriah Nichols's blog post, "Why I've had it with 'The Mighty.'"[4] It helped clarify for me why free-for-all is so important in our church. Nichols describes herself as " . . . a deaf mom who has TBI, PTSD, and bi-polar disorder,"[5] and also has a child with Down syndrome. She is critical of well-meaning parents who explain their child's disability through their own lens, believing they are telling the stories of people with disabilities:

> You see, no one knows what another person's life is truly like. You just don't. Your interpretation of an event, an expression, an utterance, is all based on your own experience, history, personality, perceptions. You simply cannot tell someone else's story for them, you can't explain their life for them.
>
> In gender terms, that's called "man-splaining," in racial terms, it's "white-splaining," and in disability terms, it's "able-splaining"—when an able-bodied person is attempting to explain our experience, often *to us*.[6]

We have to hear from each other in order to know what following Jesus is like for each of us. In free-for-all, power is decentralized, and no one gets to speak on behalf of everyone. We have the chance to object when our perspective and experience has been overlooked or "-splained."

Additionally, authority is not divorced from the gathered community's ability to discern. Disciples need to learn to function without the preacher/pastor mediating reality for them, and free-for-all gives us the chance to develop this skill together.

I assume the Spirit is in our midst and leading us as a congregation. Because of my experiences at Ponsonby Baptist, I cannot see how the Spirit can do that if we don't hear from many voices when we gather. Time and time again, the call to follow Christ that ushers us out the door and rings in our ears all week hasn't been issued by me. It's come from the floor.

Interacting over Scripture

A question remains: free-for-all is a lovely notion, but what has that got to do with preaching? Preaching involves a trustworthy voice, recognized by the

---

4. Nichols, "Why I've had it with 'The Mighty,'" n. p.
5. Nichols, "Me," n. p.
6. Nichols, "Why I've had it with 'The Mighty,'" n. p.

community—someone who has taken the responsibility to pray and study and think and formulate, and then has a specific gift to offer: the sermon.

I do not disagree, and I should add that Ponsonby Baptist is a fairly conventional Baptist church that values good preaching. I'm simply suggesting that the practice of free-for-all and giving space to all voices can add to (rather than detract from) preaching. It can operate as a community process of engagement. The (well-prepared) sermon is often refined and enriched by the interaction of many voices: the responsibility to engage God, Scripture, and life, does not belong to one or few.

In order for this to work, the preacher has to learn (and keep learning) to be non-defensive and non-anxious. In our gatherings each Sunday there are smarter thinkers, broader readers, heavier cross-carriers, better-practiced meditators, sharper observers, deeper feelers, and more hopeless hopers than me. There are professors with full Bible commentaries on their iPhones, there are rough sleepers snoozing in a pew while I spout platitudes about compassion. There are people who hear disturbing voices crying out to them while desiring to hear the voice of God.

Someone may have an insight or an illustration that develops and extends my points, or a new perspective that helps those who didn't connect with my ideas. Some preachers have to imagine the concerns of the congregation and how to address them. I don't. I hear them each Sunday. Better still, we all do.

Barbara K. Lundblad advocates preachers engaging with congregants weekly over the sermon text:

> It's even better if you can go beyond imagining the voices to actually hearing a few. In the parish I met with members each week for text study at an Indian restaurant near the church. Sometimes there were three of us, sometimes twelve. It wasn't so much a teaching session as a conversation with the Sunday texts. I heard the text in a new way as I listened to others. Someone noticed something I'd never seen; someone was confused about something I'd assumed was absolutely clear. Now I'd be more intentional about inviting different people over a year's time: a group of students during Advent, retired people who could meet over lunch during Lent, new members who might stay for Sunday brunch after Easter. You might be thinking—who has time for this? I know how limited time is for parish pastors—if I had time for only one text study group each week, I'd choose to meet with a group of lay members rather than other clergy. If you have time for both, that's great![7]

---

7. Childers, *Birthing the Sermon*, 124.

While it's true I could write a better, more polished sermon if I heard from people before the fact, free-for-all achieves the same purpose, with the benefit of the insights being heard directly from those who have them. Free-for-all opens up the discussion to everyone.

David Lose advocates for interaction over the sermon, and his ideas for developing this skill in a congregation are helpful. He suggests starting with smaller opportunities like preachers getting to know people's life contexts and using examples from them as illustrations, asking people to respond with a show of hands to a question posed during the sermon, writing something down in response to the sermon.[8] One benefit of free-for-all is it allows people to test the waters of sharing; contributions can be as simple as introducing a visitor or requesting donations for a school craft activity.

I also give plenty of thought to setting people up to contribute meaningfully. We have recently done a series on "Ordinary Time" where I have targeted people in our church who we tend not to hear much from, and asked them a series of questions springing from one of the miracle stories in the Gospels. I still did plenty of sermonlike preparation on the text—reflecting, reading, praying, crafting a series of questions relating to the extraordinary miracle in the text, and the ordinary life and faith of the person I was interviewing.

We heard things from people that were pedestrian yet profound because of who was saying it. One person, working in an acute mental health ward, spoke on Jesus calming the storm: "try to be a calm presence for others."

Another, who described himself as not being able to work since his "nervous breakdown," told us about the value of friendship and community in relation to the paralyzed man lowered through a roof to Jesus, and said "don't sweat the small stuff."

Another, who lived for a number of years in Africa with his family, talked about the abundance of water turned to wine: the joy of seeing and being part of the body of Christ as it moves and breathes.

I could perhaps have thought of these things. God could have given me these insights. But to hear them from each particular person, with their particular experiences, was infinitely more useful.

Once, in response to an earnest sermon from me, someone talked about what it was going to be like for him to go home from church that day and interact with the recently released prisoner who would be waiting for him on his doorstep. A great balance to my take on the passage that day—not that I was wrong—I just didn't have the entire picture. I can't remember what my sermon was about but I remember vividly this reflection in response.

8. Lose, *Preaching at the Crossroads*, 108.

Another person in our congregation is the master of the thirty-second comment to broaden our biblical horizons. In one sermon I was preoccupied with the unnamed bleeding woman. This person commented in free-for-all: "Amazing to think of Jairus, such an important man, a leader in the synagogue, on his knees begging Jesus for help." His comment was that brief—yet it added an important perspective to our reflections on the text that I had completely overlooked.

People learn, directly and indirectly, in this kind of context, that there is not only one way of reading a text. We discover by listening to each other's observations and experiences that Scripture is not merely a compilation of truth statements, but a living document that beckons us into complexity, conversation, struggle, and transformation.

This leads David Lose to challenge preachers to find ways to shift from a "performative homiletic," where they are the main or sole interpreter of Scripture, to a "participatory" homiletic.[9]

> . . . it's not that a performative homiletic is wrong; artful interpretation of the text is only to be esteemed. Rather, the performative homiletic is simply insufficient in and of itself to the demands of the day and therefore must be supplemented by a homiletic that invites, nurtures, and expects a lively interaction between hearer and text.[10]

Perhaps in other settings, God does give the preacher all that needs to be spoken about the Scripture that day, with the remaining work happening in the minds and hearts of the hearers. But I believe, and am thankful, that in our setting God spreads what needs to be said among us.

We Have to Listen

There's always the concern that by including many voices we end up with a "pooling of ignorance." I do not deny this risk.

There's a lot to be said for having a few trustworthy voices in the congregation who can leaven the conversation, and I believe I am one such voice in our church. But my voice is better for the possibility of answering back: checks and balances, breadth and depth.

The practice of free-for-all helps us to resist the temptation to categorize people and treat them accordingly. Deciding if someone is "to be respected" or "to be pitied," has "something to offer" or is "someone in need,"

---

9. Lose, *Preaching at the Crossroads*, 105.
10. Ibid., 106.

becomes unimportant when the real task is to pay attention to what the person has to say, then and there, and where God might be in that.

We don't always know who someone is, how they are doing, what their education consists of, how long they've been a Christian for, what their socioeconomic status is, and so on, when they talk. We have to learn to discern what is being said, not rest on a preconceived value judgement of who is saying it.

Of course many of us know each other well and have background information when someone starts to talk. But the fundamental principle remains: anyone can say anything, and therefore we have to listen.

People surprise me. I can't presume: I have to listen. We all do. Every time. Just because someone said something ridiculous last week doesn't mean they won't say something incredibly insightful this week.

Preaching is proclamation that transforms. Free-for-all develops our ability to listen to the transforming voice of God in our midst.

Bibliography

Carlyon, Jenny, and Diana Morrow, *Urban Village*. Auckland: Random House, 2008.

Childers, Jana, ed. *Birthing the Sermon: Woman Preachers on the Creative Process*. St. Louis: Chalice, 2001.

Collins English Dictionary. Glasgow: Harper Collins, 1995.

Lose, David. *Preaching at the Crossroads: How the World and our Preaching is Changing*. Minneapolis: Fortress, 2013.

Nichols, Meriah. "Me." http://www.meriahnichols.com/meriah-nichols-4.

———. "Why I've Had it with 'The Mighty.'" http://www.meriahnichols.com/why-ive-had-it-with-the-mighty.

PART IV

Preacher

Spiritual Practices for Preachers

*Making Space for a Continuing Conversation
with the Living God*

Lynne M. Baab

We hear a lot these days about the significance of stories in preaching, so I want to begin with a story. When I was twenty-one years old, studying at a university in Oregon, I went to a weekend conference sponsored by InterVarsity Christian Fellowship. The conference was called "Bible and Life," and the goal was to help students learn to study the Bible in depth and apply it to their lives. We spent the entire weekend studying the six verses of Psalm 1. Until that time, I had no idea a person could spend that much time on six short verses.

I came away from the weekend having memorized the psalm simply from studying it so long. The first three verses read:

> Happy are those
> who do not follow the advice of the wicked,
> or take the path that sinners tread,
> or sit in the seat of scoffers;
> but their delight is in the law of the Lord,
> and on his law they meditate day and night.
> They are like trees
> planted by streams of water,
> which yield their fruit in its season,
> and their leaves do not wither.

In all that they do, they prosper. (Ps 1:1–3)[1]

The psalm goes on to describe the wicked, comparing them to "chaff that the wind drives away" (verse 4).

At that point, I had been a committed Christian for only two years. The psalm gave me language for what I wanted to be—that green, fruitful tree. I wanted to learn how to put my roots deep into the living water that comes from God. The psalm became a guiding light for my life as I finished university and joined the staff of InterVarsity Christian Fellowship, working with students at the University of Washington in Seattle.

During my first year of student work, I studied Jeremiah. To my surprise, I found a passage in Jeremiah 17 that echoes Psalm 1. The Jeremiah passage begins with those who don't follow God, and describes them differently than in Psalm 1:

> Cursed are those who trust in mere mortals
> and make mere flesh their strength,
> whose hearts turn away from the Lord.
> They shall be like a shrub in the desert,
> and shall not see when relief comes.
> They shall live in the parched places of the wilderness,
> in an uninhabited salt land. (Jer 17:5–6)

Jeremiah goes on to describe the faithful, again comparing them to a tree. The blessed people are described a bit differently, and this time the tree flourishes and continues to bear fruit even in a time of drought:

> Blessed are those who trust in the Lord,
> whose trust is the Lord.
> They shall be like a tree planted by water,
> sending out its roots by the stream.
> It shall not fear when heat comes,
> and its leaves shall stay green;
> in the year of drought it is not anxious,
> and it does not cease to bear fruit. (Jer 17:7–8)

During my four years of student ministry, I met and married my husband Dave, who was teaching dentistry at the university. He felt called to use his specialized skills in a country where traditional missionaries were

---

1. All biblical quotations in this chapter are from the *New Revised Standard Version*.

not welcome, so from the time we were married we prayed about going overseas. Over and over, God brought Iran to our attention, and Dave was able to get a teaching job at the university in Shiraz.

We arrived in Iran in July of 1978, just as the Iranian revolution was gaining strength, and we lived there only six months. How we left Iran at the height of the Iranian revolution and made our way to Israel is a dramatic story, but not the story I want to tell here.[2] Instead, I want to focus here on the ways Iran made Psalm 1 and Jeremiah 17 come alive.

Shiraz is at 1,500 metres (5,000 feet) and the landscape can be described as mountainous desert. In the six months we lived there it rained only twice, the first time for about five minutes with huge drops of water plopping onto the dusty roads. The second time, the rain might have lasted thirty minutes. The metaphors from Psalm 1 and Jeremiah 17 of withering leaves and shrubs in the desert were very vivid from our first day in Shiraz. My earliest impression of the city was the dusty beige/brown color of the buildings, roads, and vegetation surrounded by beige/brown mountains. Because we moved to Shiraz from Seattle, a very green part of the world, a significant mental adjustment was required.

We attended the only church in the town of several hundred thousand people. At church, we met an Iranian couple who befriended us and took us on numerous trips outside Shiraz. On these drives, the views into the rocky and barren mountains were fascinating to me because the lack of vegetation revealed the contours of the mountains. Occasionally we would pass a river or a small lake, the vivid blue of the water reflecting the cloudless sky.

On one particular trip, we drove north and east from the city. About an hour out of Shiraz, our friends stopped the car by the side of the road and said, "You have to see this." We wondered what they had in mind, especially in the forty-degree heat (104 degrees Fahrenheit). On the side of the road, we could see a small stream. They led us along a path beside the stream.

The stream was blue, reflecting the sky. Otherwise, everything was beige/brown as far as the eye could see: hillsides, rocks, dust, and dirt. Along the stream occasional small bushes sported brown leaves. The path took a turn, and there in front of us was the source of the stream, a spring coming out of a rocky hillside. And right beside the spring was a big tree with green leaves. In that beige and brown landscape, the greenness of the tree was totally unexpected, astonishing, and refreshing.

---

2. Our son, using his pen name Michael Hobbes, wrote an account of our adventure in Iran for slate.com in 2014. It is entitled "How My Parents Accidentally Got Caught Up in the Iranian Revolution: And almost stayed longer than anyone should," and is available online.

"It's the tree from Psalm 1 and Jeremiah 17," I exclaimed. We took a picture of that tree, and when we returned to Seattle, I printed and framed the picture. During our first decade back in Seattle, I was a stay-at-home mother and part-time seminary student. In the kitchen, my major work place, I wanted to be reminded of Psalm 1 and Jeremiah 17 every day. I wanted to be that tree, covered with green leaves in the height of a desert summer, as I nurtured my kids, studied, and lived all the other components of my life.

Why have I told you this story? I have numerous purposes in mind. I want you to know me a little bit, so it will be clear that what I'm saying in this chapter comes from one person's real life. In addition, the story shows the power of both stories and metaphors to communicate God's truth, a significant factor in preaching. The story illustrates the passion lying behind this chapter. I long for all preachers to be the kind of people who "trust in the Lord, whose trust is the Lord" (Jer 17:7), whose sermons are illumined by a vibrant personal relationship with the living God, and whose roots are deep in the living water of Jesus Christ.

The story also introduces the concept of spiritual practices, and this chapter focuses on spiritual practices for preachers. I memorized Psalm 1 and recalled it over and over. I pondered it, chewed on it, and tried to figure out what it meant in my life. That's what it means to meditate on Scripture. I posted a photo in a prominent place to remind myself of the psalm and the parallel passage in Jeremiah. I created space in my life for a continuing conversation with the living God about what it looked like for me to put my roots down deep into living water and live as that green, fruitful tree. These actions indicate that I engaged in spiritual practices connected with Psalm 1 and Jeremiah 17.

These spiritual practices shaped me as a disciple of Jesus Christ, and they were foundational for me as I moved into preaching roles more than a decade after we returned to the United States from overseas. Meditating on the Bible and praying based on passages from the Bible have shaped Christians throughout history and have enabled Christians to draw near to God in Jesus Christ, through the power and guidance of the Holy Spirit. In recent years, the words "spiritual practices" or "spiritual disciplines" have increasingly been used to describe the kinds of actions and relationships that Christians engage in for the purposes of intimacy with God and growth into Christ's image.

What are Spiritual Practices or Spiritual Disciplines?

Richard Foster's landmark book, *Celebration of Discipline*, was released in 1978. In it, Foster gently and vividly explores twelve classical spiritual disciplines, such as meditation, submission, service, confession, and fasting. Foster's writing and speaking sparked a resurgence of interest in the spiritual disciplines that shaped the church for most of two millennia, but which were largely forgotten in the twentieth century.

Three additional authors have shaped my understanding of what constitutes a spiritual discipline or spiritual practice. Each of these authors also provides lists that can help expand awareness of options. Marjorie Thompson, in her 1995 book *Soul Feast*, describes seven spiritual disciplines: reading of Scripture, prayer, worship, fasting, confession/self examination, spiritual direction, and hospitality. She writes that her purpose is

> to help people of faith understand and begin to practice some of the basic disciplines of the Christian spiritual life. Disciplines are simply practices that train us in faithfulness.... Such practices have consistently been experienced as vehicles of God's presence, guidance, and call in the lives of faithful seekers.[3]

Thompson's definition, that disciplines are "simply practices that train us in faithfulness," illustrates the overlap of the two words "discipline" and "practices." I use the terms "spiritual practices" and "spiritual disciplines" interchangeably.

The practices recommended by Foster and Thompson are not the only ones to consider. Tony Jones, a leader of the North American emergent church movement, describes sixteen spiritual disciplines in his 2005 book, *The Sacred Way*. Jones includes most of the spiritual disciplines mentioned by Marjorie Thompson, and adds others such as pilgrimage, meditation, and the Jesus prayer. Jones uses the analogy of learning to play a musical instrument or growing competent in a sport. He notes that proficiency requires practice:

> If there's a common theme among the great Christian spiritual writers, it's this: Seeking God will not be easy. The history of the church is the story of many faithful Christians admirably fighting back their own sins by these disciplines, only to be thwarted again and again. But, as with a sport, the more you practice, the better you get. You'll get in better "spiritual shape" as you practice, and you'll be able to run the race to completion.[4]

---
3. Thompson, *Soul Feast*, xv.
4. Jones, *The Sacred Way*, 30–31.

Jones's comparison of the Christian life to learning a sport or learning to play a musical instrument illuminates a profound truth. God, through the Holy Spirit, is in the business of transforming us into the image of Jesus Christ (2 Cor 3:18), and that transformation doesn't begin and end on the day we acknowledge Jesus as our Lord and Savior. That transformation continues over our entire lives, and we do indeed change as we practice living the Christian life. In effect, we participate in the Holy Spirit's transformation of us. Thompson's definition echoes this idea when she writes that spiritual practices "train us in faithfulness."[5]

Adele Ahlberg Calhoun describes more than sixty specific spiritual disciplines in her *Spiritual Disciplines Handbook*, also published in 2005. She includes many forms of prayer and Bible study, along with retreats, pilgrimages, and other actions that could be considered to be spiritual practices. Her list expands the possibilities for what exactly constitutes a spiritual discipline, and her definition is also helpful: From its beginning, the church linked the desire for more of God to intentional practices, relationships, and experiences that gave people space in their lives to 'keep company' with Jesus. These intentional practices, relationships, and experiences we know as spiritual disciplines."[6] The earlier definitions presented here emphasize transformation and growth; Calhoun's definition emphasizes relationship, which she calls "keeping company" with Jesus.

Calhoun's *Spiritual Disciplines Handbook*, by including so many different and specific spiritual disciplines, makes clear that many habits or practices in daily life can be considered spiritual disciplines. The mother who stands by the front door as her children leave in the morning and says a brief prayer for each child when the door closes is engaging in a practice that "trains her in faithfulness" and helps her "keep company with Jesus." In the same way, the man who has a habit of glancing at a Scripture verse on his phone when he waits for the lift at work is being trained in faithfulness and is keeping company with Jesus. No one can possibly engage in sixty spiritual practices. In fact, most people cannot engage in more than a few, but a long list helps provide an overview of the options and helps us notice—and think creatively—about the things we already do that help us keep company with Jesus or that train us in faithfulness.

Spiritual practices can be individual or communal, and most Christians engage in spiritual practices both alone and with others. Sunday worship in congregations—with singing, various kinds of prayer, the reading of

---

5. Thompson, *Soul Feast*, xv.

6. Calhoun, *Spiritual Disciplines Handbook*, 17. In 2016, a revised and expanded version was released by InterVarsity Press.

Scripture, the preaching of the word, the sacraments of baptism and Communion, and congregational fellowship afterward—enables worshippers to keep company with Jesus and provides training in faithfulness. Therefore, a practice of attending a worship service and engaging in the various components of worship can certainly be considered a spiritual discipline, or perhaps a cluster of spiritual practices. Many congregational activities, such as prayer meetings, small-group Bible studies, and home prayer groups, can also be considered spiritual practices.

Drawing Near to the God Who Calls Us Beloved

These practices help us draw near to the God who already loves us. Henri Nouwen writes:

> Every time you listen with great attentiveness to the voice that calls you the Beloved, you will discover within yourself a desire to hear that voice longer and more deeply. It is like discovering a well in the desert. Once you have touched wet ground, you want to dig deeper.[7]

Like Psalm 1 and Jeremiah 17, Nouwen uses the metaphor of water in the desert. God's words of love enliven us and refresh us like water in a dry and thirsty land.

Nouwen continues:

> The word 'digging' might not be the best word since it suggests hard and painful work that finally leads me to the place where I can quench my thirst. Perhaps all we need to do is remove the dry sand that covers the well. There may be quite a pile of dry sand in our lives, but the One who so desires to quench our thirst will help us to remove it.[8]

Spiritual practices help us return to the well over and over. They help us remove the dry sand. And, as Nouwen points out, "the One who so desires to quench our thirst" helps us return to the well and remove the dry sand. We don't engage in spiritual practices apart from the God who loves us, calls us to draw near, and empowers us to do so.

Identifying various categories of spiritual practices can help us explore creative options. Calhoun describes the way different authors categorize spiritual practices:

---

7. Nouwen, *Life of the Beloved*, 31.
8. Ibid., 31–32.

Richard Foster divides the disciplines into inward, outward, and corporate. Inward disciplines are practiced in the privacy of our intimate walk with Jesus. Outward disciplines affect how we interface with the world. And corporate disciplines are practiced with others. Dallas Willard distinguishes between disciplines of engagement and disciplines of abstinence. Disciplines of engagement connect us to the needs of others and the call to be God's heart and hands in this world. They address sins of commission. Disciplines of abstinence detach us from hurry, clutter, and busyness, and open us to being with God alone. They remind us that we are human beings, not human doings, and that God is more concerned with who we become than what we accomplish. They address sins of omission.[9]

No one system of categorizing spiritual practices works perfectly because so many spiritual practices have overlapping functions. I have found it helpful to think of three categories of spiritual practices: ways of engaging with the Bible, ways to pray, and other kinds of practices. When I teach groups about spiritual practices, I often use a white board and ask participants to call out all the ways they can think of to engage with the Bible. We usually end up with a list of fifteen to twenty different approaches to Bible study, Bible memorization, and Bible meditation. I'll ask for kinds of prayer as well and we usually create quite a long list. The category of "other" includes practices such as Sabbath-keeping, fasting, journaling, walking a labyrinth, pilgrimage, spiritual direction, simplicity, hospitality, and service. I always point out that practices in the "other" category often include components of Bible study or prayer. And I always remind people that the purpose of lists of spiritual practices is to create excitement about options, not to put pressure on people to do all of them.

I recommend to everyone that they consider having at least one spiritual practice in each of my categories: something to do consistently which is related to the Bible, at least one form of prayer that is a consistent part of life, and one practice in the "other" category. For preachers and others in ministry, I make an additional recommendation. People in ministry often study the Bible to prepare for preaching, leading devotionals, and facilitating Bible study groups. People in ministry often pray with and for congregational leaders and people in need. I suggest that people in ministry consider having at least one spiritual practice in each of my three areas that has nothing to do with ministry.

My own personal practice related to the Bible—which has little to do with ministry or preaching—is Scripture memory and then meditation

---

9. Calhoun, *Spiritual Disciplines Handbook*, 19–20.

on the verses and passages I have memorized. Psalm 1 is only one of the many passages I know by heart. I have seldom preached on the passages I've memorized, and I have seldom led Bible studies on them. Quite simply, they are for me, a child of God, who wants to have roots deep into Jesus' living water, who wants to have green leaves and bear fruit even in brutal hot summer weather. When I have felt guilt and shame, some of the passages I memorized have given me an assurance of God's pardon. In the years that I battled depression, many passages I had memorized were like anchors for me, giving me hope in the midst of discouragement. In many instances, when I was facing challenging decisions, the Scriptures I memorized were a means of guidance from God.

After everything is taken away from him, Job reflects that he came into the world naked and that he will also leave it naked (Job 1:21). I will stand before Jesus in judgment naked of my roles. I won't be a minister, preacher, lecturer, writer, wife, mother, sister, or friend. I will simply be Lynne, a child of God, reliant on Jesus' mercy and grace. I want to be sure that parts of my life are lived that way every day, even when I have leadership, preaching, and teaching roles in the church. I want the roots of my life to stretch deep into Jesus' living water so that my ministry will thrive, but also so I will be nurtured by God as a precious and well-loved child.[10]

Making Space for God to Shape Us: Sabbath-Keeping

The Sabbath is one spiritual practice in the "other" category that enables me to live one day each week as a child of God. The roots of my Sabbath practice go back to that experience in the Middle East when my husband and I were young adults. Dave and I had to leave Iran in haste because of the Iranian revolution. We had been planning a vacation in Israel, so we made our way to Israel to try to figure out what to do next. Because of a series of unexpected and God-ordained relational connections, Dave was offered an eighteen-month position chairing a department in the dental school at Tel Aviv University. Because the future in Iran looked so precarious, he took the position.

I had always wanted to visit Israel, believing that a firsthand experience of the biblical sites would strengthen my faith. Indeed, I loved seeing the settings for many stories from the Old and New Testaments. The Bible did come alive in new ways. However, the biggest impact on my faith was our experience of the Jewish Sabbath.

---

10. Some of the material in this section on spiritual practices is excerpted from my book *Joy Together: Spiritual Practices for Your Congregation*.

We lived in a flat two buildings away from the main road going north out of Tel Aviv. All week long, busses, trucks, and cars thundered along that six-lane road. The first thing we noticed on the Sabbath was the relative silence because the traffic was reduced to a fraction of the weekday volume. On the Sabbath day, with our windows open in the warm Mediterranean air, we could hear people's footsteps on the footpath, and we could hear children calling, "Abba! Ima!" (Daddy! Mummy!).

The Sabbath began at sunset on Friday, so Friday afternoon was full of bustle. Streets and shops were crowded. At sunset, everything closed, and I mean everything: shops of all sizes, petrol stations, museums, restaurants, and movie theatres. For our first few months in Israel, I carefully made arrangements for things to do on the Sabbath. We didn't have a car, and the busses didn't run, so I looked for people our age at church who might pick us up in their cars to go on an outing somewhere.

It took some months for us to fall into a comfortable rhythm for Sabbath days. Eventually we began to enjoy the quiet day, and I stopped the frantic arranging of outings to fill the scary emptiness. Dave would take his binoculars across the big road to a field and watch birds. I would write long letters to my parents and friends in the United States. We talked, walked, read, prayed, and ate in a leisurely, unstructured way. Our first son was born in Israel, and after his birth, the Sabbath was a lovely day to be a family and enjoy relaxed walks and easy companionship.

When we returned to the United States after eighteen months in Israel, we tried to talk about our Sabbath experience, but our friends were not at all interested. The Sabbath for Christians simply wasn't on the radar screen in 1980. We quietly decided to replicate the Jewish Sabbath as best as we could in a North American city. We moved our Sabbath to Sunday. We went to church and spent the rest of the day as a family. My husband didn't bring his work home. I didn't do what I call "the work of motherhood": house cleaning, shopping, or laundry. I was a part-time seminary student, and I didn't open a textbook on Sundays. We pretended all the shops and paid entertainment options were closed, just like they had been in Israel. We went to a park or stayed home and played with our kids.

After ten years, I finished my master's degree and began to work part-time as a writer and editor for Presbyterian Church Publications. Now my Sabbath included a new discipline: I didn't walk into my home office on the Sabbath day. Later, when our children were close to being out of the nest, I was ordained as a Presbyterian minister, and we moved our Sabbath day to Monday. Mercifully, my husband wasn't working on Mondays at that time so we could continue to have a Sabbath together.

Our Sabbath day and our Sabbath patterns changed a bit over time.[11] Despite the small changes, the constant rhythm of six days of work and one day of rest has shaped us. More than anything else I've done, the Sabbath has imprinted on my heart that God is God and I am not. This is an essential perspective for people engaged in any kind of ministry. The ministry belongs to God and not to us.

The two versions of the Sabbath command in the Ten Commandments help illuminate these truths. You'll remember that when Moses brought the tablets of the law down from Mount Sinai, he found the Israelites worshipping the golden calf, so he threw down the tablets in anger, and they broke (Exod 32). Later God gave him a second set of tablets. Nine of the commandments are almost identical in the first and second versions, but the Sabbath command has numerous interesting differences.

The first version, in Exodus 20:8–11, reads like this:

> Remember the Sabbath day, and keep it holy. For six days you shall labor and do all your work. But the seventh day is a Sabbath to the Lord your God; you shall not do any work—you, your son or your daughter, your male or female slave, your livestock, or the alien resident in your towns. For in six days the Lord made heaven and earth, the sea, and all that is in them, but rested the seventh day; therefore the Lord blessed the Sabbath day and consecrated it.

The Sabbath command is a profound statement of social justice, because every human is included, whatever their social status. The Sabbath command is a profound statement of the value of creation, because even the animals get to rest. The reason for the Sabbath command in this first version of the Ten Commandments is that God rested at creation, and we are invited to follow God's model. We are to remember creation on the Sabbath day, and many people in ministry find it soothing and refreshing to get out in nature on the Sabbath: walking, hiking, biking, swimming, or simply sitting on a bench in a garden.

Reconnecting with creation helps to remind us that the earth and all that is in it belongs to someone else. We are creatures, charged with stewarding creation and obeying God to be sure, charged with working hard to bring about God's kingdom, but ultimately God is God and we are not.

In the second version of the command, the reason for keeping the Sabbath is entirely different: "Remember that you were a slave in the land of Egypt, and the Lord your God brought you out from there with a mighty

---

11. I recount our Sabbath experience in more detail in my book, *Sabbath Keeping: Finding Freedom in the Rhythms of Rest*.

hand and an outstretched arm; therefore the Lord your God commanded you to keep the Sabbath day" (Deut 5:15). God freed the Israelites from slavery in Egypt, and post-resurrection we know that in Christ God has also freed us from slavery to sin, death, and the devil. When we stop working one day each week, we remember that we are not slaves any longer because of God's great gift to us in Jesus Christ.

Christian ministry can be so compelling that we give our heart and soul to it. We often find it easy to feel indispensable, and we find it hard to stop serving. Our loving service can morph into a kind of slavery to other people's needs, to our own expectations of excellence, and to our need to be needed. The Sabbath, week after week, helps breaks that slavery.

God has given us so much, and we are called to live in response to God's generosity. The Sabbath highlights God's gifts of a bountiful creation to enjoy and freedom from many kinds of slavery. In recent years, the word "receptivity" has been a guiding light for me. In many ways, being a Christian is a lifelong process of learning how to receive the gifts God wants to give us. Spending a day each week experiencing God as Creator and Redeemer helps us grow as receivers. We need to learn receptivity as people in ministry: our ministry originates in God, is empowered and guided by God, and belongs to God. We also need to learn receptivity as children of God, resting in the arms of God, taking comfort in the amazing truth that we are beloved. The Sabbath helps us dwell in the truth that we are beloved of God not because of our own deserving, but because of God's bounty.

Making Space for God to Shape Us: Listening

A listening stance is another spiritual practice that puts us in a place of receptivity. In order to know that we are beloved, we have to listen to God's voice in Scripture. In order to receive the gifts of human relationships, given to us to mirror the communal nature of the Triune God, we must listen to others. The ability to listen well depends on the acquisition of specific listening skills as well as an attitude of humility that believes that other people can contribute to our life. Also necessary is a heart of compassion that cares about the emotions that lie behind people's words. What I'm calling a listening stance refers to all of these: the willingness to grow in listening skills, the belief that God is at work in others and I will learn as I listen, and the commitment to show compassion through listening because God has called us to do so.

Lutheran Bishop Craig Satterlee uses the term "holy listening" to describe the kind of listening that I view as a spiritual practice:

> Holy listening demands vigilance, alertness, openness to others, and the expectation that God will speak through them. Holy listening trusts that the Holy Spirit acts in and through our listening. We discern and discover the wisdom and will of God by listening to one another and to ourselves. From a Christian perspective, holy listening also takes the incarnation seriously; it dares to believe that, as God was enfleshed in Jesus of Nazareth, so God is embodied in other people and in the things around us.[12]

The notion that intentional listening takes the incarnation seriously lays a theological foundation for a listening stance. We listen because we expect to see, hear, and experience God's presence in others, and as people in ministry we model that kind of expectation to others.

This stance is deeply significant for preachers. For many preachers, preparing a sermon is largely a cognitive exercise where we think analytically about the central point of a biblical passage and the kinds of everyday stories, metaphors, and ideas that will help bring the passage to life in a way that is relevant for the community to whom we are preaching. Of course we know that some degree of listening is necessary in order to know our community well enough to preach to them. Of course we hope we are listening to God's guidance as we prepare the sermon. We may be aware that the best sermons seem to come from somewhere beyond ourselves, shaped by listening to God and to others, but it is all too easy to engage in sermon preparation largely as an intellectual and individual exercise.

For my book on listening,[13] I conducted interviews with sixty-three ministers and lay leaders of congregations. Numerous interviewees reflected on the similarity between listening to people and listening to God. Both forms of listening, they said, require slowing down long enough to pay attention to something beyond the swirling thoughts and the to-do lists that crowd our minds. Both forms of listening require an attitude of acknowledging I have something to learn, and both require an effort on my part to be vigilant, alert, attentive, and careful.

I have argued that the Sabbath is a spiritual practice that primarily nurtures my life as a beloved child of God. Yes, the Sabbath gives me rest and renewal so I can accomplish my ministry. The Sabbath is not, therefore, irrelevant to my life of service and work, but primarily the Sabbath positions me one day each week as a child resting on the lap of a loving and nurturing parent. In a similar manner, a listening stance is a spiritual practice that

12. Satterlee, "Holy and Active Listening," n. p. Adapted from Craig Satterlee's book, *When God Speaks through Change: Preaching in Times of Congregational Transformation*.

13. Baab, *The Power of Listening*.

nurtures both ministry and the personal life of a child of God. Good preaching is impossible without listening to God and to people. We must listen to the congregation to understand what to preach and how to illustrate it, and we must listen to congregational leaders to preach in a way that builds on their concerns as leaders. We must listen to the community beyond the congregation in order to preach in a way that helps our congregation members know how to engage beyond the church door and in a way that is welcoming to any members of the wider community who visit the congregation. Listening is a foundational skill for ministry in a complex world.

At the same time, a listening stance is essential for us as children of God. Listening to God plays a significant role in knowing we are beloved, welcomed into God's presence for who we are and not just for what we do. Healthy relationships with family members and friends are also impossible without listening, and our relational God has called us to participate enthusiastically in human relationships that shape us, nurture us, and support us in many ways.

I mentioned earlier that Tony Jones compares spiritual practices to learning to play a musical instrument or learning the skills associated with a sport.[14] These comparisons shed light on the spiritual practice of listening, because growing in listening skills is a lifelong journey just like playing a musical instrument or engaging in athletics. Even the best listeners I know are eager to improve, because they know good listening is difficult and complex.

For those who desire to improve as listeners, two directions for pondering and learning may be helpful. One of them is exemplified by *The Spirituality of Listening* by Keith Anderson, which focuses on a receptive attitude of the heart toward God's voice. A second focus for learning is specific listening skills, which are described in many interpersonal communication textbooks and which I summarized in my book, *The Power of Listening*.[15] Specific listening skills include:

- non-verbal communication
- silence
- words and short phrases to encourage people to keep talking
- perceptive open-ended questions
- reflecting back what we've heard

---

14. Jones, *The Sacred Way*, 31.

15. In addition, I have many blog posts and articles about listening skills on my website: www.lynnebaab.com.

- empathy

A small amount of effort to improve these skills usually results in significant payoff.

Adele Ahlborg Calhoun emphasizes spiritual practices as a way to keep company with Jesus.[16] Listening to others helps us walk with Jesus because we get to hear their stories about the ways God has worked in their lives. We get to express compassion as we listen, companioning with Jesus in showing care to hurting people. We dare to take the incarnation seriously when we listen, expecting to find Jesus in interactions with others. As we grow in listening skills with human beings, as we learn to set aside our swirling and tumultuous thoughts in order to focus on someone else, we grow in the very skills that help us listen to God.

Making Space for God to Shape Us: Communal Discernment

Congregational culture changes when people in leadership demonstrate and talk about the importance of listening to God and to others. Committees and board meetings shift in the direction of a desire to seek God's will to meet diverse needs within the community, rather than functioning with a business model. Congregation members increasingly try to hear God's voice in their lives, and they listen to each other with the expectation that God will be present in conversations. This kind of congregational culture is a significant blessing to the person who preaches. In this atmosphere, the preacher is simply one more person seeking God's will and using his or her gifts to serve. The preacher serves the congregation by using gifts of study, imagination, and speaking while others are using their gifts to serve the community in other ways. All are partners in seeking to hear and follow God's voice.

In recent years, many leaders of business organizations have begun to talk about decisions by consensus rather than voting. Congregational leaders have adopted the language of consensus as well, and often talk as if consensus and discernment are the same. In fact, they are quite different. Consensus decisions try to address the concerns of the greatest number of people involved and are often the right strategy for many kinds of decisions in congregations. However, in contrast, discernment is an attempt to hear God speak.

---

16. Calhoun, *Spiritual Disciplines Handbook*, 17.

Tim Challies, a Canadian pastor who has written widely on discernment, proposes numerous definitions of discernment, and I like this one:

> Discernment is a process of prayerful reflection which leads a person or community to understanding of God's call at a given time or in particular circumstances of life. It involves listening to God in all the ways God communicates with us: in prayer, in the scriptures, through the Church and the world, in personal experience, and in other people.[17]

As Challies points out, discernment can be exercised individually or communally. Both settings for discernment build on each other. People who are committed to individual discernment will be eager to exercise it in groups, and people who experience communal discernment will be more motivated to exercise discernment in their own lives. The significance of listening is visible in Challies's definition, and the spiritual practices involving the Bible and prayer undergird discernment in significant ways.

Several of the interviewees for my listening research talked about the characteristics of congregations that value communal discernment. One of the interviewees described a church where she had been involved for many years. "In that congregation," she said, "listening to God is in the fabric of how it is. You have to make intentional choices, but it's simply assumed that that everyone will try to listen for God's voice." She used the word "multi-factorial" to describe the ways that congregation nurtures this listening posture. Some of those factors—or practices—are:

- an intentional commitment to listening to God, stated in numerous settings
- sermons that model and discuss listening to God
- prayer, including periods of listening, at meetings
- collaborative leadership and openness to hearing God's voice through different people
- leadership groups stopping to talk about vision and mission, making sure specific strategies are rooted there
- parish council retreat days
- encouragement for lay leaders to listen to God and to each other
- encouragement for all members to seek God's guidance about where God is calling them to serve

---

17. Challies, "Defining Discernment," n. p.

A congregational climate that nurtures communal discernment changes the balance of power. It is so easy for preachers to come to believe on some level that they have a more significant role than others in the congregation. This ego-driven perspective must be addressed, and the spiritual practice of a listening stance, which flows into a commitment to congregational discernment, can help. Martin Copenhaver, in a review of books on discernment, writes,

> Spiritual discernment, rightly understood, is truly countercultural. It uses silence, it requires that we take our time, it redefines our precious sense of individualism. One other implication of spiritual discernment is a potential redistribution of power. If you must listen to each person with attentiveness because you never know who the Holy Spirit will choose to speak through at any given moment, then we must listen with as much care to a stranger as to a longstanding church member, we must listen as attentively to a young person as to a mature adult. Because you never know.[18]

Listening to others—even the quietest and least dominant people in a group—with the expectation that God will speak through them and that God will be present in the conversation is a spiritual practice that undergirds preaching in many ways. Not only does the practice of communal discernment liberate preachers from the burden of feeling that they are the sole mouthpiece for God, it can also sharpen a congregation's sense of hearing as it listens to and reflects on the preached word.[19]

Making Space for a Continuing Conversation with the Living God

In this chapter, I could have talked about numerous other spiritual practices that make space for a continuing conversation with the God who calls us "beloved" and who longs for our company. Ministers have told me about a variety of prayer practices and diverse ways of engaging with the Bible that help them meet God personally in Scripture, ranging from analytical engagement with critical biblical scholarship to contemplative practices like *lectio divina*. Many ministers have told me about the significance of journaling, where they write out prayer needs, listen for God's response, make lists of things they're

---

18. Copenhaver, "Decide or Discern," 31.
19. Some congregations make a practice of discussing the sermon after it is preached. For an example of this, see chapter 6.

thankful for and slow down enough to experience keeping company with Jesus. They have also told me about spiritual direction, fasting, pilgrimages to places where they experienced God in the past, and hospitality experiences where they have encountered God in a guest. All of these practices can shape us as beloved children of a generous God, and all of them can impact our preaching in ways that make sermons more vivid and authentic. Any of those practices would have been appropriate in this chapter, and any of those practices can help preachers nurture a posture of receptivity.

I chose to focus on Sabbath because so many ministers have talked to me about the Sabbath as a way to experience being a child of God. I focused on listening and communal discernment because those two practices would not be the first to come to mind for many people when they consider spiritual practices that undergird preaching. I see them as formative because they help us receive from God and others. These three practices, plus many others, train us in faithfulness and also help us keep company with Jesus in a spirit of receptivity. They also help us preach with authenticity.

"To be authentic is to be clear about one's own most basic feelings, desires, and convictions, and to openly express one's stance in the public arena."[20] This description, from the *Stanford Dictionary of Philosophy*, motivates me to be sure that my most basic feelings, desires, and convictions are being influenced daily by my life with God. I want my sermons to reflect something of my own journey in putting my roots deep into the living water that comes only from Jesus Christ through the power and guidance of the Holy Spirit. I want my sermons to show forth the deep and lasting joy of being a tree planted by a stream of living water, which continues to bear green leaves and fruit even in a drought. I want to trust in God, and I want God to be my trust, in my ministry roles and in my life as a beloved child of God. I long for all preachers to be fruitful trees with green leaves, speaking in an authentic and enthusiastic voice about God's grace shown to us in Jesus Christ through the empowering presence of the Holy Spirit. One way to achieve those goals is to pay attention to spiritual practices.

---

20. "Authenticity," *Stanford Dictionary of Philosophy*, n. p.

Bibliography

Anderson, Keith. *The Spirituality of Listening*. Downers Grove, IL: IVP Academic, 2016.

Baab, Lynne. *Joy Together: Spiritual Practices for Your Congregation*. Louisville: Westminster John Knox, 2012.

———. *The Power of Listening: Building Skills for Mission and Ministry*. Lanham, MD: Rowman and Littlefield, 2014.

———. *Sabbath Keeping: Finding Freedom in the Rhythms of Rest*. Downers Grove, IL: InterVarsity, 2005.

Calhoun, Adele Ahlberg. *Spiritual Disciplines Handbook*. Downers Grove, IL: InterVarsity, 2005.

Challies, Tim. "Defining Discernment." http://www.challies.com/articles/defining-discernment-0.

Copenhaver, Martin B. "Decide or Discern." *The Christian Century* (December 28, 2010) 29–31.

Foster, Richard. *A Celebration of Discipline*. San Francisco: Harper & Row, 1978.

Jones, Tony. *The Sacred Way: Spiritual Practices for Everyday Life*. Grand Rapids: Zondervan, 2005.

Nouwen, Henri. *Life of the Beloved*. New York: Crossroad, 1992.

Satterlee, Craig. "Holy and Active Listening." https://alban.org/archive/holy-and-active-listening/.

———. *When God Speaks through Change: Preaching in Times of Congregational Transformation*. Bethesda, MD: The Alban Institute, 2005.

Thompson, Marjorie J. *Soul Feast: An Invitation to the Christian Spiritual Life*. Louisville: Westminster John Knox, 1995.

Depleted No More

Practices that Sustain and Invigorate Preaching Ministries

Philip Halstead

Many pastors find it extremely difficult to maintain preaching ministries over time. This is not surprising. Queues of never-ending demands puncture enthusiasm and impinge upon sermon preparation time. Successes are not celebrated due to the pressures of the next deadline. Indestructible internal and external critics conspire to silence. Parishioner gratitude is not forthcoming, distractions entice, and life-giving activities are set aside. All of this fuels stress and causes pastors to preach on empty. In light of this scenario, it is important to identify established practices that can prevent burnout and lead to a sustainable way of living, practices that will enable pastors to maintain effective preaching ministries over the years.

In this chapter I first describe some of the common challenges preachers face today. I then spotlight a number of key principles that four pastors recommend and employ to nourish their time-proven preaching ministries. The final section depicts three key pastoral counseling insights that have been successfully utilized to help preachers mitigate stress, recover from burnout, and find new inspiration for their preaching. In this way, I hope to motivate preachers to utilize practices that will enable their preaching ministries to flourish over the long-term.

Setting the Scene

For reasons unbeknownst to me, I purchased a fifteen-volume series of Charles Spurgeon's sermons shortly after I became a Christian in 1982. Each book had just over fifty sermons in it and within a year I had read half of the fifteen volumes. I was mesmerized. Quotes like this stirred my spirit: "Paul preached Christ, and nothing but Christ. He lifted up the cross, and extolled the Son of God who bled there. His one and only calling here below was to cry, 'Behold the Lamb!'"[1] They also energized my delusion of grandeur in which I was destined to become the Spurgeon of my generation, who would singlehandedly change the world for God and for good via my exemplary preaching!

Ten years later my opportunity arrived. A wonderful, benevolent pastor invited me to preach on the last Sunday evening of each month at the church my wife and I attended. I was very excited, but also encountered some serious problems. The first sermon took three weeks to prepare as did all of the ensuing talks. My wife noted that I emotionally checked out of our marriage as I prepared my sermons, which meant that I was unavailable for three weeks of every month! This was clearly not helpful for our fledgling marriage, but I was seemingly powerless to change my approach. A parishioner advised me after my second homily that I ought to move around more when I preached. Adopting his feedback, another congregant commented after my third sermon that I moved around too much! A different person politely asked me after my fourth or fifth talk if I had ever taken a homiletics course. I presume my response of asking him what homiletics meant answered his question. I also received an uninvited letter from a friend after each address in which he itemized my pronunciation and grammar errors; he said "I do this to support you." Preaching had become a challenge!

My practice of offering a sermon at the end of each month carried on for a few years. The preparation time I required and my acute performance anxiety never abated. Fortunately, I was put out of my misery when the evening service was moved to our larger mother church's premises where the senior pastors did all the preaching.

I have subsequently learned I am not the only person who finds the preparation and delivery of sermons burdensome. Andrew Picard, for example, writes, "preaching was often bad for my health. At the worst of times it became a robber. I allowed it to rob me of health, sleep, and sanity, and I allowed it to rob my family of a husband and a dad."[2] Statistics echo these

---

1. Spurgeon, *Spurgeon's Sermons Volumes 9–10*, 247.
2. Picard, "Is Preaching Bad For Your Health?" n. p.

sentiments. The *New York Times*, for instance, reported that forty percent of pastors are suffering from burnouts, frantic schedules, and/or unrealistic expectations. Seventy-five percent experience severe stress causing anguish, worry, bewilderment, anger, depression, fear, and alienation. And ninety percent of pastors work more than fifty hours per week.[3]

Regardless of the precise veracity of these claims, no one would deny that the stress of regular preaching and pastoring can dilute the enthusiasm, passion, and cutting-edges of preachers. Charles Hewlett encapsulates this point well:

> It's so easy to lose excitement when you're a leader. You come into the job as a young pastor, ready to change the world—a risk-taker, a pioneer, an adventurer. You're energetic, fired up, and excited. And then you slowly change. You get wiser, you take a few knocks, criticism comes your way, you learn to pace yourself, you learn about self-preservation. We become self-aware, self-contained, self-conscious.[4]

Burnout is an all-too-common consequence of preaching and pastoral ministries. It can be defined as,

> The index of the dislocation between what people are and what they have to do. It represents erosion in value, dignity, spirit, and will—an erosion of the human soul. It is a malady that spreads gradually and continuously over time, putting people into a downward spiral from which it's hard to recover.[5]

Stated differently, burnout is a serious, chronic, and debilitating condition.[6] It often involves preachers losing their normal zeal and ability for preaching and as a result their frustration mounts when the expected rewards associated with prolonged effort fail to eventuate.[7]

Since the demands of preaching can lead to burnout and numerous other negative corollaries, it is imperative that preachers establish helpful practices that protect them from harm whilst prospering their teaching. To identify such practices I contacted five respected pastors who had time-proven preaching ministries to ask if they "have any advice or pearls of wisdom for me and/or us as a family as I/we start out on this next phase

---

3. See Vitello, "Taking a Break from the Lord's Work," n. p.; "Pastor Burnout Statistics," PastorBurnout.com.

4. Hewlett, "Conversations with James," 76.

5. Maslach and Leiter, *The Truth about Burnout*, 17.

6. Guy, "Burnout," 167–68.

7. Davies, "Stress," 817–18.

of our journey?" I thought this might help to prepare me for my new role of pastoral care and counseling leader at St. Paul's Symonds Street, Auckland.[8] All five pastors kindly replied and as I read their responses I realized I had unwittingly unearthed a treasure trove of insights that could not only greatly assist me but also numerous other preachers and pastors. The problem, however, was the pastors had specifically shared their insights with me privately and at that stage I had no platform from which to share their pearls. These obstacles were overcome eight years later when I followed up with the pastors and asked if they would allow me to share their insights at a conference on preaching. Four of the five responded and each of them expressed their pleasure in being able to assist other preachers via the dissemination of their learnings.

The Pastors' Insights

Pastor A[9] is a passionate preacher who loves nothing more than to preach weekly. The first insight he shared with me was "to work within my groove" by which he meant "for some people preaching is their sweet spot and for others it is not." What counts, he believes, is knowing your specific role (i.e., one's "groove" or "sweet spot") in the body of Christ, remaining in that role unless shown otherwise, and doing everything possible to become the best you can be in that role. By adhering to these principles, Pastor A reasons you will experience passion, life, and energy as you prepare and deliver your sermons. Conversely, if preaching is not your sweet spot, to preach regularly would lead to a loss of enthusiasm, exhaustion, and a lack of vocational fulfillment.

There are a number of paths to determine if preaching is "within your groove." One involves praying, receiving feedback from trusted individuals, assessing one's enjoyment of preaching, and completing inventories that assist persons to identify their gifts and interests. A second entails probing constructs within oneself such as perfectionism, fear, and/or a reluctance to undertake training, which might cause people to conclude erroneously that preaching is not for them. What counts is establishing if you are called to preach.

---

8. I commenced my role of pastoral care and counseling leader at St. Paul's in November 2008 and held it through to my resignation and departure in January 2016.

9. Given that some of the pastors wished to remain anonymous and the others were happy to follow my lead, I have chosen to identify them as Pastor A, B, C, and D for the sake of consistency. Quotation marks are used to delineate their direct quotes.

The second piece of advice Pastor A passed on to me was simply to enjoy preaching and pastoring. He wrote, "For me this is the best thing I have ever done with my life . . . it beats selling widgets! You will have bad days but what you are doing has an eternal aspect!" By reflecting on these words, I have been reminded that deep satisfaction can be gained by serving God and joy is a *fruit* of such service; yet, I have also fathomed that longevity in preaching can be fueled by persons implementing rituals that enhance their enjoyment of speaking publicly. Examples include pausing to give thanks after sharing a homily, relaxing in a hot bath post-sermon, and/or enjoying a leisurely coffee with a friend as a well-earned reward after the conclusion of a service. Practices of this nature help preachers to pause, bring closure, regroup, recreate, connect with God, and enhance joy.

A further word of wisdom Pastor A advanced was that pastors ought to build a supportive leadership team around them. These people must not be subservient "yes" women and men, but rather individuals who believe in the essential role preaching fills in God's wider mission and who provide honest feedback to their pastors about their preaching, ministries, and lives. This support is necessary, because preachers are regularly isolated from church attendees, they frequently make themselves vulnerable via their teaching, and churchgoers can be quick to criticize.

Of the five pastors I consulted, Pastor B had the longest history of preaching and pastoring. From this basis, he exhorted me firstly "to keep seeking after Jesus—to know him, understand him, and draw close to him." He continued, "I know it sounds silly but with ministry and church it is very easy to slip into 'Pastoral Mode,' yet there is a very subtle trap that I have found with many of my pastor friends over the years—very few ever talk about Jesus!" He explained, "When we have pastors' gatherings and conferences the discussion is largely around 'Church Growth' or this system or program. However, if we are ever seeking after Jesus—just to know him and love him—then I think we express it in our ministry." Reflecting on these insights, Pastor B added "the further I go in ministry—and the more difficult it has become over the years—the more I just long to know Jesus. Above family, congregation, ministry, and anything else." He then quoted Carson Pue's words about getting elevated "in Christian leadership responsibility past the point of getting accurate feedback—and we are allowed to continue without anyone ever asking the question, 'Where are you in your relationship to Jesus?'"[10]

This powerful exhortation ought to be heeded by all preachers, especially as we are urged to come to Jesus (Matt 11:28), remain in the vine (John

---

10. Pue, *Mentoring Leaders*, 40.

15:5), seek first his kingdom (Matt 6:33), love the Lord above all else (Matt 22:37), and practice what we preach (Rom 2:21). That is to say, Jesus is the primary source of spiritual strength, life, passion, inspiration, and endurance.[11] An alternative reading of Pastor B's appeal is that a preacher's love for Jesus, or lack thereof, is an excellent barometer of her or his spiritual health.

The second piece of advice Pastor B passed on was to "develop a friendship—not with a mentor or a spiritual advisor, though you might have those, too—but with a friend, a mate you can laugh with, someone you can be silly with, talk to, and express your thoughts and anguish with from time to time." Such friends are not "always easy to find" but they "are very important." Pastor B elaborated on this by saying "I have a friend like this and although he is a pastor we are good mates. I find it grounds me somehow and he is always willing to speak to me if he is concerned about anything. I may not see him for a few weeks, but we speak on the phone at least once per week. Having him 'there' is a real strength."

Lynne Baab echoes these sentiments and states that "friendship is a spiritual practice, a place where we live out the things we believe in. Friendship is a space where our values and commitments take flesh."[12] Baab also sees friendship as a verb, which accentuates the point that preachers who wish to have great friendships will need to initiate, serve, love, and pray for their friends. This describes Pastor B's understanding. Speaking from his wealth of experience he declared that all preachers who wish to excel in their preaching need to prioritize key friendships.

First Corinthians 12 was the source of Pastor B's final pearl. Where Pastor A used this passage of Scripture to emphasize working in your groove, Pastor B exercised it to counsel me not to compare myself with anyone else. He argues that every preacher (and person) "is unique and gifted and God will use them in his own way." Thus, preachers must not make the mistake of measuring themselves against other preachers, for this practice leads to destructive feelings of inferiority or superiority. What they should do is look to Jesus and measure themselves against their own God-given potential.

Pastor C was the youngest pastor whom I consulted. Reflecting on what he would do differently if he was starting out in a new pastoral leadership role he first said that he would "maintain an 'aggressive' reading programme." He explained, "I did a lot of reading for next Sunday's sermon or next month's church meeting, but I didn't keep up a steady diet of uncommitted reading (i.e., reading for pleasure, or for my own personal

---

11. Lewis, *The Business of Heaven*, 307.
12. Baab, *Friending*, 12.

development as a pastor, leader, and preacher, without any immediate project in mind)." Pastor C believes that

> This sort of reading is so important for nourishing the soil in your mind and heart. Out of it sprout new ideas and energy, without which ministry can become so much drier and harder. The problem is that this kind of work doesn't fall into the "urgent" category, so it often gets dropped down the to-do list.

This sterling advice highlights a critical question every preacher needs to ask themselves: How can I best nourish the soil in my own mind and heart to invigorate my preaching? Personally, I think it would be difficult to find a richer response than that of combining Pastor B's recommendation of seeking first to know Jesus with Pastor C's suggestion of maintaining an "uncommitted" reading program of perhaps thirty minutes per day.

Another piece of wisdom Pastor C shared was to "expect to suffer and die." This sobering warning arose from his painful experience "that church leadership means facing a unique level of criticism and rejection." He expounded on this by explaining "every time someone left the church I died a little death. Often when someone spoke harshly against the church, its strategic direction, [or my preaching], I felt bruised and bloodied. This is one of the crosses that pastors—and their spouses and children—are called to bear." Accordingly, he recommended "chatting about this as a family earlier rather than later." Significantly, all of the four other pastors I surveyed also alerted me to this same troubling dynamic.

To be forewarned about the inevitability, regularity, and severity of parishioner critique and the resultant suffering is to some degree to be pre-armed against it. Other helpful ways to process critique and mitigate the suffering associated with it include discussing the incidents in supervision, deconstructing the critic within,[13] grieving effectually,[14] drawing one's strength and value from Jesus, and judiciously confronting one's critics. On occasions, there is also a place for accepting and not resisting the suffering.

Since a common cause of hurt for congregants comes from leaders who make unilateral decisions and/or rush change, Pastor C advises leaders who are "called to initiate change of any kind" to take their "time in setting new directions and consult widely and thoroughly before" initiating change. Personalizing this advice, he added "give your people an opportunity to speak into the process, and demonstrate that you really do believe that their opinions and concerns matter to you." Wisdom of this nature is priceless for

---

13. See, for example, Appendix A.

14. Sometimes the only way to move beyond critique and suffering is to acknowledge and grieve the very real losses that have occurred.

preachers, as it may prevent them from hurting people and experiencing the resultant anguish and passion-puncturing phenomenon of preaching to antagonistic parishioners.

Living by clearly defined principles and foundations makes a difference. They bring stability, strength, vocational clarity, inspiration, and much more besides. Pastor D argues that every preacher and pastoral leader ought to create a personal theology of ministry that serves as an underpinning of their work. Such theologies can be fashioned by asking questions like "What is your image of a preacher?" "What is your picture of ministry?" "What do you like and not like about being a pastor?" "What has God asked you to do through your preaching?" And, "How do you measure success?"[15] By engaging with questions like these, preachers will not only craft a theology of preaching, but they will also increase their self-knowledge, illuminate their expectations, and develop touchstones that can be returned to in times of stress and decision-making. In thinking about this, I am reminded of Jesus' (paraphrased) admonition: "These words I speak to you are not incidental additions to your life, homeowner improvements to your standard of living. They are foundational words, words to build a life on. If you work these words into your life, you are like a smart carpenter who built his house on solid rock."[16]

Pastor D also promoted the importance of developing a theology of self-care. One reason why self-care should be mandatory for preachers is that if they fail to look after themselves, if they refuse to heed their bodies' (i.e., their primary places of residence) warning signs, their preaching ministries *will* prematurely end. Parker Palmer makes a similar point: "Self-care is never a selfish act—it is simply good stewardship of the only gift I have, the gift I was put on earth to offer others. Anytime we can listen to true self and give it the care it requires, we do so not only for ourselves but for the many others whose lives we touch."[17]

There are numerous components to holistic self-care that preachers should consider if they wish to sustain their ministries over the years and not lose their enthusiasm for public speaking. Jesus, for example, grew in wisdom and stature and in favour with God and people (Luke 2:52). Similarly, the *Te Whare Tapa Whā* health model stresses the importance of *taha tinano* (physical health), *taha wairua* (spiritual health), *taha whanau* (family health), and *taha hinengaro* (mental health).[18] And Philip Culbert-

---

15. Adapted from Hunter, *Desert Hearts and Healing Foundations*, 136–38.
16. Peterson, *The Message*, 28.
17. Palmer, *Let Your Life Speak*, 30.
18. New Zealand Ministry of Health, "Maori Health Models," n. p.

son identifies spiritual, volitional, emotional, social, physical, and mental components of wholeness that should be considered in a self-care scheme.[19]

To experience such wholeness and create a more balanced life, Pastor D encourages preachers to establish pragmatic steps and principles. Examples of practical steps include scheduling regular holidays, Sabbath rests, and breaks from preaching; planning frequent family escapades, life-giving hobbies and activities, supervision sessions, and exercise; limiting preparation time for sermon writing each week; and undertaking professional development. Helpful principles include determining to address conflict situations and financial stresses immediately. In other words, preachers ought to be proactive rather than reactive in regards to their self-care.

Pastor D also urges preachers to take sagacious risks. For, after all, preaching effectively does require preachers to undertake the *risky* enterprises of wholeheartedly following Jesus, surrendering their lives to a greater cause, preaching the truth in love, and denying themselves on occasions. To navigate one's path successfully between the concepts of risk and self-care will no doubt require prayerful consideration and the counsel of trusted others.

A well-known adage states that the best advice is to seek the advice of wise people. Clearly, if preachers were to implement some or all of the pastors' ideas identified above the likelihood of them developing sustainable lifestyles and fruitful preaching ministries would be greatly enhanced.

Insights from My Pastoral Counseling Room

In the course of my work as a pastoral counselor, a number of preachers from a range of denominations have informed me that they have lost their passion for preaching and would like to recapture it. In trying to help these persons I have noticed three intersecting issues—namely, the perils of busyness, the preachers' own shadows, and the struggles of effecting meaningful change in their parishioners' lives.

The problem of rampant busyness in the lives of so many preachers today needs to be addressed if they and their ministries are to survive and prosper. Thomas Merton claims that "to allow oneself to be carried away by a multitude of concerns, to surrender to too many demands, to commit oneself to too many projects, to want to help everyone in everything, is to succumb to the violence of our times."[20] Peterson concurs and adds: "A sense of hurry in pastoral work disqualifies one for the work of conversation

---

19. Culbertson, *Caring for God's People*, 5.
20. Merton, *Conjectures of a Guilty Bystander*, 86.

and prayer that develops relationships that meet personal needs . . . the pastor must not be 'busy.' Busyness is an illness of spirit."[21]

So why, then, do innumerable preachers succumb to busyness, this violence of our times, this illness of spirit? There are many plausible reasons. One could spotlight the preachers' good hearts. Ministers of the word long to reach everyone with the good news of Jesus, help the hurting, effect positive change in the world, and fulfill their potential. A second collection of causes points to the never-ending demands of pastoral work, the ever-unfolding needs of people, and the urgency of new programs and opportunities. Society's liberal dispersal of accolades upon busy and entrepreneurial individuals also motivates preachers towards over-involvement, as do a raft of yet-to-be-healed internal ills. Examples of such internal issues include the *need* of preachers to rescue people; the *difficulties* preachers have in setting boundaries, saying no, delegating, and trusting others to do the work; and their *lack* of self-worth and self-knowledge. We will discuss these further later in the chapter.

Cheryl Richardson outlines one helpful response to busyness. She explains:

> People who feel overworked, overburdened, or under pressure ask me to share time-management secrets, or strategies for being better organized, so they can get a handle on their chaotic schedules. My response is always the same: You can't make sanity out of an insane situation . . . the key to reclaiming your life [and hopefully your zeal for preaching] has a lot more to do with what you *remove* from your life than how you organize it.[22]

To do this, Richardson teaches people how to say the word *no* in a gracious yet firm manner. She also encourages people to create absolute *no* lists. Examples from her own list include: "Saying no to anything that we can't give an absolute yes to"; "No longer taking phone calls during meals"; "No longer feeling the need to check e-mails multiple times a day"; "No longer keeping anything in our homes that we don't love or need"; and "No longer dealing with difficult life situations alone."[23] I have observed that reductionism of this nature has helped many preachers to regain their fervor for preaching.

A second beneficial antidote to preachers' busyness is to help them apprehend more fully the beauty and purpose of the body of Christ (1 Cor 12). C. S. Lewis adroitly captures an aspect of this: "At first it is natural for a baby to

---

21. Peterson, *Five Smooth Stones of Pastoral Work*, 61.
22. Richardson, *The Art of Extreme Self-Care*, 43.
23. Ibid., 43–49.

take its mother's milk without knowing its mother. It is equally natural for us to see the man who helps us without seeing Christ behind him. But we must not remain babies. We must go on to recognize the real Giver."[24] Yet, at the same time, people (or organs) *form* the body of Christ.[25] As such, preachers may need assistance to *see* Jesus and to absorb the fact that other people might be better equipped to fulfill certain tasks than they are. They may also need hands-on coaching to develop teams, delegate tasks, and release people into ministry opportunities. As they do, their workloads will reduce, their energy reserves will rise, and their fervor for preaching will increase.

The second observation to emerge from my work with preachers who had lost their passion for preaching was their shadows had emerged and gotten in their way. I am often asked what I mean by shadows, so let me explain. Everyone has shadows, but where do they come from? We are all born relationally dependent. Our very survival depended on our primary caregivers' favor; thus, if our key caregivers disapproved of any of our characteristics for any reason we typically discarded these traits in order to maintain their favor.[26] Similarly, if certain characteristics were welcomed by our caregivers we tended to exaggerate these attributes. Most people have repeated this pattern of rejecting and/or inflating aspects of themselves throughout their lives in order to preserve the favor of significant others. It is these socially-shaped characteristics of our beings which we try to hide, deny, or suppress that comprise our shadows.[27]

Shadow work is mandatory for preachers, as the unexamined aspects of their shadows *will* detrimentally affect them, their preaching, and their listeners. Consider the following examples: A preacher accuses several parishioners of being hostile when the real issue is not the parishioners or their hostility, but rather it is that the preacher was not allowed to express anger in his family-of-origin; as a result, the preacher disowned his anger and consequently projects his anger onto others. If the preacher were to face his hidden rage, many of the formerly so-called hostile parishioners would suddenly respond warmly to him. Stated differently, since what we resist persists,[28] preachers *will* project the disowned aspects of themselves onto others who in turn will mirror back to the preachers what resides in the preachers' internal lives. This is why Debbie Ford reasons we do not

---

24. Lewis, *The Business of Heaven*, 307.
25. Ibid., 307.
26. Wilber et al., *Integral Life Practice*, 41–45.
27. Ford, *The Secret of The Shadow*, 197–205.
28. The well-known axiom—"what we resist persists"—is typically attributed to Carl Gustav Jung.

need "to guess how we really feel about ourselves at the deepest level. All we have to do is look at how the outer world treats us."[29] Tolle puts it this way: "Awareness is the greatest agent of change."[30]

Here is another example: A preacher deems that Christians need to work and not rest. Therefore, she labors ceaselessly, condemns parishioners for their frivolity, and preaches a works-based gospel. Unsurprisingly, she is not popular and accounts for this by labeling it "the cross I bear for being a preacher of truth." However, the real issue is that during her upbringing influential individuals taught and modeled to her that Christians have to labor tirelessly. Accordingly, the preacher disowned her need to rest, laugh, and recreate; instead, she projects these needs onto congregants and labels those who express these traits as obdurate, lazy, and ungodly.

For reasons such as these it is imperative that preachers examine, befriend, and integrate their shadows. This vital work may entail some pain as old patterns are dismantled; however, it will also involve joy as potential is liberated, energy is released that had previously been employed to repress disowned characteristics, and the world is viewed and experienced more positively. (Appendix A outlines a step-by-step model for healing our shadows.)

The third issue that emerged from my work with preachers centered on the lack of change they perceived in their listeners' lives as a result of their preaching. Interestingly, these preachers were not particularly interested in exploring related themes such as the accuracy of their perceptions, their definitions of change, the concept of seasons in people's lives, and their expectations of different stages of faith. Neither did they want to explore God's role in effecting change, the relationship between prayer and change, and their own contributions to the situation. (Only in certain instances were some of these notions considered.) What these preachers wanted was to be taught counseling skills and modalities that they could adapt to their preaching contexts to initiate change.

Oftentimes, my first response was, therefore, to elaborate on Covey's masterful "Principles of Empathic Communication."[31] A bedrock of Covey's three-phase model is that personal credibility (Stage One) along with the desire to understand others and convey that understanding (Stage Two) must precede any advice-giving (Stage Three). Thus, if preachers wish to effect meaningful change in people's lives their first task is to demonstrate their trustworthiness and congruency and their second task is to get to know their congregants by listening to them carefully. When these two

29. Ford, "The Shadow Process," n. p.
30. Tolle, *A New Earth*, 99.
31. Covey, *The 7 Habits of Highly Effective People*, 235–60.

objectives are achieved, parishioners are far more likely to respond to the appeals of preachers. This insight ought to come as no surprise to preachers given Jesus' emphasis on love and relationships, as well as the fact that change, healing, and growth usually only occur in relational contexts.[32]

Another idea I suggested hearkens back to the first two years of my Christian life in which the man who introduced me to Jesus met with me weekly to lead me through a series of prescribed Bible studies. He always concluded our meetings by asking me to articulate a personal application based on the study. Generalities were never good enough for him; he would keep pushing me until I identified a concrete, achievable task. Given that preachers tend to get what they preach after, some of the preachers I have worked with have chosen to follow my former mentor's example and urge their parishioners regularly to make tangible applications from their sermons. The preachers have also begun to share their own applications, which has brought forth transformation and change.

David Forman's five-phase selling-cycle has also generated helpful discussion and change.[33] The cycle first involves *establishing a need*. For example, preachers might talk about the inevitability of being hurt by other people and lead listeners to reflect on whether they have processed their interpersonal wounds adequately. The next task is to *create want* which could entail outlining the consequences of not processing one's wounds. Then, the goal is to *present a method* to forgive effectively, for example. This is followed by the preacher disarming the expected *resistance barriers* of people, which invariably arise when they learn how to forgive, change, heal, and/or grow. For instance, to defuse the cry that "I can't work through this pain alone" preachers might state that the pastoral care team members have been primed to accompany persons on their journeys. The final step is to *close for action* by helping listeners to take a concrete step that contributes to change such as committing to meet with a caregiver to talk about forgiveness.

A further helpful model for facilitating change that I have pointed preachers to is *The Decision Based Motivational Tool*.[34] The model is highly accessible and creatively empowers people to make their own informed choices. This is very significant, because individuals are more likely to follow through on what they have chosen themselves to do as opposed to what they are told to do. Preachers can use the motivational tool in a variety of

---

32. Atwood, "Credo and Reflections," 139.

33. Forman, *The Selling Model*.

34. Peter Thorburn from ABACUS Counselling, Training, and Supervision, Herne Bay, Auckland, New Zealand, introduced and demonstrated *The Decision Based Motivational Tool* to Carey Baptist College's *Introduction to Pastoral Care* (MM561) class on June 13, 2016.

ways. For instance, they might provide a live demonstration of the model as part of a sermon and/or teach their listeners how to use it in their own time to determine what they wish to change. Appendix B demonstrates the model in action.

Of course, nothing can replace the need for preachers to develop and nourish a robust theology of preaching. This is absolutely vital to sustaining a fruitful and faithful preaching ministry over the long haul. However, with that theological foundation in place, there is enormous profit to be gained from drawing on the wisdom inherent in these pastoral counseling principles and models.

Summary

While there are many styles of preaching—deductive, inductive, topical, and narrative to name but a few—and an even wider range of preachers, a common thread runs through all of this diversity: Every authentic preacher aims to lead their listeners and themselves deeper into God's story and mission. Yet, experience also reveals that an alarmingly high percentage of gifted preachers fail to achieve this admirable goal due to the challenges of life and ministry, exhaustion, loneliness, critique, and other adversaries. Still, hope remains. It is a psychological fact that it is far better to set a goal that stretches you a little and yet is achievable than to set a goal that is impossible to reach, as unreachable goals lead to dejection and inertia. Thus, if preachers were to adopt and persist with just one of the time-proven principles and practices outlined in this chapter, they may well replenish their tanks and find the strength and inspiration to preach the good news of Jesus for years to come.

Appendix A

Wilber et al. outline a helpful method for healing our shadows.[35] First, they invite people to identify a difficult person in their lives who repels them. For example, a preacher may state "Bob disturbs me greatly."

Next, the preacher is asked to *face it,* which means he needs to observe the disturbance closely and describe it in the third person. Thus, he says, "Bob never responds to my challenges from the pulpit. *He* always opts for safety. *He's* clearly crippled with fear."

---

35. Adapted from Wilber et al., *Integral Life Practice,* 50–55.

Then, the preacher *talks to it* whereby he enters into a hypothetical dialogue with Bob in the second person. For example, he voices "Bob, why are *you* unwilling to take a risk and go on the mission trip?" Bob responds, "I am willing to risk, pastor, it's just that I happen to like the present status quo and I don't believe that God is asking me to step aside from my managerial responsibilities in this season."

Finally, the preacher is to *be it*. Hence, he declares in the first person, "*I* want to be safe and responsible (like Bob)" and then adds "*I* am safe and responsible." In this way, the preacher (theoretically) fathoms that he had disowned his personal need for safety to such an extent that he reacted to Bob's perceived desire for safety. He will also have integrated the traits of safety and responsibility further into his life. This integration in turn liberates the preacher to be able to choose to risk or to be safe and responsible in accordance with the circumstances of the moment.

It is not difficult to comprehend how variations of this exercise could transform the lives and ministries of preachers. Similarly, it is easy to grasp how people's shadows can become their teachers and guides.

Appendix B

The first task of *The Decision Based Motivational Tool* involves determining what topic is to be explored and creating a two-column chart where the word "Good" is written at the top of the lefthand column and the phrase "Not so good" at the top of the right column.[36]

Next, counselees (or parishioners) are invited to identify three or so "Good" points about the topic being studied. In my experience, there is always some good to be found. For example, Belinda might nominate that her use of methamphetamine makes her feel accepted by her friends who use drugs, happy, and care-free. Counselors (or preachers) must not make judgement statements about the good that the counselees identify, but they will note opportunities for possible interventions in regards to the points, such as Belinda might benefit by learning to accept herself, make new friends, find happiness in safe ways, and forsake her burdens.

Continuing with this example, Belinda is then invited to write in the right-hand column of the chart three (or thereabouts) "Not so good" aspects of her drug use. Examples include: it costs a lot of money to purchase the drugs, using methamphetamine could lead to trouble with the police and criminal convictions, and using this drug can compromise one's health. The counselor's next task is to ask Belinda to share a personal story about

---

36. Thorburn, *The Decision Based Motivational Tool*.

each of the points she has listed in the "Not so good" column such as "last time I used meth I was violently ill the following day and I ran out of money mid-week." Ideally, the counselor would then add some statistics or additional stories to expand upon each of the not-so-good points. For instance, research reveals that tolerance to methamphetamine develops very quickly, which means higher doses are needed by people to achieve the same effects. This in turn increases the financial cost and the risks of experiencing methamphetamine psychoses.[37]

The counselor's next task is to step back from the chart and invite Belinda (or whomever) to reflect on what has been written. In this way, the process elicits engagement, treats persons with respect, provides individuals with important information, and offers Belinda (and by extension, others) choices. And as we have seen, providing people with options increases the prospects of meaningful change occurring.

37. NZ Drug Foundation, "Methamphetamine," n. p.

Bibliography

Atwood, George E. "Credo and Reflections." *Psychoanalytic Dialogues: The International Journal of Relational Perspectives* 25:2 (2015) 137–52.

Baab, Lynne. *Friending: Real Relationships in a Virtual World.* Downers Grove, IL: InterVarsity, 2011.

Covey, Stephen. *The 7 Habits of Highly Effective People: Restoring the Character Ethic.* New York: Free Press, 2004.

Culbertson, Philip L. *Caring for God's People: Counseling and Christian Wholeness.* Minneapolis: Fortress, 2000.

Davies, Gaius. "Stress." In *New Dictionary of Christian Ethics and Pastoral Theology,* edited by David J. Atkinson et al., 817–8. Downers Grove, IL: InterVarsity, 1995.

Ford, Debbie. *The Secret of The Shadow: The Power of Owning Your Whole Story.* New York: HarperOne, 2002.

———. "The Shadow Process." http://www.soulfulliving.com/the_shadow_process.htm.

Forman, David. *The Selling Model Based on The Buyer's Cycle of Motivation.* Auckland: David Forman Excellence in Business Performance, 2000.

Guy, James D. Jr. "Burnout." In *Baker Encyclopedia of Psychology & Counseling,* edited by David G. Benner and Peter. C. Hill, 167–68. 2nd ed. Grand Rapids: Baker, 1999.

Hewlett, Charles. "Conversations with James on Leadership: What can we Learn about Leadership and Personhood from People with Severe Cognitive Disability?" In *Theology and the Experience of Disability: Interdisciplinary Perspective from Voices Down Under,* edited by Andrew Picard and Myk Habets, 73–77. New York: Routledge, 2016.

Hunter, Victor L. *Desert Hearts and Healing Foundations: Gaining Pastoral Vocational Clarity.* Atlanta: Chalice, 2003.

Lewis, Clive S. *The Business of Heaven: Daily Readings from C. S. Lewis.* Edited by Walter Hooper. London: HarperCollins, 1984.

Maslach, Christina, and Michael P. Leiter. *The Truth about Burnout: How Organizations Cause Personal Stress and What to Do About It.* New York: John Wiley & Sons, 2008.

Merton, Thomas. *Conjectures of a Guilty Bystander.* New York: Image, 1968.

New Zealand Ministry of Health. "Maori Health Models—Te Whare Tapa Wha." http://www.health.govt.nz/our-work/populations/maori-health/maori-health-models/maori-health-models-te-whare-tapa-wha.

NZ Drug Foundation. "Methamphetamine." https://drugfoundation.org.nz/methamphetamine.

Palmer, Parker J. *Let Your Life Speak: Listening for the Voice of Vocation.* San Francisco: Jossey-Bass, 2000.

"Pastor Burnout Statistics." PastorBurnout.com. http://www.pastorburnout.com/pastor-burnout-statistics.html.

Peterson, Eugene H. *Five Smooth Stones of Pastoral Work.* Grand Rapids: Eerdmans, 1992.

———. *The Message: New Testament with Psalms and Proverbs.* Colorado Springs, CO: Christian Art, 1996.

Picard, Andrew. "Is Preaching Bad for Your Health?" http://kiwimadepreaching.com/2010/12/andrew-picard-is-preaching-bad-for-your-health/.

Pue, Carson. *Mentoring Leaders: Wisdom for Developing Character, Calling, and Competency*. Grand Rapids: Baker, 2005.
Richardson, Cheryl. *The Art of Extreme Self-Care: Transform Your Life One Month at a Time*. Carlsbad, CA: Hay House, 2012.
Spurgeon, Charles. *Spurgeon's Sermons Volumes 9–10*. Grand Rapids: Baker, 1996.
Tolle, Eckhart. *A New Earth: Create a Better Life*. London: Penguin, 2016.
Vitello, Paul. "Taking a Break from the Lord's Work." *New York Times* (August 2 2010) http://www.nytimes.com/2010/08/02/nyregion/02burnout.html/?_r=0
Wilber, Ken, et al. *Integral Life Practice: A 21st-Century Blueprint for Physical Health, Emotional Balance, Mental Clarity, and Spiritual Awakening*. Boston: Integral, 2008.

Upgrading Our Preaching

Professional Development for Preachers Today

John Tucker

For some years now I have been haunted by these words from the pen of N. T. Wright:

> The various crises in the Western church of our day—decline in numbers and resources, moral dilemmas, internal division, failure to present the gospel coherently to a new generation—all these and more should drive us to pray for Scripture to be given its head once more, for teachers and preachers who can open the Bible in the power of the Spirit, to give the church the energy and direction it needs for its mission and renew it in its love for God.[1]

What does it take to become a preacher like this, a preacher who can open the Bible in the power of the Spirit? David Lose argues that "[any] practice worth giving your professional life to will not be mastered during one's years at seminary, let alone in a single course." Consequently—he insists—it is imperative that students develop "the awareness that their course work at seminary is merely the good beginning of a lifelong journey."[2]

I believe this. Preaching is such a personally and theologically demanding discipline and we preachers—at least in the West—must live and work in an increasingly inhospitable cultural climate. The call to preach is, therefore, "a call to live a different kind of life."[3] It is the call to a lifelong

---

1. Wright, *The Last Word*, 140–41.
2. Lose, "Teaching Preaching as a Christian Preaching," 50.
3. Johnson, *The Glory of Preaching*, 191.

journey of ongoing personal and professional development. This chapter will attempt to map the primary contours for an effective program of lifelong learning among preachers.

In recent years some teachers of homiletics have shown that literature in the field of educational theory can contribute significantly to our understanding of how preachers learn and grow.[4] Educational theories tend to fall broadly into two categories: those that begin with the individual and those that begin with the environment.[5] Theories that start with the individual emphasize the student's internal motivations or personality or particular learning style, drawing on instruments like the Myers Briggs Type Indicator. In contrast to these individualistic approaches to learning, social learning theories start from the idea that learning is fundamentally relational. Geoffrey Stevenson has shown that social learning theory has considerable value for our thinking about the training and development of preachers.[6] Drawing on his work, and the work of David Lose, I want to argue that for preachers to acquire, nurture, and sustain the skills, character, and convictions required to discharge their ministry in a challenging world they will need to give attention to five important relationships.

A Learning Community

In their pioneering study on situated learning, Jean Lave and Etienne Wenger argue that learning involves a deepening process of participation in what they call a "community of practice." They considered studies of apprenticeships in a range of contexts: Yucatec midwives in Mexico, Vai and Gola tailors in Liberia, quartermasters in the United States navy, butchers in American supermarkets, and "non-drinking Alcoholics" in Alcoholics Anonymous. They observed in each of these apprenticeship situations that learning is not just a matter of acquiring certain forms of knowledge or mastering particular skills. It is a process of "learning to speak, act, and improvise in ways that make sense in the community."[7] It is "a process in which the learner comes to understand their identity and their place or membership in the community of practice."[8]

---

4. See, for example, Long and Tisdale, *Teaching Preaching as a Christian Practice*, and Stevenson, *The Future of Preaching*.
5. Tenant, *Psychology and Adult Learning*, 3.
6. Stevenson, "Forming Future Preachers," 190–205.
7. Lave and Wenger, *Situated Learning*, 49.
8. Stevenson, "Forming Future Preachers," 193–94.

This concept of learning certainly applies to preaching. It takes a village to raise a preacher. Preachers are formed by their participation within the wider Christian community, with its shared traditions and convictions about what constitutes faithful Christian preaching and why it is fundamental to the church's life and mission. Preachers grow and are sustained in their calling by imbibing—through conversations, lectures, books, and conferences—the church's accumulated wisdom regarding the nature and dynamics of preaching. These theological convictions are essential for preachers in any age, but especially important in view of the many challenges facing preachers in the West today.

In early 2016 I interviewed seven New Zealand Baptist ministers. These ministers had all trained for pastoral leadership at the same theological college. They had all been serving in full-time ministry for at least three years. And they had all, since graduating, participated in a preaching cluster facilitated by Carey Baptist College's School of Preaching. I asked these pastors a series of questions about their development as preachers. When I asked them what have been the greatest challenges they have faced in their preaching, some of them talked about issues of technique. Kathryn, for example,[9] talked about the challenge of preaching narrative sermons. Taylor said he struggles with the "still highly mysterious realm of contemporary, cultural exegesis."

For all of these preachers, however, it was clear that the greatest challenges were not primarily technical. The greater challenge was environmental: they were too busy. Scott, for instance, said to me, "[If I want to read for my sermon I have to] get out of the office," and "[the only time when I can write my sermon is] late . . . at night." Sermon preparation, he said, has been "relegated" to the edges of my working week because of "the pressures of . . . church life." Scott lamented, "When [you're] here on site . . . people want to talk with you" and "you've got a myriad of managerial . . . things [to do]. . . . Senior pastors today, I think, are expected to be the CEO before they're the preacher."

Scott's reflections extended beyond ministerial expectations to the distractions of digital media. He said there are "so many streams of thought and influence [coming] into your life through blogs, through social media . . . there's actually too much noise for a good preacher today . . . like you just look at the Carey Graduate [School] Facebook page. My word. I wonder [what] those guys . . . do with their day." We live and preach in what

---

9. This is not her real name. I have assigned pseudonyms to my interview subjects in order to protect their identities.

Ellsworth Kalas calls "the Age of Distraction."[10] For these preachers, then, the primary challenges are not technical. They are environmental.

They are also internal. The preachers in my study spoke candidly about their struggles with self-doubt, pride, fear (of offending people), and discouragement. Kathryn talked about a sense of frustration that her preaching was not changing lives like she had hoped. She said, "[You're preaching and you think], 'This is what God wants you to hear,' and then you see that person is falling asleep!" You think, "How could you fall asleep?! . . . [W]hy isn't the whole church alive?" Kathryn confessed, "I sometimes can feel quite frustrated. You know that God's just doing stuff, but you want everyone to be on board and serving and to see it outwork in service, to see it outwork in people having the joy of the Lord, just to see them excited about mission." Taylor talked about how "every sermon seems like an incredibly difficult, impossible task." He said, "It just feels like such grinding, grueling work and the temptation [is] to escape it" by doing something else, anything else.

When I asked these preachers, "So how do you keep doing it? What sustains and encourages you in your preaching," they talked essentially about their theological convictions. Kathryn said, "For me it's only the word of God that changes and transforms people. So I could do a whole number of things, but if I'm not preaching the word and people aren't hearing the word, they won't be transformed." Evan also pointed to his "convictions around God and Scripture" and said "that's why . . . [it] is so important to keep revisiting [these convictions]," something which he conceded he might not do if it were not for the preaching cluster. I think William Willimon was right when he wrote that "contemporary homiletics has expended too much energy on issues of style, technique, rhetoric" and not enough on theology.[11] "The essential secret," John Stott said, "is not mastering certain techniques but being mastered by certain convictions."[12] And this happens through ongoing participation in a learning community with its theological traditions. It happens through reading books, attending conferences, engaging in conversations. One of the greatest services that theological colleges and denominational leaders can perform in our day is to develop the resources, events, and networks that will enable preachers to nourish and nurture their theology of preaching.

---

10. Kalas, *Preaching in an Age of Distraction*.
11. Willimon, *Proclamation and Theology*, 3.
12. Stott, *I Believe in Preaching*, 92.

Role Models

According to social learning theorists, people largely learn through observation and imitation of those around them. David Lose writes that, "An implicit conviction of . . . practice-oriented education is that it is difficult to do what you cannot imagine and even more difficult to imagine what you have not experienced." Consequently "frequent exposure to exemplary practice is crucial to the teaching and learning of any discipline."[13] This is evident in many fields. What is the easiest way to learn a second language? The way we learned out first: by immersion, by listening at great lengths to those who speak the language fluently. How do Suzuki students learn to play the violin? Immersion. Before they set bow to string, they spend hours listening to excellent performances of the music they will eventually attempt to play. In much the same way, preachers are formed by the examples and exemplars they have observed:

> Anyone who has gone to church with any regularity has preaching ancestors—preachers who have modeled, for good or ill, what a sermon is supposed to sound like: how long, how loud, how laced with Scripture references, how esoteric, or how heart-rending it should be. Whenever you stand up to begin a sermon, there is a cloud of unseen witnesses behind you. . . . They are present. And they are not silent.[14]

In my recent study of New Zealand Baptist preachers, one of the questions I asked was this: "What were the highlights of your training?" A number of them said that they appreciated the weekly chapel services where they got to see some (mostly) good examples of preaching. This was deeply formative. Others pointed to their placement in different churches each year, and the benefit of being exposed to a range of different preachers. But several also talked about the negative impact of bad preaching. For instance, Felix said, "for me the first year [at Carey] was [all about forgetting] what I knew." He had to "unlearn" what he had picked up from preachers "back home."

With any discipline, bad examples can have a very negative and enduring impact. In the field of music, for example, "some theorists believe that tone deafness is not the result of a physical defect of the ear or brain but rather the result of repeated exposure to an out-of-tune musical gamut. The solution, in such a case, is to overwhelm the history of negative examples with positive ones."[15] Maybe the reason so many emerging preachers never

---

13. Lose, "Teaching Preaching as a Christian Preaching," 45.
14. Schlafer, *Your Way with God's Word*, 196.
15. Lose, "Teaching Preaching as a Christian Preaching," 46.

really fulfill their potential is the simple fact that they have heard—and continue to hear—so much bad preaching that it overwhelms any good homiletics instruction they might have received. To grow—and to keep growing—as preachers, we need to be exposed to a steady stream of excellent sermons.

For the preachers I interviewed, one such stream has been the preaching cluster they attend. They meet every two months for three hours at a time. The first hour is given over to lunch and discussion of a preaching book which they are reading together. Then two members will preach to the group. Reflecting on this cluster, Kathryn said, "You get to see other people's giftings come out really clearly." You get to see "how other people approach the same text in a completely different way [and you think], 'Actually, I could do that. Maybe I'm in a rut here.'" Scott agreed: "[A]ll of my training . . . was very valuable, but watching other preachers and listening consistently to other very good preachers. . . . I think what enhances a good preacher is being able to see others preach and engage with their preaching."

Growth in a discipline like preaching involves frequent exposure to examples of excellent practice. It is of value not just for skill development, but also for character formation and theological convictions.[16] As part of their ongoing professional development, preachers should be encouraged to identify their role models and commit to regularly listening to them, watching them, or reading them—and reflecting on what they have observed. They should also be encouraged to attend preaching clusters where they can discuss their role models with other preachers and so expand the range of exceptional voices with which they can engage. Preachers should also consider consciously imitating some of the outstanding sermons they witness. By this I do not mean direct plagiarism or behavioral imitation, but copying such things as the structural form, illustrative techniques, or the literary devices. As Stevenson reminds us, "Teachers of preaching from Augustine to the present have recognized and recommended imitation as of *prima facie* value to the preacher who desires to learn from others."[17]

Mentors

This brings us to another relationship, the relationship between preachers and their mentors—those who are consciously and deliberately investing

---

16. Stevenson, "Forming Future Preachers," 197.

17. Ibid., 197. John Wesley reportedly gave his preachers collections of his sermons with the instruction that they should not attempt to prepare their own sermons until they had first preached their way through his model sermons.

in their formation. The central conviction animating much contemporary educational theory is that students learn by doing. David Lose notes that this challenges:

> the Enlightenment and modernist penchant for privileging the theoretical over the practical. All too often, the actual practice of a discipline has been seen as merely the application of previously derived theory. What is called for is a more organic sense of the relationship between theory and practice, emphasizing the necessary interdependence between the two, in that while theory informs practice, practice in turn not only assesses, validates, and extends theory but is often the source of theory in the first place. That is, often it is only by participating in a practice *and reflecting on that participation* that we can deduce its internal logic.[18]

A good mentor can assist enormously with this reflection, as the preachers in my study confirmed. Evan recounted how one mentor helpfully "pulled him back to the basics" after he preached: "I remember [him] coming back again and again: 'Show us how the point that you're making [comes from] the text.' [He kept hitting] the simple things . . . like a drummer. Just kick drum, snare and high hat; just do that and then we'll talk about cymbals and the rest later." Other preachers reflected on the value—during their formal theological training—of being placed each year in a different church where, as interns, they could benefit from exposure to a range of different pastors and preaching mentors.

Many denominational training schemes assign to student preachers a mentor who can provide feedback on their preaching. These programs, however, are usually subject to two weaknesses. First, by assigning or imposing a mentor they fail to recognize that a positive mentoring experience often depends on "personal chemistry" or personality. The result is that some student preachers end up frustrated, like the one who said to me of the instruction he received: "I was trying to force my gumboot feet into his stilettos." The second weakness is that the mentors are often not competent to provide incisive homiletical advice to their charges. They might be capable pastoral leaders but not particularly gifted as preachers, or not familiar with recent homiletical literature. And, of course, most of these mentoring arrangements extend only until the students complete their formal theological training or ministry internship. If student preachers are to experience lifelong learning and development in their calling, then they need mentors throughout their ministries, mentors who can provide them with incisive

---

18. Lose, "Teaching Preaching as a Christian Preaching," 49.

feedback on their preaching ministry. If denominations are to be effective communities of practice they should identify prospective mentors, provide them with training in homiletical best practice, and encourage pastors to link up with a mentor who fits them and their personality.

Peers

Geoffrey Stevenson also observes that one of the weaknesses with many denominational mentoring programs is that the mentor is often expected to provide evaluative reports that can materially affect the student's career progress.[19] This severely compromises the relationship and, therefore, the learning. In the words of David Lose, "Learning is a discretionary activity. That is, it will not take place until other more basic needs have been met. These include basic requirements of shelter and food (hence the success of free-breakfast programs at many schools) and the need for a sense of safety, well-being, and affirmation."[20] In my experience, that is certainly the case with preaching. Students must experience the classroom as a place of safety if they are to preach with freedom and vulnerability and then be receptive to strong feedback. Lose argues that to cultivate this kind of learning environment instructors must be clear about their expectations—both as to what constitutes effective practice and what constitutes appropriate feedback. Evaluators must commend what is strong (and worthy of emulation) and critique what is weak (and in need of correction). In other words, feedback must be both encouraging and rigorous. The learning environment must be both safe and demanding.

That is a difficult balance to strike. Supervisors who act as gatekeepers are not seen as safe. Congregational members, who have received no instruction in homiletics, often struggle to provide feedback that is demanding. The one group that seems to hold the greatest potential in terms of ongoing learning are a preacher's peers. A group of peers makes an excellent coach. On the one hand, ministry colleagues do not have the institutional power of a formal supervisor, and so they are not threatening. After years spent training together or in ministry together, colleagues can become trusted friends. On the other hand, they have spent years in college studying homiletics and years out of college practicing it. They know a thing or two about preaching—and receiving feedback on their preaching—and are perfectly poised to provide thoughtful, rigorous, and sensitive critique. The group setting is also valuable because—as Christine Blair notes—"reflection

19. Stevenson, "Forming Future Preachers," 198.
20. Lose, "Teaching Preaching as a Christian Preaching," 46.

is strengthened when adults can return to the subject matter several times in different ways."[21]

While a growing body of educational literature supports the value of peer groups for learning, the potential of peer-assisted learning for preachers is only just beginning to be examined.[22] My research, however, highlights its value for lifelong learning among preachers. The ministers I interviewed spoke highly of the weekly preaching labs which were compulsory during their training. In these labs, pastoral leadership students had to preach to their peers, with feedback facilitated by a member of the teaching staff. Kathryn reflected, "I think having to preach in front of your peers is the hardest thing, but helpful in many ways because these are your friends, these are your colleagues." Liam recalled that some of the challenging comments he'd received in a lab several years ago were still "haunting" him, influencing his practice in positive ways. Vaughan remembered that being subjected to public critique was "intense," "threatening," and "nerve-wracking." But it was "really, really helpful."

The preachers in my study also said they valued the written evaluation forms that were used in these preaching labs. The different sections on text, listeners, world, and preacher, provided a helpful lens through which to view and critique their peers' sermons. But, they said, we were much "too gracious with each other." Taylor put it like this: towards the end of their training "we were getting a bit better as we probably had more foundation of relationship, but initially [we were] kind of just tickling each other."

In the preaching cluster which they have been attending since graduating, the tickling has stopped. Over time their sense of trust has deepened. Felix describes the feedback in the group as more "honest," more "truthful," even "brutal." And because of that it has been profoundly transformative. Evan described to me how, as a result of this group's feedback, he has radically renovated his preaching style, to the delight of his congregation:

> Instead of having heavy notes that [keep me bound], I've limited myself to one A5 piece that I put in my Bible and I carry that around and it's there just to keep me on track. . . . The feedback has been incredibly positive, just recently even in the last few months. So I'm just feeling actually almost like I'm starting again really and that's because of this preaching mentoring group.

In one interview, Taylor said, "[I'm] so much . . . more . . . aware [now] of just how vital and how precious it is to have the preaching cluster where you can have people who are well-read and studied in the art of preaching,

---

21. Blair, "Understanding Adult Learners," 15.
22. Lundblad, "Designing the Introductory Course in Preaching," 218–19.

but are willing also to give . . . honest feedback that you just don't get from your average church attender."

If preachers are to keep growing over the course of their ministries, they would be wise to form or join preaching clusters where they can receive face-to-face feedback from a group of their peers. The key is to construct a safe environment where discussion is both encouraging and rigorous. This means commitment to journeying together over a period of time, a clear understanding of what is expected in terms of feedback, and ongoing reading of homiletical literature in order to resource and stimulate feedback. Denominations need to recognize the value of these peer-based structures and establish systems to encourage their organic growth.

Congregations

Stevenson claims that preachers should view their congregations not only as listeners but also as teachers. A minister arriving in a church will encounter a set of expectations about how and what to preach:

> There will be more-or-less precisely expressed customs regarding a sermon's length and its place in the service, the position of delivery, and the homiletical nature of the sermon. . . . There will be congregational expectations and understandings for the minister to discover about the rhetoric of the sermon, its intellectual level, the style of public speaking and the degree of self-revelation allowed.[23]

Informal and indirect congregational feedback does shape a preacher's theological posture, hermeneutical approaches, and rhetorical strategies. In my study Kathryn declared that her congregation had definitely molded her preaching: "The people have shaped my preaching because I know what's important to them." The congregation, she said, is "charismatic" and "evangelical," with a strong grounding in the Bible and mission. So "they expect me to have done work in the word" and not just offer them some "inspired thoughts."

As valuable as this informal feedback can be, more formal and direct feedback mechanisms can be exponentially more helpful. Several of the pastors in my study indicated that during their seminary training "the single most helpful experience" was their summer pastorate where, over a twelve-week period, they had to do the majority of the preaching in a local church—eight, twelve, or sixteen different sermons. In their words this was

---

23. Stevenson, "Forming Future Preachers," 199.

"hugely stretching" and "really valuable," particularly because their sermons were being critiqued, with different members of the congregation providing written feedback.

Since graduating, however, only one of these ministers has installed anything like a formal mechanism for obtaining rigorous feedback on their preaching. Most have not. Vaughan, for example, said, "On a Monday morning in the staffroom we'll typically kind of talk through how Sunday went, so there might be the odd thing that [emerges by way of feedback], but nothing really constructive." Liam reflected: "[My wife] lets me know in no uncertain terms without saying a thing when I've overstepped the mark and said something I shouldn't have." Most relied on this kind of informal and spontaneous feedback. However, as Evan observed:

> the feedback that you get at a local church context is either handshakes and "good sermon this morning" or sometimes more detailed than others, but usually . . . if you get any negative feedback it's often attached to a personal issue or preference. So the feedback you get is often abbreviated and it's given in unhelpful ways.

In their congregational context, then, these young preachers have struggled to develop effective systems for reflecting on their preaching.

There are many ways of gaining congregational feedback. It can be "as intimate as one or two trusted church members providing criticism and assessment, or as broad as a web-based blog where reactions to and discussions of a sermon can give the preacher considerable guidance on the effectiveness of his or her communication strategy."[24] Marc Rader, a Canadian preacher based in Sydney, Australia, has developed a powerful process for gathering informed and honest feedback from church members through confidential online tools like SurveyMonkey.[25] After surveying 100 Baptist preachers in New South Wales and the Australian Capital Territory, he suggests the following process:

- ensure that the purpose of feedback is formative not summative (i.e., it is for the preacher's development, with no disciplinary consequences). The results are their property
- identify the specific area or areas in which you as a preacher want to develop (e.g., introductions)
- read a chapter from a homiletics text on that area

---

24. Stevenson, "Forming Future Preachers," 200.
25. Rader, "Insights from Multi-Source Feedback."

- list several items to be assessed—usually these will divide into primary items (e.g., what introductions are meant to do) and secondary items (e.g., how introductions typically do it)
- make sure these items are observable (e.g., *not* "was Christ glorified?")
- rate yourself against each of these items
- select a facilitator (e.g., a trusted church elder) to facilitate the feedback process
- choose your feedback team. Confidentiality is essential, so select a team of at least three
- the facilitator should invite the team members to participate, explaining that you have asked that they be involved and what the feedback will be used for (development not discipline)
- give the team training in "what good preaching looks like" (e.g., give them a copy of the chapter you have read)
- set an appropriate rating period (anything from one to twelve months)
- ensure that the feedback questionnaire tests development over time (rather than individual sermons)
- frame questions in positive terms (i.e., instead of a value scale of "excellent" to "poor," a frequency scale is better—"most of the time" to "rarely"). Some people will not feel qualified to say whether an introduction was "excellent," but they will be able to "strongly agree" that it held their attention
- include a catch-all question: "Do you have any other comments about my preaching?"
- give these questions to the feedback team at the beginning of the period, during which they observe the preacher in the areas requested
- at the conclusion of the rating period, ask the raters to complete a survey
- the facilitator explores with the feedback team any discrepancies between ratings and obtains examples where necessary
- the facilitator and preacher discuss the results and compare them with the preacher's own self-assessment at the beginning of the period

There is enormous potential in this approach. If preachers want to keep growing in their calling, they would be wise to occasionally do something like this to obtain multisource feedback from their congregations.

Conclusion

Ray McDermott, a Professor of Anthropology at Stanford University, writes that:

> Learning traditionally gets measured as on the assumption that it is a possession of individuals that can be found inside their heads. . . . [However] learning is in the relationships between people. Learning is in the conditions that bring people together and organize a point of contact that allows for particular pieces of information to take on a relevance; without the points of contact, without the system of relevancies, there is not learning, and there is little memory. Learning does not belong to individual persons, but to the various conversations of which they are a part.[26]

A Christian approach to education, rooted in a relational understanding of human beings, would support this idea. Learning is "an evolving, continuously renewed set of relations."[27] We grow through relationships. This is as true of preachers as anyone else. Yet, as Stevenson says:

> the preacher often ploughs a lonely furrow. The minister, priest, or pastor is frequently the primary occupant of the pulpit in his or her church, with little contact with or experience of the preaching and sermons of others. Trial and error puts a lot of preachers, and their congregations, through unnecessary pain. Where are the communities of practice to help?[28]

Where, indeed? This is an urgent question. The church is a creature of the word. It grows and is renewed by God's word. We see this throughout history. O. C. Edwards claims that "Most of the significant movements in the history of the church have involved preaching in their development and expansion."[29] Conversely, if periods of revival or reform have been heralded by renewed preaching, "the decadent periods and eras in the history of the church have always been those periods when preaching had declined."[30] Edwin Charles Dargan, in his magisterial history of preaching, concurs:

> Decline of spiritual life and activity in the churches is commonly accompanied by a lifeless, formal, unfruitful preaching, and this is partly as cause, partly as effect. On the other hand, the great

---

26. McDermott, "On Becoming Labelled," 167.
27. Lave and Wenger, *Situated Learning*, 50.
28. Stevenson, "Forming Future Preachers," 194.
29. Edwards, *A History of Preaching*, 828–29.
30. Lloyd-Jones, *Preachers & Preaching*, 24.

revivals of Christian history can most usually be traced to the work of the pulpit.[31]

We would do well to take these words to heart. Preachers in the West today are under enormous pressure. Too many never fulfill their potential as heralds of God's word. Too many fail to honor their calling as stewards of the gospel. And the people of God starve. There are many prescriptions for church renewal on offer today, but I would contend that what we need more than anything else are pastors who will give themselves to their calling as preachers. Pastors who will commit to a lifelong program of growing in their preaching.

This will mean participating in a learning community with its accumulated wisdom and traditions regarding the nature and dynamics of preaching. It will mean reading books, attending conferences, engaging in networks in order to sustain our theological convictions concerning preaching. It will mean committing to regularly watch or listen to exemplary preachers, role models who we can imitate. It will mean committing to receive regular feedback from qualified mentors. It will mean interacting rigorously with peers in preaching clusters. And it will mean listening to the congregations we serve by installing mechanisms to receive informed and honest feedback. The churches we serve, and the gospel we proclaim, deserve nothing less.

---

31. Dargan, *A History of Preaching*, 13.

Bibliography

Blair, Christine Eaton. "Understanding Adult Learners: Challenges for Theological Education." *Theological Education* 34.1 (1997) 15.

Dargan, Edwin Charles. *A History of Preaching: From the Apostolic Fathers to the Great Reformers, A.D. 70—1572*. Vol. 1. New York: Hodder & Stoughton, 1905.

Edwards, O. C. Jr. *A History of Preaching*. Nashville: Abingdon, 2004.

Johnson, Darrell. *The Glory of Preaching: Participating in God's Transformation of the World*. Downers Grove, IL: IVP, 2009.

Kalas, J. Ellsworth. *Preaching in an Age of Distraction*. Downers Grove, IL: IVP, 2014.

Lave, Jean, and Etienne Wenger. *Situated Learning: Legitimate Peripheral Participation*. Cambridge: University of Cambridge Press, 1991.

Lloyd-Jones, Martyn. *Preachers & Preaching*. Grand Rapids: Zondervan, 1971.

Long, Thomas G., and Leonora Tubbs Tisdale, eds. *Teaching Preaching as a Christian Practice: A New Approach to Homiletical Pedagogy*. Louisville: Westminster John Knox, 2008.

Lose, David J. "Teaching Preaching as a Christian Preaching." In *Teaching Preaching as a Christian Practice: A New Approach to Homiletical Pedagogy*, edited by Thomas G. Long and Leonora Tubbs Tisdale, 41–57. Louisville: Westminster John Knox, 2008.

Lundblad, Barbara K. "Designing the Introductory Course in Preaching." In *Teaching Preaching as a Christian Practice: A New Approach to Homiletical Pedagogy*, edited by Thomas G. Long and Leonora Tubbs Tisdale, 218–19. Louisville: Westminster John Knox, 2008.

McDermott, R. P. "On Becoming Labelled—the Story of Adam." In *Learners, Learning and Assessment*, edited by Patricia Murphy, 167. London: Paul Chapman, 1999.

Rader, Marc. "Insights from Multi-Source Feedback for the Development of Preachers and Preaching." DMin thesis. Australian College of Theology, 2013.

Schlafer, David J. *Your Way with God's Word*. Cambridge, MA: Cowley, 1995.

Stevenson, Geoffrey. "Forming Future Preachers." In *The Future of Preaching*, edited by Geoffrey Stevenson, 190–205. London: SCM, 2010.

Stevenson, Geoffrey, ed. *The Future of Preaching*. London: SCM, 2010.

Stott, John R. W. *I Believe in Preaching*. London: Hodder & Stoughton, 1982.

Tenant, Mark. *Psychology and Adult Learning*. 2nd ed. London: Routledge, 1997.

Willimon, William H. *Proclamation and Theology*. Nashville: Abingdon, 2005.

Wright, N. T. *The Last Word: Scripture and the Authority of God—Getting Beyond the Bible Wars*. San Franciso: Harper, 2005.

PART V
Christ

Preaching Christ Crucified

Cruciformity in Content and Delivery

MARK KEOWN

IT IS ESTABLISHED THAT Paul's theology is profoundly cruciform.[1] At the center of his thought is Christ and him crucified. This Christ-centeredness is seen in Paul's experience—a vision of the raised Christ blew to smithereens his belief that a crucified Christ is an oxymoron; he converted in an instant when he met Jesus on the Damascus Road. The cross shapes his soteriology—the cross of Christ the moment when Jesus absorbed to himself human sin. As a result, sin was destroyed in his body of death, enabling God through his Son to justify, reconcile, redeem, adopt, regenerate, and seal by his Spirit those who are "in him" by faith. The cross provides the supreme example of God's character and human living—believers in Jesus are empowered by the Spirit to live lives of humility, sacrificial service, suffering, and love as they live the Christian life. Through the power of the Spirit, in Christ, they are transformed to be more and more like Jesus, *the imago Dei* (Rom 8:29; Col 1:15). The cross provides the way he shapes his approach to Christian life and mission. In this essay, I explore how, in 1 Corinthians 1–2, Paul calls the Corinthians back from the brink of complete fragmentation to cruciform lives. In so doing, Paul refers to his cruciform approach to preaching, a proclamation shaped by the cross in both content and

---

1. The leading writer in this area is Michael J. Gorman. For example, *Inhabiting the Cruciform God: Kenosis, Justification, and Theosis in Paul's Narrative Soteriology*, among others.

delivery. As we consider a contemporary estern world with somewhat similar trappings to ancient Corinth, it is my view that we must allow Paul's approach to inform us regarding both what we preach and how we deliver it.

The Church and Culture of Corinth

In 1 Corinthians 1:10–4:21, written from Ephesus sometime during spring in the years AD 53 to 55, to his church planted some three to five years earlier (Acts 18),[2] Paul is dealing with the Corinthian church fragmenting over their preferences for certain preachers. Some from the whanau[3] of a certain woman Chloe have reported this to him,[4] telling him that members of the church are gathering around their favorite preachers—Paul, Apollos, and Cephas (1 Cor 1:12).[5] Further, this is no mere friendly rivalry but is dividing the church.[6] Faulty understandings of preaching and preachers lie at the core of the Corinthian problem.

The Paul group likely includes those who were converted by Paul or members of their families. They remember him fondly, perhaps for his simple preaching of the cross through which God saved them. It likely includes those whom he baptized, perhaps including some from the homes of Sosthenes, Crispus, Titius Justus, Gaius, Crispus, and Stephanas (Acts 18:7, 8, 17; 1 Cor 1:1, 14, 16).

The supporters of Apollos would likely include those whom Apollos led to Christ and baptized during his trip from Ephesus sometime after Paul left Ephesus. Luke describes Apollos as a "man of words" (*anēr logois*), likely meaning he was eloquent and educated (Acts 18:24).[7] As such, they were perhaps deeply impressed with his fervency of spirit,[8] his boldness of

---

2. On dates see the thorough discussion in Thiselton, *The First Epistle to the Corinthians*, 29–32. Based in part on the Gallio inscription, Paul likely planted the church in autumn to early summer AD 52, and 1 Corinthians was likely written in AD spring 54 or 55.

3. A New Zealand Maori term for the household which was the extended family.

4. Chloe may be a businesswoman from Asia Minor (see Fee, *The First Epistle to the Corinthians*, 54), although she could equally be from Corinth, (see Garland, 1 *Corinthians*, 44).

5. For a full discussion of the range of views in each of the groups see Thiselton, *The First Epistle*, 124–33.

6. The "I am . . ." formulas may indicate slogans or a rhetorical caricature of their fragmentation, (see Mitchell, *Paul and the Rhetoric of Reconciliation*, 83–86).

7. Litfin, *St. Paul's Theology of Proclamation*, 123.

8. Literally "boiling (*zeō*) in spirit," so metaphorically of a highly passionate

preaching,⁹ and his public refutation of the Jews in synagogues and other contexts (Acts 18:23–24, 28; 19:27–28). It is probable, then, that he was a rhetorician more like those familiar to the Corinthians from their history of celebrating traveling speakers, whether Sophists, Stoics, Cynics, or other philosophers.¹⁰ In addition, some of those initially converted by Paul may have become enamored by Apollos's brilliant oratory and shifted allegiance to him as a result.

The existence of a Cephas group suggests Peter had visited Corinth sometime after Paul left the city, perhaps with his wife (cf. 1 Cor 9:5). With his mission focus on the circumcised (Gal 2:7–10), those supporting him were likely Jewish converts and believers. While not Judaizers who impose Judaism on Gentile converts, for there is no evidence of a Judaizing problem in the letter, they are likely believers who lived out of the Jewish culture.

There may be a fourth group, perhaps the super-spiritual who attach themselves to Christ alone¹¹ and look down on the others with their attachment to merely human preachers. However, it is more likely that the "I am of Christ" group represents Paul's perspective; a somewhat ironical or even sarcastic launch of his response to the Corinthian disintegration.¹² It may have the sense, "You follow these humans! Really? Well, I follow Christ as should we all!"

The Corinthians' attachments to their preferred missionaries went further than mere preference. It is likely that these groups offered patronage to these preachers which Apollos and Peter may have accepted—as was their right (1 Cor 9:1–14). However, as we read in the letter, Paul refused Corinthian financial support—he did not want to be a puppet in their political games (1 Cor 9:15–18). When compared with Galatians, 2 Corinthians 11, and Philemon 3, there is no indication of a theological dimension to these

---

communicator. See on the verb in Oepke, "ζέω," in *Theological Dictionary of the New Testament*, 2.875–76.

9. The Greek for boldness *parrēsiazomai* means to "speak freely, openly, fearlessly." See *A Greek-English Lexicon of the New Testament and Other Early Christian Literature*, 782.

10. To get a feel for this, read Dio Chrysostom, *Corinthian Discourse*, which speaks of his reception in the city.

11. Fee, *The First Epistle*, 58 notes a range of possibilities for those who consider there is a Christ-group, including those who honored his preaching, Jewish extremists, Gnostics who cursed Jesus but affirmed Christ as the true "Spiritual man, enthusiasts, Corinthian *pneumatikoi* with a hyper-spiritual Christology which avoids the cross."

12. See for example Hurd, *The Origin of 1 Corinthians*, 105; Branick, "Source and Redaction Analysis of 1 Corinthians 1–3," 251–69; Mitchell, *The Rhetoric*, 82 n. 1010; Garland, *1 Corinthians*, 49.

divisions.[13] Neither did Paul criticize Apollos or Cephas as if the preachers themselves were involved.[14] None of the preachers initiated or endorsed the groups—the preachers were pawns in the Corinthians' political games as they pursued status. These people were gathering around their favored preachers based on style.

In a culture where honor and reputation mattered above all, the members of these different factions likely thought that associating themselves with these missionaries would gain them honor and, conversely, shame their opponents. They were probably seeking "to legitimate their power by appealing to renowned figures in the church."[15]

Corinth had a particular culture in the Greco-Roman world. Having been destroyed by the Romans in the battle of Corinth in 146 BC and rebuilt in 44 BC under Julius Caesar's instruction, the city was relatively young. It was in the midst of a building boom at the time. Without an established aristocracy and the same degree of ancient tradition and hierarchy as other Roman cities, and as a key trade center between Rome and the east, Corinth had real possibilities for social mobility. It was a place where people could make some real money and rise up the social pecking order. Anthony Thiselton notes that the core city values were "those of trade, business, entrepreneurial pragmatism in the pursuit of success."[16] David Garland observes that "[t]hese values fed the zeal to attain public status, to promote one's own honor, and to secure power."[17] Social status was of key importance to the citizens of the city, and it was keenly sought after. Garland further adds, "[t]he scramble for scarce honor was as intense as the scramble for scarce wealth."[18]

There were various means to gain honor including providing patronage for new cults or public societies (*collegia*, of which Christianity would be one), and through the demonstration of philosophical and rhetorical brilliance.[19] Another means of gaining esteem was social attachment to the highly venerated, as in the case of these three preachers. Wayne Meeks writes, "[m]ost individuals tend to measure themselves by the standards of some group that is very important to them—their reference group, whether or not they belong to it—rather than by the standards of the whole society."[20] Social status then was

---

13. Much of the language is political. See Pogoloff, *Logos and Sophia*, 99–100.
14. Garland, *1 Corinthians*, 50.
15. Welborn, *Politics and Rhetoric in the Corinthian Epistles*, 24.
16. Thiselton, *The First Epistle*, 4.
17. Garland, *1 Corinthians*, 4.
18. Ibid., 5.
19. Stansbury, "Corinthian Honor, Corinthian Conflict," 87.
20. Meeks, *The First Urban Christians*, 54.

gained by "who you know." By social attachment and lavish patronage, they could themselves gain honor. Conversely, using political enmity, they could demean the other. Garland draws parallels to the current American scene: "schmoozing, massaging a superior's ego, rubbing shoulders with the powerful, pulling strings, scratching each other's back, and dragging rivals' names through the mud—all describe what was required to attain success in this society."[21] The recent presidential election battles in the USA bring this home vividly. Being attached to Paul, Apollos, and Cephas, then, was in effect using these preachers for their own political gain.

Paul's Cruciform Preaching

Paul responds to this problem through to the end of chapter 4 with rhetorical skill, and touches on it again in a mention of disunity at the Lord's Supper (1 Cor 11:17–22). Beginning in 1 Cor 1:10 he urges unity of mind and thought. He argues christologically,[22] starting with "I follow Christ," questioning whether Christ—into whom they were all baptized—can be divided. The implied answer is, no! They should all be following Christ—not Paul, Apollos, or Cephas, even if they did baptize them.

In 1:17 he states, "For Christ did not send me to baptize but to preach the gospel, and not with *wisdom of word* (*sophia logou*), lest the cross of Christ be emptied of its power." Paul here confirms his commission from Christ to preach the gospel (*euangelizomai*). The singular *logou*, the genitive of *logos*, here indicates "message," "preaching," or "proclamation." The head noun *sophia* has the sense of "wisdom," "brilliance," or "eloquence." Put together we come up with something like "eloquence of preaching," "sophisticated speech,"[23] or more loosely, "rhetorical brilliance."[24] As Ben Witherington says, "he [Paul] also resolved not to declaim the gospel (2:1), that is, not to use Sophistic or ornamental rhetoric in his missionary preaching, lest the audience focus on form rather than content."[25] So then, Paul was not sent to preach with sensational delivery, "lest the cross of Christ be emptied of its power."

---

21. Garland, 1 *Corinthians*, 5.

22. In effect Paul begins in 1 Cor 1:9, where he stresses that the Corinthians have been called by the faithful God into the *koinōnia* of his Son and Lord Jesus Christ—the fellowship in Christ cannot be riddled with status-seeking and division.

23. Pogoloff, *Logos and Sophia*, 110.

24. See the discussion in Garland, 1 *Corinthians*, 55–58.

25. Witherington, *Conflict and Community in Corinth*, 46.

"The cross of Christ" here is a summary of the content of the gospel message he preaches; Christ crucified. For Paul, Christ lies at the center of his preaching, especially his death and resurrection. Christ's death is the means by which God saves humanity. Jesus "died for our sins" (15:3) to deliver humanity "from the present evil age" (Gal 1:4) "so that in him we might become the righteousness of God" (2 Cor 5:21). Further, the "Christ-life" becomes the basis of Christian ethics; Christians are called to emulate Christ's voluntary self-emptying and self-humbling. Empowered by the Spirit (Rom 8:1–17; Gal 5:16–6:9), they are to live a totally selfless life of sacrifice and suffering for the salvation of humanity (Phil 2:6–8). Paul does not want this message of Christ's self-emptying to be emptied of its power.[26] Power here speaks of God's ability—by his Spirit, through the agency of the proclaimed word concerning his Son preached and heard—to bring about the birth of faith in the receptive human heart. Paul does not want the brilliance of his presence and delivery to obscure or compromise the message so that the message of the cross can be heard without distraction.

In 1 Corinthians 1:18–25, Paul continues his argument, first addressing the effect of the message of the cross—for those perishing the message (*logos*) of the cross is hogwash; for those who are being saved, it is God's power to convert. Through this *apparently* "foolish" message of a seemingly powerless crucified Christ, God, through Paul's preaching, saved the Corinthians and other believers. God called them through this supposedly weak and contemptible message, which is, in fact, wiser and stronger than anything humanity can contemplate.

He goes on in 1 Cor 1:26–31, urging the Corinthians to recall the moment(s) of their own calling, when they, mostly from humble origins, were chosen by God to be his people. As such, they who are using the preachers as tools in their machinations must hear the voices of Jeremiah 9:23–24 and 1 Samuel 2:10 and renounce all self-arrogation other than boasting in Christ (cf. Jer 9:23–24; 1 Sam 2:10, LXX).

In chapter 2, Paul reminds them of his proclamation on his visit on his second Antiochian mission (Acts 18:1–17). He did not proclaim the mystery of God[27] with *hyperochēn logou* hē *sophias*—"excellence of rhetoric

---

26. See Keown, "An 'Aha Moment,' 1 Cor 1:17," n. p.

27. Alternatively, this is "testimony of God." Some texts have *mystērion*, "mystery," others *martyrion*, "testimony." While *martyrion* is favored in some popular translations (e.g., ESV, NIV, NET), has some contextual relevance (cf. 1 Cor 1:6), and has wide support (ℵ^c B D G P Ψ 33 81 614 1739 *Byz* it^d, g vg syr^h cop^{sa} arm eth Origen *al*), *mystērion* (as in the NRSV) is preferable in context (cf. 1 Cor 2:7), and also has early support (P^{46vid}? ℵ* A C 88 436 it^r, 61 syr^p cop^{bo} Hippolytus Ambrosiaster Ephraem Ambrose Pelagius Augustine Antiochus). See Metzger, *A Textual Commentary*, 480.

or wisdom." Paul here refers to both form and content. *Hyperochēn logou* speaks of "excellence of rhetoric." The genitive construction picks up the same sense as 1:17, which I have already discussed. The genitive of *sophia*, "wisdom," speaks of content—the message of Christ and his death defies the wisdom of Jew and Greek alike. How is it that a crucified, so-called cosmic monarch, would die the most humiliating death imaginable in the Roman world? Surely, he is a pathetic loser. Of course, for Paul and for those who "get it," it is the supreme demonstration of God's love, the means by which God deals with the problem of sin and corruption, humanity's salvation, and is the example par excellence of what it means to be human.

In 1 Corinthians 2:3, Paul goes further. He reminds them that "I came to you in weakness and in fear and in much trembling." Such attitudes of vulnerability were anathema to a polished rhetorician in the Greco-Roman world. Such emotions were to be held at bay, no evidence of shakiness given. The delivery was to be uncluttered, as this was the primary means of persuasion. However, Paul is unashamed to admit to his fear. Some scholars seek to find reasons for Paul's concerns, such as the reputation of Corinth, his supposed failure in Athens, the crowds, the expectations of a rhetorician, the weight of responsibility as the apostle to the Gentiles, and so on.[28] While there is truth to such ideas, Paul's inclusion of this reference to his struggles is not merely to remind them of his anxieties but to recall how he *embodied in his proclamation approach the example of Christ*. Just as Christ died in "weakness, fear, and trembling" in the torment of the cross from which he cried, "My God, my God, why have you forsaken me," so Paul was unashamed as a rhetorician to embody his anxieties. We might say today that he wasn't afraid to be vulnerable or authentic. For him, such things are of no concern, for the power of the message of a crucified Christ is what does the converting, not the polished confidence of the eloquent rhetorician.

In verse 4 Paul continues, "and my *logos* and my *kerygma* were not in persuasive wisdom, but in a demonstration of the Spirit and power." *Logos* and *kerygma* can refer to the content (*logos*) and form (*kerygma*) of his preaching,[29] yet the converse can also be the case; *logos* indicating form and *kerygma* content. Then again, the two terms can both represent form and content and so it is likely that they are emphatic and interchangeable. As Roy Ciampa and Brian Rosner write, "[t]ogether they encompass all of Paul's speaking as an apostle."[30] If so, his proclamation in form and content

---

28. See Ciampa and Rosner, *The First Letter to the Corinthians*, 115 for a neat summary.

29. Fee, *The First Epistle*, 94: "message and preaching."

30. Ciampa and Rosner, 1 *Corinthians*, 116.

was "not in persuasive wisdom" or "persuasive words of wisdom."[31] This construct reiterates his earlier emphasis on a form of preaching that does not obscure the proclamation of the cross in 1:17 and 2:1—he did not employ dynamic eloquence.

Rather (*alla*),[32] he preached "with a demonstration of the Spirit and power." Abstracted from context, this can refer to miracles which accompanied the preaching of the gospel.[33] However, there is nothing in the setting to suggest that Paul has this in mind. Instead, the power here is the power of God by his Spirit, as the word of Christ and the cross are proclaimed, to generate faith in the human heart.

Using a characteristic purposive *hina*,[34] verse five speaks of the purpose of this approach to preaching which renounces rhetorical brilliance as a means to convince people to believe. Paul does so, "so that your faith may not rest on the wisdom of people (*anthrōpos*) but on the power of God." For Paul, faith (*pistis*) is the human response by which a person experiences salvation (Rom 3:22, 25–26, 28; 5:1; 9:30; Gal 2:16, 20; 3:22, 24, 26; Phil 3:9; Eph 2:8). For those being saved, faith is generated by the Spirit as the word is preached (cf. Rom 10:14–17; Gal 3:2). Paul does not want the medium to obscure the message. Otherwise, people's faith will be based on the "wisdom of people" rather than the "power of God." Paul is well aware that such a faith premised on the mere rhetorical persuasion of preachers, no matter how brilliant they may be, is at best shaky and unable to be sustained. If based on God's creation-power, it is a deep-rooted faith that has the capacity to stand the tests that will come as the new believer lives life in Christ.

In sum then, when Paul came to Corinth, he intentionally chose not to seek to emulate the Sophists and other philosophical preachers and utilize the tools of dynamic delivery, brilliantly crafted rhetorical masterpieces, and commanding presence to convince the Corinthians that Jesus Christ is Lord. One would have thought he *would* do so, for this would contextualize the message to the preferences that the Corinthians and other Greeks and Romans had for such rhetoric. Surely, when among the Greeks he would be

---

31. There are eleven variants for this clause (*en peithoi[s] sophias [logois]*). The primary question is over *peithois*, an adjective without precedent in Greek literature. This could indicate a scribal error copying *peithoi sophias*. If so, it reads "not in persuasive art of wisdom." While UBS4 and NA28 prefer "in persuasive words of wisdom," the shorter reading is more likely—"in persuasion of wisdom." See Garland, 1 *Corinthians*, 89; Fee, *The First Epistle*, 88 n. 2.

32. The choice of *alla* over *de* emphasizes the contrast.

33. See the discussion in Fee, *The First Epistle*, 95.

34. See P. Lampe, "ἵνα," in *EDNT*, 2.190 who notes 83 percent of Paul's uses of *hina* are purposive (final). As such, the conjunction introduces the purpose for the previous statement.

as a Greek to win the Greeks (cf. 1 Cor 9:19–23). Yet, in this case, Paul did not choose to do so. Why? Because he knew to do so in a place like Corinth would potentially empty the gospel of its latent God-given power to convert the human heart. Rather, it would be *his* rhetorical persuasion that would be doing the converting, as if that was possible. Such a "conversion" would be at best be shallow and limited. The faith would not be the deep-rooted faith that comes to the open human heart by the Spirit when the gospel of a crucified Messiah is heard and understood.

Counterculturally, Paul chose to preach without resorting to the rhetorical techniques of the age, resisting the impulse to "play the game." He sought to embody the message in his preaching style by embracing his fear and weakness, speaking out of it, and so portraying Christ as crucified and allowing God's message to do its work by the Spirit.

We can say that his preaching content and style was cruciform. Paul's whole theology is premised on cruciformity. Christ is the center of his salvation experience. Christ crucified is the basis of his message of salvation. As we read in Philippians 2:1–8, Christ and Christ crucified provides the basis for Christian ethics; what I call the Christ-pattern: humility, selflessness, service, sacrifice, suffering, and love, even to the point of death. This pattern should shape our lives and our churches. Paul's frequent references to suffering and desire to live the Christ-life speak of his commitment to cruciform living (e.g., Phil 3:10). The cross shapes his life; he lives "on Easter Friday" by the power of Sunday. Here, we see that cruciformity shapes his preaching in both content and form. It is well known that the cross is the center of Paul's preaching—he seeks before his hearers' eyes to publicly portray Jesus Christ as crucified (Gal 3:1). However, he goes further than cruciform *content*, also embodying the cross in the way he preaches, in his cruciform *delivery*. He not only makes Christ and his crucifixion the center of his message, but he seeks to embody Christ crucified in his approach. So when we read in 2 Corinthians 10:10 that his critics say of him, "His letters are weighty and strong, but his bodily presence is weak, and his speech of no account," they do not understand Paul's MO. While no doubt capable of forceful rhetoric (as his letters show), he intentionally took a path less traveled in his speech, renouncing the cultural speech patterns, speaking Christ crucified plainly, knowing God does the work. Little wonder in 2 Corinthians 10–12 that he responds to his critics with ironical boasting of his participation in Christ's sufferings. The *stigmata* of Jesus which he bears give witness to his expression of cruciformity (Gal 6:17).

Two more comments need to be made. First, we can consider Paul's response to Apollos. Apollos likely took a different approach to Paul, perhaps utilizing a more dynamic Greco-Roman style to which the Corinthians could relate. While Paul veers away from such an approach, he does not criticize Apollos for doing so. Clearly, Paul was comfortable with Apollos's content even if he chose a different delivery style. However, one wonders if Paul had had the chance, whether he would have counseled Apollos to tone it down to ensure it was Christ in the limelight and not Apollos. Second, we must not imagine Paul did not preach without real conviction. In 1 Thessalonians 1:5 he writes: "our gospel came to you not only in *logos* (word) but also in power and in the Holy Spirit and with full conviction (*plērophoria*)." *Plērophoria* is a noun rarely found in the comparative literature. It technically means "fill completely" and so can either indicate that he preached with "full conviction" or "fully," i.e., he gave them the complete gospel. However, most scholars prefer the interpretation "full conviction," "full assurance." So, while Paul veered from rhetoric in his proclamation, he did preach with real confidence in the gospel. The overall point is that he did not resort to technique which obscured the message but he did preach with conviction. So should we.

Contemporary Preaching

I find Paul's cruciform approach to preaching profoundly challenging. We live in an age which celebrates the dynamism of delivery from our so-called "celebrities." We delight in the witty radio and television celebrities who speak with great rapidity and flair, full of humor, overflowing with confidence and even arrogance, and who are masterful in the art of persuasion. Yet, the content of much of what they say is at best, vacuous. Or, when they say something profound, it is often lost in the din of their repartee. In my admittedly limited experience, the Protestant churches which are full in our nation tend to be those whose stages and pulpits are peopled with brilliant worship teams supported by superb sound systems and technology, good looking and dynamic preachers who, with engaging delivery, can speak with great "relevance" in cultural terms. Without wanting to generalize, their messages are often bereft of the word and of Christ and him crucified. They are strong on delivery and capture the itchy-eared crowds rooted in a consumptive culture, but the profound message of the cross is (again to generalize) rare. Even where the message of the cross is central, often delivery is still the means of persuasion. The power of God to convert is so heavily packaged that it becomes unclear who is doing the converting. Perhaps this leads to the not uncommon problem that the "conversions" are short-lived with some back doors as wide as the front.

Many other preachers in struggling local parishes dwarfed by sister churches down the road feel pressured to ensure that their proclamation follows glorious polished singing that "prepares the heart" for the message, even if a good number of the songs are as spiritually nourishing as cornflakes. Preachers feel pressured to use humor, show rhetorical skill, and seek to live up to the dynamic orators down the road. We utilize the latest technologies to ensure the package is consumptively pleasing. We employ video clips and other resources to keep the attention of the flock so easily distracted by their cell phones. We do all we can to ensure that the delivery is relevant, dynamic, and holds the attention of the sheep shaped by a consumptive society with its brilliant packaging. I wonder too whether those of us in seminary contexts focus too heavily on sermon delivery technique rather than encouraging authentic cruciform proclamation.

I believe Paul in this passage challenges us to consider another way. Certainly, we should seek to do all things well including preach the gospel. We must prepare carefully, immersed in prayer and Scripture, searching for suitable metaphors and analogies—Paul loved those things (e.g., sport, religion, business, etc.). However, the real questions are these: "Are we preaching Christ and Christ crucified?" Are we embodying Christ crucified in our lives and in our preaching styles—unafraid of being real, less concerned about brilliant delivery of the gospel message to be absolutely sure that it is God who is doing the transforming and not us with our rhetorical skill? We want people to attach to Christ and not to *us*. Are we so worried about numbers and attraction that we renounce the power latent in the message for technique? Sure, this may fill our churches up, but are we making real converts? Or better, is God making real converts through us?

Paul challenges us to have the same confidence in the message of the gospel that he had. As preachers, we don't need all that stuff. Rather, we need to immerse ourselves in God's story which is christological, christocentric, and christotelic. We need to sit in the presence of the crucified one and allow him to shape our hearts and minds. We need to embrace cruciformity in our beings, our message, and our rhetorical style. We need to bring the focus back to Jesus and off ourselves and our media techniques and well-crafted songs and sermons. We need to draw the limelight off ourselves and onto Jesus, again and again and again. As the great preacher John the Baptist once said, he must become greater and we less (John 3:30).

This study is profoundly challenging because it calls for us to dwell deeply in the Christ-story. This is indeed the full story of Scripture with him at beginning, center, and end, so that we go deeper and deeper into the mystery of Christ, and he pours forth from us and through us by his Spirit. In an age of shallow faith, such a focus and approach will see real faith birthed in our churches, and this is what will bring about a faith that lasts. It may not produce huge churches, but that is not the point. Jesus was happy with some twelve, then seventy-two, and then 120 with whom he changed the world. We must remember too that after the initial explosion of the Jerusalem Church (which was soon dispersed), the first churches were not large. Instead, believers gathered in small groups crowded into homes, whether apartments (*insulae*) or the atriums of Roman villas. Is it really about size or deep cross-centered discipleship?

I think Paul's example challenges us as preachers to reflect on the level of our presence in the pulpit. Recently, I observed a dynamic preacher leading a communion. I was troubled with what was going on but could not work out what was getting to me. As I pondered, I realized that the commanding presence and brilliant oratory of the preacher were actually drawing attention away from the table to himself. It was clearly unwitting because he is a naturally-gifted speaker. However, this moment reveals a challenge. It is this: the more dynamic and charismatic a preacher is, the more commanding his or her presence, the more that person needs to take heed of Paul's words. Are people being drawn to me as the preacher? Or are they being drawn to Christ? Is the preacher the point of attraction or is it Christ?

I am extremely challenged by all this myself. As a relatively tall, confident speaker, I have always sought to be a preacher who is cruciform in content but dynamic in delivery. That seemed right to me as I tried to contextualize the message. In fact, up until not that long ago I never gave it a second thought. I had thought that if I could just combine something of the brilliance of delivery of those speakers whose rhetoric draws the crowds (not that I managed it much) while investing it with really good cruciform content, this would enable more people to come to Christ. I am now questioning this, for the danger of being concerned with delivery and packaging is that we no longer hear the brilliance of God's wisdom, the wisdom of a crucified Messiah. A crucified Messiah and its implications for all of life are still the same radical culturally-subversive idea the world needs and does not get. In fact, in an age where empires are on the rise and where charisma matters above all (forget substance) we need to hear it more. As such, I am now on a journey to find cruciformity in delivery. I am not entirely sure what that looks like, but if I let the cruciform Spirit do the leading, I will find out. As I go on this journey, I find myself as a preacher increasingly committed to discover more of what this all means concerning proclaiming today. I am profoundly challenged. I hope you are too.

Bibliography

Branick, V. P. "Source and Redaction Analysis of 1 Corinthians 1–3." *JBL* 101 (1982) 251–69.

Ciampa, Roy E., and Brian S. Rosner. *The First Letter to the Corinthians*. Pillar New Testament Commentary. Grand Rapids: Eerdmans, 2010.

Fee, G. D. *The First Epistle to the Corinthians*. The New International Commentary on the New Testament. Grand Rapids: Eerdmans, 1987.

Garland, David E. *1 Corinthians*. Baker Exegetical Commentary on the New Testament. Grand Rapids: Baker Academic, 2003.

Gorman, Michael J. *Inhabiting the Cruciform God: Kenosis, Justification, and Theosis in Paul's Narrative Soteriology*. Grand Rapids: Eerdmans, 2009.

Hurd, John Coolidge. *The Origin of 1 Corinthians*. New York: Seabury, 1965.

Keown, Mark J. "An 'Aha Moment,' 1 Cor 1:17." http://drmarkk.blogspot.co.nz/2013/08/an-aha-moment-1-cor-117.html.

Litfin, Duane. *St. Paul's Theology of Proclamation: 1 Corinthians 1–4 and Greco-Roman Rhetoric*. Society for New Testament Studies Monograph Series 83. Cambridge: Cambridge University Press, 1994.

Meeks, Wayne A. *The First Urban Christians: The Social World of the Apostle Paul*. New Haven, CT: Yale University Press, 1983.

Metzger, Bruce M. *A Textual Commentary on the Greek New Testament, Second Edition a Companion Volume to the United Bible Societies' Greek New Testament*. 4th ed. London: United Bible Societies, 1994.

Mitchell, Margaret. M. *Paul and the Rhetoric of Reconciliation: An Exegetical Investigation of the Language and Composition of 1 Corinthians*. Louisville: Westminster John Knox, 1993.

Pogoloff, Stephen. M. *Logos and Sophia: The Rhetorical Structure of 1 Corinthians*. Society of Biblical Literature Dissertation Series 134. Atlanta: Scholars, 1992.

Stansbury, H. A. "Corinthian Honor, Corinthian Conflict: A Social History of Early Roman Corinth and Its Pauline Community." PhD diss., University of California, Irvine, 1990.

Thiselton, Anthony C. *The First Epistle to the Corinthians: A Commentary on the Greek Text*. The New International Greek Testament Commentary. Grand Rapids: Eerdmans, 2000.

Welborn, L. L. *Politics and Rhetoric in the Corinthian Epistles*. Macon, GA: Mercer University Press, 1997.

Witherington, Ben. *Conflict and Community in Corinth: A Socio-Rhetorical Commentary on 1 and 2 Corinthians*. Grand Rapids: Eerdmans, 1995.

Disturbed Words

The Holy Spirit and Preaching

WILLIAM H. WILLIMON

I HEARD FROM A former parishioner the other day. Her letter was a bit disarming in its beginning: "Thank you for messing up my life for good." She went on to say that she had made a major life move, "Because of that sermon you preached in the fall of 2010."

Though I barely could remember the sermon, she attributed her great lurch in life to that sermon. She reported that her life, though now more demanding than it had been before, was fulfilling. "I'm living for the needs of other people, rather than my own. Don't you think that's a rather amazing achievement for somebody in our culture? Anyway, thanks for the sermon."

My point in recalling her letter? *I didn't do that.*

Not only is the Holy Spirit the "more" of Christian preaching, because the Holy Spirit is the spirit of Jesus, it's the invasive, disruptive agency of preaching. I could preach, without having a nervous stomach, if I knew how to keep my sermons safe from the threat of incursions by the Holy Spirit. Trouble is, on more Sundays than not, in spite of our locked doors, the Holy Spirit rips the sermon out of my hands and says more than I meant, disrupting a church that I—by theological training and natural inclination—intend to sedate.

The Holy Spirit's work in preaching is a particular challenge for us modern, Western types. The major point of modernity was the promise of control. Through modern mechanisms of making sense of the world we can predict, determine patterns, discover laws of nature, make plans, all in the interest of control. Trouble is, it is the nature of the Holy Spirit to wrench our lives out of our control and to give us more interesting futures than we would have had without a God who is determined to have us in order to love us.

Eugene Peterson, in his autobiographical *The Pastor: A Memoir*,[1] presents himself as an unintentional pastor. Peterson wandered into ministry, one day waking up, to his surprise, as a Presbyterian pastor, founding a thriving congregation that he didn't really intend, sharing with the church a rendition of Scripture that sprang spontaneously out of his personal love of the Bible. Peterson's account at first struck me as disingenuous. Come on now, Gene, you really are an amazingly competent, compelling linguist, skilled pastor, and eloquent writer. That just happened?

Then I realized that Peterson was pointing to a truth at the heart of all faithful ministry—*we are out of control*. Luck has little to do with it. It's not about our discernment of some alleged plan that God has mapped out for us, not about our skillful turning of our lives into our projects; it's about divine agency. Providence. We cannot be certain, step-by-step, how the story of us and God will play out in each of our lives, but we can hope because our lives are not our own. A living God surprises, enjoys commissioning us for outrageous assignments, calls betrayers to be disciples, and likes nothing better than to create something out of nothing, to preach where we have failed, and to address people we had no intention, on our own, of addressing. By God's grace, we are out of control.

The first question of the Heidelberg Catechism: "What is your only comfort in life and in death?" The answer: "That I am not my own, but belong with body and soul, both in life and in death, to my faithful Saviour Jesus Christ."[2]

"I am not my own," because the reconciling, atoning Savior is also the calling, summoning, commissioning God. Paul, chastising the Corinthians for their sexual escapades, could have urged more responsible use of their bodies. Instead Paul asks, "Do you not know that your body is a temple of the Holy Spirit within you, which you have from God, and *that you are not your own*?" (1 Cor 6:19, italics mine).

Losing control of our lives, "body and soul" due to divine, gracious intrusion is a consolation of the Christian faith. When millions attempt uncalled lives, unaware of external authorization or commendation, it's a wonderful time to recover the homiletical implications of the truth that God is not only Father and Son, but also Holy Spirit, and that these three are one.

---

1. Peterson, *The Pastor*.

2. Online: http://www.heidelberg-catechism.com/en/lords-days/1.html#sthash.EMkBoBFO.dpuf.

Rainer Maria Rilke was asked by an aspiring young poet for advice on success in the poetic arts.[3] Rilke advised, "turn inward"—don't listen to critics, introvert, develop your subjectivity, create from within. Look upon nature only after you have looked at yourself; study your perceptions of the world rather than the world.

The older poet seems unaware that his counsel to turn inward and listen to nothing external is advice arising from somewhere other than the young poet's subjectivity. Here is the modern way of knowing: Attend to no voice other than your own. Self-construct your life to avoid being claimed "body and soul" by anyone other than yourself. Was there ever a time when young people needed counsel to be self-centered?

Because of the Holy Spirit's intrusions and interaction with creation we are able to look back upon a life, a ministry, or a sermon and say in all honesty and humility, "I didn't do that."

The Holy Spirit as the Agency of God

Christians are nothing without the Holy Spirit. Little in the Christian faith is self-derived. Jesus commands us to venture courageous, countercultural, demanding lives—ordering us to love one another, to pray for our enemies, to take up the cross and follow—but never by our own devices.

That's why the historic core of the service of ordination is the *Veni Creator Spiritus*, "Come, Creator Spirit." The church in its wisdom knows that preaching ought not be attempted alone. Just as the Spirit brooded over the waters at creation, faithful sermons are conceived and birthed by the Holy Spirit. Preparation for preaching requires the discipline of regularly standing before God empty-handed, mute, brashly begging God for words we cannot say on our own.

James Kay characterizes sermon prep as human work undertaken in concert with the Holy Spirit:

> All sermon preparation therefore must be a prayer for the Holy Spirit to take our ordinary words, however eloquent or inarticulate, and make them the bread of life. Here the sermon, on analogy with the Lord's Supper, is always a matter of *epiclesis* or invocation. . . . Come Creator Spirit![4]

When we pray, "Come, Holy Spirit!" it's as if we dare to ask, "Bring it on, Holy Spirit! Shake our foundations, send us forth, kick us out, set us on

---

3. Rilke, *Letters to a Young Poet*, 17.
4. Kay, *Preaching and Theology*, 67.

fire, and give us something more interesting to say than we would have said on our own!"

If not for continuing Pentecostal commotion, we would have nothing to say that the world couldn't hear as well through exclusively worldly means. That's why seminary homiletics courses are susceptible to the charge of a-theism—tempting students to substitute merely human rhetorical technique for empty-handed, pneumatological dependence. The church speaks not by savvy, worldly wisdom, strategies for church growth, or helpful psychological advice, but prophetically, in all times and places, driven by the prodding of the Spirit.

Preaching is based upon the character of God. We know from Scripture that God—Father, Son, and Holy Spirit—is relentlessly revealing. When someone hears gospel, Luther's *verbum externum* (the external word we cannot say to ourselves), it's a practical, mundane validation of Scripture's claims of God's determined self-revelation. If a preacher manages to assert anything faithful in a sermon, it's a Holy Spirit-induced miracle; a public, practical demonstration that God has refused to be God without us.

When Christians say *Holy Spirit* we are talking about *God*. More pointedly, we are saying *Trinity*: Father, Son, and Holy Spirit, who are one. When you are third in a list, for instance, like the Apostles' Creed, third can seem an afterthought. The Father creates, the Son redeems, and the Spirit—well, *what does the Spirit do?*[5]

The Holy Spirit is more than personal, vaguely spiritual experience; the Holy Spirit is who God is and what God does as the Trinity, whether we feel it or not, God's anything-but-vague self-presentation. Thus, in a sermon on the Holy Spirit, Gregory Nazianzen says that we ought never compromise the unity of the Trinity when we talk about the Holy Spirit. The Holy Spirit ought only be distinguished from Father and Son by a title: *proceeding*. Gregory explains that "ingenerate" belongs to the Father, "begotten" to the Son, and "proceeding" to the Spirit.[6] *The Holy Spirit is the means by which God the Father and Son proceed into human history.*

God shows up, invades, self-reveals, impregnates, and becomes incarnate as Jesus Christ, in the power of the Holy Spirit. Looking back on decades of experience with the Holy Spirit messing with my sermons, I would like to testify to a spiritual gift that Paul fails to mention in 1 Corinthians 12:8–10, perhaps because it was so obvious to him personally—*disruption*.

---

5. This is Eugene Rogers's formulation of the question in his book *After the Spirit: A Constructive Pneumatology from Resources outside the Modern West*, 19.

6. See Norris, *Faith Gives Fullness to Reasoning*; Gregory, *Holy Spirit*, 31.7.

A Christian is someone who has submitted to an unbalanced, instable life, a life out of control, driven by and accountable to someone more interesting than ourselves or even our church, i.e., the third person of the Trinity, God in action.

It's a widely acknowledged truth that our lives cannot be in our control because we all will die. Death is about as out of control as one can get. Much of our pretense to know so much about the world in order better to secure and protect ourselves is rather silly when we face our finitude and the deeply contingent quality of our lives.

Yet naturalistic truisms about our mortality and contingency are not my main concern. My thesis is more countercultural, more biblical, and more specifically Christian. We are out of control because, as the psalmist affirms, "It is [God] that hath made us and not we ourselves" (Ps 100:3, KJV). We are neither self-created nor self-preserved. To be even more specific about our contingency, *we are not self-directed*. We are out of control because we live in a realm circumscribed by an active, commanding, interventionist, summoning God. "All our steps are ordered by the Lord; / how then can we understand our own ways?" (Prov 20:24). We cannot have balance, control, peace, and stability, not because we are overworked and mortal, but *because of God*.

I'm sure that's a major reason why I enjoy teaching in a seminary. It is invigorating to be cast with people whose lives are out of control due to the intrusive vocation of God. Though Schleiermacher said it was impossible to preach Genesis 22 to modern people come of age, I can testify that there are still those whose lives are analogous to Abraham, risking subordination of success, family, and future due to the conviction that God refuses to be God alone, that God not only loves but commands, enlists and speaks through ordinary people like us.

As Karl Barth said, "Preachers dare." Preachers dare that silent, solitary Abrahamic walk every week when we trudge into our studies and open the book and lay all we have on the altar in faith that God will make of our sermons more than we could on our own, that God will provide. Preachers' words are not so much out of control as under control.

God in Action

The Jesus drama is instigated by the Holy Spirit's disruptive impregnation of Mary, who, "became pregnant by the Holy Spirit" (Matt 1:18). Just as the Spirit brooded over the waters at creation (Gen 1), so the fecund Spirit continues to create—God for us—whether we asked for so interesting a God or not.

As Jesus came up from the water the heavens were opened, "and he saw the Spirit of God coming down like a dove and resting on him" (Matt 3:16). Describing the Holy Spirit as "resting" on Jesus could be misleading were it not for John the Baptist's warning that whereas he baptized with water, Jesus's baptism was of "the Holy Spirit and fire" (Luke 3:16). As I heard Barbara Brown Taylor say in a sermon, this dove has claws.

Because the Holy Spirit is the Spirit of the Son, the Holy Spirit is as disruptive, as demanding, and as communicatively aggressive, as Jesus. Thus right after baptism, Jesus "full of the Holy Spirit" (Luke 4:1) is driven into the wilderness (Mark 1:12) for head-to-head homiletical competition with the devil. "Filled with the power of the Spirit," (Luke 4:14) Jesus bursts forth into Galilee. With his premier sermon, Jesus immediately incites an otherwise serene Sabbath-keeping congregation to murderous riot because, "The Spirit of the Lord is upon me, . . . to preach" (Luke 4:18).

The question, "What can the Spirit do that Christ cannot do better?" finds its answer in Luke 4. The Spirit teaches Jesus to preach.

Disruption is a gift of the Holy Spirit, given for the sake of all who attempt homiletics. To all the sweet people who come to church murmuring, "I want to be more spiritual," the church responds not only with, "Have some bread, take some wine," but also with, "listen to the truth about God delivered by someone who looks suspiciously like you without killing her for saying it. If that works, we'll baptize you and make you subject to the same Spirit who has emboldened the preacher."

The advocate, the Holy Spirit, is sent, not to give us a warm feeling of peace, but rather to, "teach you everything, and remind you of all I have said to you" (John 14:26); everything, even the offensive commands of Christ that we have tried so hard to forget: turning the other cheek, praying for enemies, and letting the dead bury the dead, etc.

That the Holy Spirit "will teach you everything, and remind you" of all that Jesus said is a bit threatening. Here is truth we cannot teach ourselves, truth that is not only a great mystery to us but also truth so demanding that we, in our human sin, cannot attain on our own, truth that we have martialed some of our best intellectual resources to avoid.

That the Holy Spirit teaches is also reassuring. We preachers don't work alone. The truth about God makes a way for itself, in the power of the Holy Spirit, boring into the hard hearts and thick skulls of our listeners in ways we do not control. We preachers thus take heart that, when it comes to speaking, hearing, and obeying God's word, in speaking to and listening to God, we are not left to our own devices. As Paul says, "The Holy Spirit comes to help our weakness" (Rom 8:26).

The Spirit Upon Us—To Preach

Luke introduces us to Jesus in action at his hometown synagogue (Luke 4). There, what does Jesus do? In the power of the Holy Spirit he preaches. The disruption of the Holy Spirit tends to be disturbance of silence, the temptation to say nothing and silently acquiesce to the powers and principalities. The disturbing, commotion-producing Holy Spirit tends to generate uppity speech:

> When he came to Nazareth, where he had been brought up, he went to the synagogue on the sabbath day, as was his custom. He stood up to read, and the scroll of the prophet Isaiah was given to him. He unrolled the scroll and found the place where it was written:
>
> > "The Spirit of the Lord is upon me,
> > because he has anointed me
> > to bring good news to the poor.
> > He has sent me to proclaim release to the captives
> > and recovery of sight to the blind,
> > to let the oppressed go free,
> >
> > to proclaim the year of the Lord's favor." (Luke 4:16–17, NRSV)

The Acts of the Apostles makes clear that the Holy Spirit-induced disruption embodied in the preaching of Jesus now accelerates, goes worldwide, infecting his followers, pushing them out of their comfort zones, driving them to talk all the way "to the ends of the earth" (Acts 1:8). The body of Christ, the new visible presence of the Trinity, is God in motion into the world bringing God's truth to speech.

In the Power of the Holy Spirit, God Speaking

On Pentecost, Jews from all nations were convened in one place. Suddenly a sound from heaven like the howling of a fierce wind filled the entire house, flames of fire alighting on each. Filled with the Holy Spirit, they began to speak in other languages, enabled by the Spirit (Acts 2:1–4). They spoke of God's deeds of power. Parthians, Medes, Elamites, and all the rest of the far-flung Jewish Diaspora heard in their own languages a new "thing." That new creation by audition would bear the name *church*.

That the birth of the church by the Holy Spirit entailed the gift of languages is not accidental. At Babel humans had tried to reach to the heavens so that they might be as gods. Speaking one language gave them the presumption that they were in control of communication, in charge of their destiny.

In response to their attempt to be like God, they were punished by being separated from one another by different languages. Unable to communicate amid the babble, they became strangers, enemies. At Babel the violence begun with Cain's fratricide of Abel (Gen 4) became the new normal in a world with no common language and many barriers to community.

Pentecost brought peace, not by healing differences through the technique of English-only institutionalization of one language to replace the many, but through a multilinguistic community called church. Christians would be forced, by baptism, to learn the language of the stranger, Christ, making them strangers to the world as a people of peace in a world of violence. Driven by the Holy Spirit into the world, they would be forced to learn the language of others in order to spread the news that God has destabilized present arrangements in a continuing revolution called the kingdom of heaven.

Some who witnessed the gift of tongues at Pentecost mocked those who were possessed by the Spirit as drunk, under the influence, out of control. Peter, however, denied they were drunk, saying it's "only nine o'clock in the morning!" (Acts 2:15).

Then, under the power of the Spirit, Peter preached, drawing on the prophet Joel's dramatic apocalyptic imagery to indicate that a new age was breaking out. His sermon would become the model for Christian preaching in Acts, proclaiming that Israel's messianic hopes were now fulfilled, even expanded, in Jesus Christ.

Remember where we left Peter in Luke's Gospel? Peter was unable to say one faithful word when confronted by the maid in the courtyard before Jesus's crucifixion (Luke 22:54–62). Now Peter boldly preached! No exclusively human explanation accounts for Peter's homiletical courage. Peter's preaching is solid evidence of the work of the Holy Spirit.

According to Peter, the giving of the Spirit was nothing less than the advent of a new age inaugurated by the Holy Spirit. In former days, the Spirit was given to a few individuals, that is, prophets who were empowered to speak God's truth. But there would come a day, prophesied Joel, when God's Spirit would be poured upon all. That Spirit flood would result in prophetic sons and daughters, visionary young persons, and old folks daring to dream. Even slaves, men and women alike, would prophesy. All, even those who were previously voiceless and hopeless, would be enabled to speak up and speak out in God's name. Thus Peter boldly proclaimed that the work of the Spirit is no different from the work of Christ. To have the Spirit is to have Christ. The Holy Spirit does not enable us to say more than Christ; the

Spirit enables us to speak of Christ (Acts 2:37–39), leading us to say things we would not venture on our own.

The Holy Spirit descends to us where we are and communicates God to us in ways we can comprehend, healing the chaos and confusion of Babel. While a new age is inaugurated, bringing into existence a new people, the essential mission of the Spirit remains the same: the Spirit disrupts settled power arrangements, mocks official modes of explanation, and kicks down boundaries we have erected between one another. The primary mode through which this divine commotion is accomplished is through uppity, brash proclamation.

The church, says Chris Holmes, is subject to a "permanent Pentecost." By the Spirit the church is gathered in order to utter the cry toward which it lives: "Come, Lord Jesus" (Rev 22:20).[7] Unfortunately, the church is often comfortable in its captivity and cultural servilities. Therefore, in the power of the Holy Spirit, Pentecost keeps happening, a preacher rises to speak, the Spirit descends, shakes up the congregation, and it's Luke 4 and Jesus in the pulpit at Nazareth all over again.

As I sought to offer consolation to an Alabama pastor after a fire destroyed his church, the pastor surprised me by saying, "We lost a lot in that fire. A hundred years of memories. Still, maybe God was in it."

"How do you mean?" I asked.

"We had talked about moving up on the highway, talked about how we ought to merge with the African-American congregation up the road. Nothing ever came of it. Maybe we loved this old building too much," he explained. "I ain't saying that the Holy Spirit was behind the fire that took our building, but it is the kind of thing God might do if God really wanted us to move rather than sit here. God's done it before."

Before venturing an epiclesis, be sure you can handle what happens if your prayer should be answered!

The first time we hear Jesus preach in Mark, it's on a Sabbath in Capernaum (Mark 1:21–28). The congregation is settling in to once again hear the sweet bromides and platitudes they crave. Everyone is centering, achieving greater balance, quietly keeping Sabbath.

Then Jesus begins to preach.

"I know who you are Jesus!" shouted a possessed man. "You are from God, come to destroy us."

Mark gives not a word of Jesus' sermon, perhaps because the explosion was not due to what Jesus taught but rather how he taught. Jesus spoke as "one with authority," that is, speaking under the compulsion of external

---

7. Holmes, *The Holy Spirit*, 195.

authorization. That same Spirit that had descended upon Jesus at his baptism, that had driven him into the wilderness with the devil, had now driven him to speak in a way that caused demons to stir and all hell to break loose, destroying the faithful's Sabbath. In Jesus, in the power of the Holy Spirit, heaven has opened and, among the faithful, all hell breaks loose.

Jesus is crucified and entombed (in a vain attempt to shut him up and hold him in one place). In the interim between his death and resurrection, according to 1 Peter 3:19–20, Christ descended and preached to the dead, harrowing hell during the sermon.

First Peter's claim is so in keeping with Jesus' character to disrupt, liberate, dislodge even the dead. (I have found comfort in this text when I've had to preach in some moribund congregation.)

After decades, I'm still invigorated by the homiletical task. I still question why God called somebody like me, to whom the status quo has been so good, to preach this discombobulating good news. Oh, but what joy to cast my words into the silence on the wager that God might use my Southern-accented, scratchy voice for purposes greater than I intended.

The faithful gather seeking consolation for their aches and pains, confirmation of their illusions about themselves, a purpose-driven life, additional aid in their preservation of the status quo or whatever it is they worship rather than Jesus. And then I rise to preach, the Holy Spirit slips into our moderate, Methodist meeting, the place begins to shake, I smell smoke, demons are let loose, the Holy Spirit intrudes, and I step aside and watch the fireworks.

Fellow preachers: I don't care how demanding it can be to work with the Holy Spirit, a less interesting God wouldn't be worth our efforts.

Summoned to Deliver a Word We Didn't Devise

Any ambivalence we may have about our being summoned to the preaching vocation pales before Jeremiah's periodic anger at being called *in utero* to be "a prophet to the nations" (Jer 1:5).

When Jeremiah attempted to beg off and thereby regain some control of his life, God responded: "Do not say, 'I am only a boy'; / for you shall go to all to whom I send you, / and you shall speak whatever I command" (1:7). "See, today I appoint you over nations and over kingdoms, / to pluck up and to pull down, / to destroy and to overthrow, / to build and to plant" (1:10) with nothing more than words. A person would be a fool not to be intimidated by so violent, creative, and dangerous a vocation. Still, it is greater foolishness to attempt to evade the long arm of God.

I'm sure that's why every preacher's favorite Flannery O'Connor story is "Revelation"[8]:

Ruby Turpin sat in a crowded doctor's waiting room. And as Ruby often did she spent her time looking around and one-by-one, in her mind, measuring herself by the people seated before her. As she evaluated herself on the social ladder, Ruby always came out more than a notch above everybody else—particularly that scowling teenage girl seated across from her, unkempt, sullen, and sour. She said to the girl's mother, after having tried vainly to illicit some response from the girl, "What is your daughter's name?"

The mother looked up and said, "Mary, her name is Mary Grace."

"Well Mary Grace" says Ruby, "I always think it is just great to sit up in your chair, and posture is so important, and er . . . " The girl sullenly glared at her. Ruby continued to chatter to herself—loud enough for everybody in the waiting room to hear. She talked about the relative goodness of poor black workers compared with "poor white trash." Lazy white workers had to be paid a full day's wage. And you had to pick them up and then take them home after work. Ruby said she knew white trash that lived worse than "our pigs that Claude and me has got."

She prattled on until the unkempt teenager fixed her eyes on her like "steely drills" and glared, making Ruby very uncomfortable. The girl had been reading a big book. Ruby squinted her eyes and saw that it was *Human Development*. She could only imagine the lurid things in that book. Suddenly the girl hurls the huge book across the waiting room, cold cocking Ruby across the forehead. Ruby sprawls in the middle of the floor. Mary Grace is on top of her hissing, "Go back to hell where you belong, you old wart hog."

It is for Ruby unexpected, undesired revelation, difficult grace. Before the story ends, she is given a vision of eternity. (In this faith, grace, revelation often come when a large book smacks you between the eyes.)

You can imagine with whom I most identity in the story. I am Mary Grace on a weekly basis. I'm a preacher; someone elected—in the disrupting power of the Holy Spirit—to whop a congregation up-side the head with a great big book.

And yet in my sermon preparation, I'm more Ruby Turpin than Mary Grace. To be both the recipient and the donor of unsought, unexpected revelation isn't an easy job, God knows. But it is the vocation to which God has called Mary Grace, Ruby, and me.

---

8. O'Connor, *A Good Man Is Hard to Find*, 88–91.

As Ruby lies upon her bed at twilight, attempting to recover, she mutters, "I am not a wart hog. From hell." O'Connor says that her, "denial had no force."

"She had been singled out for the message, though there was trash in the room to whom it might justly have been applied. . . . There was a woman there who was neglecting her own child but she had been overlooked. The message had been given to Ruby Turpin, a respectable, hard-working, church-going woman. The tears dried. Her eyes began to burn instead with wrath."

To be "singled out for a message," when the news is meant not only for everyone but also aimed at you, a word that is death-dealing, life-giving, out-of-control gospel, well, that odd vocation elicits joy in the preacher and sometimes wrath. God only knows why God has chosen to assault and to recreate the world through preaching. God only knows what good it does.

Ah, but what a wonderful way to go.

Bibliography

Holmes, Christopher R. J. *The Holy Spirit*. Grand Rapids: Zondervan, 2015.

Kay, James F. *Preaching and Theology*. St. Louis: Chalice, 2007.

Norris, Frederick W. *Faith Gives Fullness to Reasoning: The Five Theological Orations of Gregory of Nazianzen*. Translated by Lionel Wickham and Frederick Williams. Leiden: E. J. Brill, 1991.

O'Connor, Flannery. *A Good Man Is Hard to Find: and Other Stories*. New York: Signet Books, The New American Library, 1961.

Peterson, Eugene. *The Pastor*. New York: HarperCollins, 2011.

Rilke, Rainer Maria. *Letters to a Young Poet*. Translated by Charlie Louth. New York: Penguin, 2013.

Rogers, Eugene. *After the Spirit: A Constructive Pneumatology from Resources Outside the Modern West*. Grand Rapids: Eerdmans, 2005.